Transnational Television Worldwide: Towards a New Media Order

edited by Jean K. Chalaby

I.B. TAURIS

LONDON · NEW YORK

To Felicity

Published in 2005 by I.B.Tauris & Co. Ltd
6 Salem Road, London W2 4BU
175 Fifth Avenue, New York NY 10010
www.ibtauris.com

In the United States of America and in Canada distributed by Palgrave
Macmillan, a division of St Martin's Press, 175 Fifth Avenue, New York
NY 10010

ISBN 1 85043 547 2 hb 1 85043 548 0 pb
EAN 978 1 85043 547 1 hb 978 1 85043 548 8 pb

A full CIP record for this book is available from the British Library

A full CIP record for this book is available from the Library of Congress
Library of Congress catalog card: available

Set in Monotype Dante by Ewan Smith, London
Printed and bound in Great Britain by MPG Books, Bodmin

Contents

Tables

Acknowledgements

The idea for this book came as I was listening to a presentation by African Broadcast Network at Rhodes University, in South Africa. I realized that cross-border TV channels were expanding everywhere and that it would be a worthwhile endeavour to compare their development in different world regions. I would like to thank Kevin Robins for his advice at an early stage of the project, and my wife Jane for her precious help with various parts of the manuscript. I would also like to thank Philippa Brewster, senior commissioning editor at I.B. Tauris, Deborah Susman, editorial controller, and Chris Parker, Ewan Smith and Janet Law for expertly producing this volume. Above all, I am grateful to the authors for their wonderful contributions and patience with all my requests.

CHAPTER I
. . . .
Towards an Understanding of Media Transnationalism

Jean K. Chalaby

§ FOR much of its history, television has been closely bound to a national territory. Broadcasters exchanged programmes and set up international associations, but operated within national boundaries. Their signal covered the length and breadth of the country, from the nation's capital to the remotest parts of the countryside. Foreign broadcasters were not allowed to transmit on national territory and attempts to do so were seen as breaches of sovereignty. Television was often tied up with the national project and no other media institution was more central to the modernist intent of engineering a national identity.[1] State broadcasting monopolies – enshrined in the law of many nations until the 1980s – were in place to ensure that nobody would interfere with this design. The close relationship between the nation and television has been unravelling over the past two decades. Causes for this disjuncture are complex and numerous,[2] but few are more potent than the emergence of cross-border TV channels.

The rise of transnational television lies at the heart of the current regional and global reshaping of media industries and cultures. Today, following two decades of expansion, hundreds of cross-border TV channels occupy transponder space on communications satellites that can beam a signal across a whole continent. Over the years, they have grown in diversity – including some of the most innovative and influential channels of recent times – and quantity. A crop of trans-border TV channels has played a determining role in the transformations of media cultures in their region. In the Middle East, satellite ventures have introduced the most innovative TV formats and driven wider changes in Arab television. MBC (now Al-Arabiya) has raised standards of broadcasting journalism and Al-Jazeera, whose independent voice has unsettled governments, has introduced the controversial talkshow (Chapter 4). In South Asia, Zee TV and Star TV have accompanied sweeping cultural change and radical transformations in the television industry (Chapters 6 and 7).

This volume offers the first overview of transnational television throughout the world. It takes a global approach to a worldwide phenomenon, bringing together contributors covering the world's main geocultural regions: Europe, the Middle East, Africa, South Asia, Greater China and Latin America. The authors bring to the book a diversity of perspectives – they are spread over five continents – and a wealth of expertise. Their contributions benefit from an intimate knowledge of their field, nourished by contacts in the industry and interviews with viewers, providing a unique source of information on the topic. In this chapter I have outlined the most salient issues in contributors' writing and the key themes brought to the fore by the volume's global perspective.

The first matter that this book brings to light is the sheer variety of existing cross-border TV channels. These channels are usually grouped under the single 'transnational' category, which is useful only when distinguishing them from those that remain within national boundaries, as it tends to mask their extraordinary diversity. International channels cover every possible television niche market, ranging from sport to movies and religion to adult entertainment. Above all, they present several types of transnationality and differ in terms of ownership, objectives, reach, cross-border strategy, resources and audience.

Every type of broadcaster has launched trans-border TV channels, whether they are public service corporations such as France Télévisions, state organizations such as Egypt's ERTU, or private concerns. Certain channels have been launched by governments trying to reach expatriate populations, while others belong to global media corporations aiming to increase the percentage of out-of-home-market revenue in their total turnover. Some channels address an audience of migrants with a common linguistic and cultural background, others target the cosmopolitan corporate elite. In terms of reach, some are distributed in a handful of countries, others on a pan-regional basis. A handful have achieved near global coverage. Some satellite feeds consist of recycled content originally produced for the home market of a terrestrial broadcaster; in other cases they are specifically produced for a multinational audience. There are channels produced and packaged in one place, while others are operated from a multinational network of production centres. These myriad differences point to the extraordinary range of cross-border television.[3]

Several contributors have begun to look at corporate practices to understand the variety of ways in which TV channels can cross borders. It has long been assumed that satellite TV channels present a 'challenge' to national cultures and sovereignty. More specifically, international broadcasters face the challenge of communicating trans-nationally. As Straubhaar and Duarte, and I, explain in Chapters 10 and 3, the corporate strategy to make channels cross boundaries has evolved over time. In the 1980s and early 1990s, it was believed in corporate circles that the global was supplanting the local and it was only a matter of time before cultural differences among nations gave way to a global culture. Television executives progressively discovered that audiences preferred to watch, when available, home-made television programmes, and underestimated local companies' ability to copy international TV channel formats. This prompted them to adapt their international feeds to local tastes, leading to the emergence of practices of localization.

Straubhaar and Duarte analyse the different levels of market adaptation in Latin America, since not all companies share the same commitment to localization. Practices of adaptation include an array of methods ranging from multilingual services (dubbing or subtitling), local programming inserts and local opt-outs. The need for localization has led to the formation of international TV networks, which consist of the creation of local channels around a core broadcasting philosophy. Chapter 3 gives an account of the development of these networks in Europe since the mid-1990s.

The practices of adaptation differ according to channel type and region. Entertainment channels that appeal to mass audiences need to localize more than international news channels aimed at a corporate elite. This book also points out regional differences in the deployment of these practices. Joseph Chan shows that regional players in Greater China must not only adapt to local cultures and languages but also take into account recalcitrant governments that remain wary of foreign cultural influence (Chapter 8). Similarly, Page and Crawley observe that transnational broadcasters 'need to be on good terms with governments in their key markets' (Chapter 6). In

Africa, Mytton, Teer-Tomaselli and Tudesq explore African satellite networks' strategies to overcome depleted advertising revenue and the population's low access to cable and satellite services (Chapter 5).

Another issue brought to the fore in this volume is the structure of media globalization, the most visible aspect of which is the formation of a global media system involving four key elements. The first is the *global media industry*, described by Herman and McChesney as a two-tier system.[4] In the first group sit seven vertically integrated transnational media corporations whose activities spread across the globe and span most media sectors.[5] The second tier includes multinational companies with strong regional sales or those with global reach specializing in a niche market. *Global communications networks* constitute the technology infrastructure of this system. They comprise undersea fibre-optic cables, communications satellites and the Internet, enabling media companies to promote and deliver their products almost free of geographical impediments.[6] The news and entertainment products, including films, TV series and documentaries that are distributed on a worldwide basis, constitute the system's *flow of communication*. The fourth component is the *global regulatory regime* for media and communications. This emerging legal framework being shaped by international agencies such as the World Trade Organization (WTO) and the International Telecommunication Union (ITU) is covering an increasing number of countries and aspects of the multinational cultural trade.[7]

The formation of the global media system does not in itself explain the changing nature of the international television market. Both Sinclair and Straubhaar have independently argued that this market has acquired a multilayered structure that involves up to four dimensions: the local, national, world-regional and global levels.[8] Thus the process of media globalization involves the formation of a second international layer that fits in between the national and global levels: the geocultural region. In this volume, John Sinclair explains that a region is not defined solely by its geographical contours but also by commonalities of language and culture. The Spanish-speaking minorities that have settled across the USA are also a part of the 'Latin American audiovisual space' (Chapter 9).

Regional media systems share several attributes and many have their own broadcasting associations, including the Arab States Broadcasting Union (ASBU), the European Broadcasting Union (EBU) or the Union of National Radio and Television Organizations of Africa (URNTA). These organizations frequently host a TV news exchange system and a network of programme distribution.[9] Although satellite providers are going through a round of consolidation on a global scale, communications satellite networks remain organized on a regional basis: Arabsat (Middle East), Eutelsat (Europe) or PanAmSat (the Americas). Increasingly, regions incorporate media hubs that act as clusters of expertise, creative talent and capital for the industry. John Sinclair has identified Miami as the Latin American audiovisual space and Joseph Chan points to Hong Kong in the Greater China market. To a lesser extent, Dubai (Middle East) and London (Europe), play a similar role for each respective region. Finally, corporate players have emerged that occupy a particularly strong position in a geocultural television market. These include RTL in Europe, the Saudi-owned pay-TV network, ART, in the Middle East, MultiChoice in Africa, Star TV in India, and Televisa in Latin America.

The development of transnational television fully reflects this process of regionalization and its complex relationship with globalization. As shown by the contributors, the geocultural region plays a pivotal role in the worldwide development of transnational TV. Global channels the world over employ regional feeds that may share more of their programming but have distinct schedules.[10] Above all, the majority of cross-border TV channels are pan-regional in scope, serving a geocultural region and its diasporic groups living beyond its geographical contours. This is partly explained by the fact that most of the dominant regional players mentioned above are very much involved in transnational television. The distribution of South Africa's MultiChoice spans over fifty countries, including the Indian Ocean Islands, China and the Mediterranean region (Chapter 5). Latin American corporations, such as the Cisneros Television Group, have long been involved in North America and Iberian Europe (Chapters 9 and 10). Daya Thussu shows how transnationalization is at the core of Zee TV's strategy, as the company – illustrating a 'growing reverse traffic in television flow' from the global South to the West – chases South Asian viewers worldwide (Chapter 7).

The global outlook of this book enables us to draw observations from the comparison of transnational television in different regional settings. It emerges that the size of the reception universe, largely determined by audience access to cable and satellite services, is crucial to the development of cross-border channels. According to Graham Mytton and colleagues, it remains a major issue in the sub-Saharan countries where access to these services remains very low. Europe provides one of the largest reception universes, where the number of households connected to cable and satellite stood at 107 million in 2001. Despite these large numbers international channels were struggling until the late 1990s as advertisers continued to favour the mass audiences of terrestrial broadcasters (Chapter 3).

The importance of regional cultural and linguistic homogeneity is demonstrated by Africa, where linguistic boundaries delineate the reach of trans-border channels (Chapter 5). The Middle East and Latin America are culturally and linguistically the most homogeneous regions, while Europe remains a mosaic of cultures, language and life-styles. Europe demonstrates how cultural diversity need not impede the development of cross-border TV channels, but it poses a limit to their political and cultural impact. European channels might be affluent and yet struggle for recognition beyond their niche audience. Al-Jazeera has flourished in the Middle East because its residents share a language and an interest in many social, cultural and political issues. In Europe, international news TV channels have the privilege of being watched by the business and political elite, but their audience share is so small that they do not always show up in audience surveys. During summer 2003, *Arab Superstar*, the Lebanese Future TV's adaptation of *Pop Idol*, caught the Arab world by storm because the region shares the same musical culture. By way of contrast, European cultural diversity forces broadcasters to adapt international TV formats to local audiences.

The impact of regional politics seems to differ from one region to another. In the Middle East, Naomi Sakr explains how antagonistic relations between Arab states has been the prime mover in their de-velopment of satellite channels. Conversely, in South Asia and Greater China, contributors note that cross-border hostilities between India and Pakistan, and between China and Taiwan, have hindered trans-border television (Chapters 6 and 8). Europe presents a different picture al-together as regional politics have had little bearing on international TV channels. In fact, the successful expansion but modest influence of cross-border channels stands in stark contrast to the pioneering development of transnational democracy in the region.

The regional development of transnational television also bears some common features. A certain number of channels have achieved global reach. Those in private hands include Bloomberg, CNN, CNBC, Discovery, National Geographic, Cartoon Network, Nickel-odeon, Hallmark, MTV and Zee TV. Few channels backed by public service broadcasters are distributed in all five regions, essentially BBC World, TV5, the German Deutsche Welle and Japan's NHK World.[11] Regions do not always receive a dedicated feed, which is often the case in Africa and, to a lesser extent, the Middle East. Bloomberg UK and CNBC US, for example, are made available in the Middle East (via Arabsat 3) and the sub-Saharan countries get the same Bloomberg channel and CNBC Europe via PanAmAat 7 and 10.

Several media conglomerates have developed a presence in all key geocultural regions besides or even without global channels. They have been operating regional channels and/or distributing international channels on an entirely regional basis, usually by for-ging alliances with local partners. Without contest, the dominant company in the satellite TV industry is News Corporation, which is involved in a mix of national, regional and global channels and satellite bouquets across the world, including Sky Digital (UK) and Sky Italia in Europe, Star TV (South Asia), Phoenix TV (Greater China), and Sky Latin America. In the Sky and Fox family, numer-ous channels are available internationally, ranging from Sky News and Fox News to Canal Fox and Fox Sports. News Corp also has an interest in National Geographic. AOL Time Warner, in addition to CNN, distributes regional selections of HBO, Cinemax, Cartoon Network and Turner Classic Movies worldwide. Viacom is pushing the global distribution of two music networks, MTV and VH1, and a children's channel, Nickelodeon. Disney distributes ESPN in Africa (with a dedicated feed), Asia, Latin America and selected European countries, and Fox Kids (which the company bought from News Corp in 2001) in Latin America, Europe and the Middle East.

These developments illustrate the complexity of the international television market, which is structured as an intricate web of dual and tripartite relations involving local, regional and global elements. More research is needed to disentangle these relationships and, in particular, to understand the influence of regional settings on transnational TV networks. Further comparison among regions will necessitate more data on the transnational TV industry and contextual factors such as economic development, regional governance and local regulation.

The concept of *deterritorialization* can provide some help with the puzzlingly complex relationship between transnational TV and space. The most commonly used definition of the notion is that of Néstor García Canclini, who explains it as 'the loss of the "natural" relation of culture to geographical and social territories'.[12] Culture becomes disembedded from territory and loses its connection to place. John Tomlinson has described this disjuncture as 'the weakening or dissolution of the connection between everyday lived culture and territorial location'.[13]

Ever since the advent of the telegraph, the media have been recognized as a deterritorializing force. It is the theme underpinning all the McLuhanesque theories about the globalizing influence of means of communication. Recent examples include Martin Albrow, who states that the expansion of communications technologies 'was the prime accelerator of disembedding of social relations in the Modern Age and continues to promote deterritorialization in the Global Age'.[14] Through the media, people become familiar with places they have never visited, come to like people they have never met and get to know fictional characters better than their neighbours. They learn about the performances of stock exchanges around the world and worry about events that take place thousands of miles away from their homes. Anthony Giddens calls this phenomenon 'displacement', which he defines as 'our insertion into globalised cultural and information settings, which means that familiarity and place are much less consistently connected than hitherto'.[15] Deterritorialization is also increasingly evoked in the context of migratory groups, where the disconnection between place and culture is most apparent.[16] Displaced populations use several media, and especially satellite television, to (re)create a culture that draws from several locales.[17]

International TV channels are not simply deterritorializing but deterritorialized cultural artefacts themselves. Many of their features, including coverage, schedule and patterns of production, tear apart the relation between place and television. Trans-border channels have different types of reach – from multi-territory to global – that challenge the traditional connections between national territory and broadcasting. Their schedules are also less time-specific than those of terrestrial television. The programming of national stations is based on the viewing time of a specific territory, broadcasting appropriate genres for clearly defined moments such as daytime and prime time. Global broadcasters might adapt their schedules to local times, but their programming is primarily twenty-four-hour oriented, broadcasting continuous feeds of news, documentaries or music videos. The process is particularly manifest in global news TV networks such as BBC World and CNN, which have developed facilities enabling them to break news on a worldwide basis and give round-the-clock real-time coverage of international affairs.

Many transnational TV channels are produced in more than one place. CNN has eight production centres across the world that the network can link at any time. Within a period of twenty-four hours, a CNBC channel will link up to satellite feeds in Europe, Asia and North America, depending on where the financial markets are open. Many entertainment channels mix American, regional and local material. Thus cross-border channels do not merely broadcast to a multinational audience but follow internationalized patterns of production.

Transnational TV channels are not entirely free from geographical impediment because most markets are local by definition and they must abide by national and regional regulations. To a certain extent, the practices of localization reterritorialize international feeds by adapting them to local audiences, but these channels are no longer defined by a specific place as national television used to be. Place ceases to be a 'container' to become a 'content' of corporate strategies: it can be redefined and accommodated to resources and commercial objectives.

Our final concern lies with the theoretical implications of our field of study. All the contributors agree that the cultural imperialism thesis has too many shortcomings to deal adequately with the complex reality of the contemporary international television market. In their chapter, Page and Crawley analyse the growth of the satellite sector in South Asia and its bringing of 'greater media pluralism' to the region, all but evaporating the 'initial lively concerns about Western cultural influences'. Daya Thussu shows how televisual images from India have become part of a global cultural experience, raising questions about the assumptions of the cultural imperialism paradigm on transnational media flows. Joseph Straubhaar reiterates his thesis that the technology of satellite transmission has not increased US cultural exports as much as was feared by cultural imperialists (and hoped for by American corporate executives), because people 'prefer their own culture or similar ones on television'.

We have the facts to discredit the old views on the international TV market, but have we yet built a theoretical framework suitable for the study of the new transnational media order? Can the concepts we deploy enable us to comprehend cross-border media spaces and experiences? The most pressing issue is the difficulty of stepping outside the prison-house of national perspective. The national agenda has its origin in the cultural imperialism thesis of the 1970s–80s, when its exponents believed that satellites constituted a 'threat' to the 'integrity of national cultures'[18] and wondered how nations would retain control over television 'in the face of foreign broadcasting'.[19] Cultural nationalism receded with the end of the Cold War but, as Kevin Robins and Asu Aksoy claim in Chapter 2, the literature on cross-border TV channels still displays a difficulty with disentangling itself from a nation-centric framework. They cite recently published work on media and globalization the main concern of which lies with affirming the resilience of national cultures and state power in the global age. They argue that the nation-centric discourse can no longer account for global restructuring of the media industries and the 'complex forms of cultural experience' created by transnational media. Can we find, they ask, new ways of thinking about media spaces and cultures?

Robins and Aksoy discard concepts that still draw from the national imaginary, such as 'ethnic minority', 'diaspora', 'identity' or 'transnational imagined community'.[20] They proceed to create a new conceptual space, borrowing categories from John Dewey's pragmatist social philosophy and Ulrich Beck's cosmopolitan sociology. Dewey's notion of 'experience' helps them reject collective identities and focus on the awareness and reflexivity of the human subject. For instance, they show how current analyses of migrants' television consumption place too much emphasis on the 'ethno-cultural' element and that the gratifications which transmigrants seek are 'banal' and common to most viewers.[21]

Ulrich Beck defines the cosmopolitan thesis as an attempt 'to overcome methodological nationalism and [...] build a frame of reference to analyse the new social conflicts, dynamics, and structures of Second Modernity'.[22] The German sociologist asserts that 'methodological nationalism' fails to grasp the ramifications of the process of globalization, which 'not only alters the interconnectedness of nation-states and national societies but the internal quality of the social'.[23] Sociology should break with the territorial bias of the nation-centric discourse because the 'principles of territoriality, collectivity and frontier are becoming questioned' and 'the assumed congruence of state and society is broken down'.[24]

Beck's thesis can provide a theoretical underpinning to our understanding of media transnationalism. This volume shows how television's relationship to place can no longer be taken for granted, but must be questioned and examined. In all events, national broadcasting cannot be taken as a point of reference and as the benchmark against which all types of broadcasters should be measured. Since the remapping of media spaces and markets at regional and global levels, the national is only one part of an intricate set of relationships involving many dimensions. The cosmopolitan perspective can help us think beyond a territorial and national mindset and analyse the emerging media cultures and experiences created by the transnational media. As Robins and Aksoy write, the new transnational media order will not materialize automatically, but 'we will have to think it into existence' against the 'gravity field of the national imaginary'.

Notes

1. Hilde Van den Bulck, 'Public Service Television and National Identity as a Project of Modernity: The Example of Flemish Television', *Media, Culture and Society*, 23(1) (2001), pp. 53–69. For the British case, see Paddy Scannel, *Radio, Television and Modern Life* (Oxford: Blackwell, 1996). See also David Morley and Kevin Robins, *Spaces of Identity: Global Media, Electronic Landscapes and Cultural Boundaries* (London: Routledge, 1995), pp. 10–25; David Morley, *Home Territories: Media, Mobility and Identity* (London: Routledge, 2000), pp. 105–27.

2. See, for example, Monroe E. Price, *Media and Sovereignty: The Global Information Revolution and Its Challenge to State Power* (Cambridge, MA: MIT Press, 2002).

3. For a typology of cross-border TV channels, see Jean K. Chalaby, 'Deconstructing the Transnational: A Typology of Cross-border Television Channels in Europe', *New Media and Society*, 6 (2004). See also Hamid Naficy, 'Narrowcasting in Diaspora: Middle Eastern Television in Los Angeles', in Karim H. Karim (ed.), *The Media of Diaspora* (London: Routledge, 2003), pp. 51–62.

4. Edward S. Herman and Robert W. McChesney, *The Global Media: The Missionaries of Global Capitalism* (London: Cassell, 1997).

5. In the early 2000s, they included AOL Time Warner, Walt Disney, Viacom, Bertelsmann, Vivendi Universal, Sony and News Corp. Their media

turnover averaged US$19.7 billion in 2001. Sources: company literature; European Audiovisual Observatory, *Yearbook Volume 1: Economy of the European Audiovisual Industry* (Strasbourg: European Audiovisual Observatory, 2002).

6. See, for example, Heather E. Hudson, *Global Connections: International Telecommunications Infrastructure and Policy* (New York: Van Nostrand Reinhold, 1997).

7. Dwayne Winseck, 'The WTO, Emerging Policy Regimes and the Political Economy of Transnational Communications', in Marc Raboy (ed.), *Global Media Policy in the New Millennium* (Luton: University of Luton Press, 2002), pp. 19–37.

8. John Sinclair, Elizabeth Jacka and Stuart Cunningham, 'Peripheral Vision', in John Sinclair, Elizabeth Jacka and Stuart Cunningham (eds), *New Patterns in Global Television: Peripheral Vision* (Oxford: Oxford University Press, 1996), pp. 22–3; Joseph Straubhaar, 'Distinguishing the Global, Regional and National Levels of World Television', in Annabelle Sreberny-Mohammadi, Dwayne Winseck, Jim McKenna and Oliver Boyd-Barrett (eds), *Media in Global Context: A Reader* (London: Arnold, 1997), p. 286.

9. Stig Hjarvard, 'TV News Exchange', in Oliver Boyd-Barrett and Terhi Rantanen (eds), *The Globalization of News* (London: Sage, 1998), pp. 202–26.

10. For instance, CNN and TV5 (the francophone channel) have six and eight regional feeds respectively.

11. A category of channels has achieved near global coverage with one or two blind spots. These include Euronews, Fox Kids, VH1, Globo International, Russia's ORT, the Korean Arirang, Hong Kong's Phoenix TV, and many more in News Corp's family of Fox and Sky satellite channels.

12. Néstor García Canclini, *Hybrid Cultures: Strategies for Entering and Leaving Modernity* (Minneapolis: University of Minnesota Press, 1995), p. 229.

13. John Tomlinson, *Globalization and Culture* (Cambridge: Polity Press, 1999), p. 128.

14. Martin Albrow, *The Global Age: State and Society Beyond Modernity* (Cambridge: Polity Press, 1996), p. 115. See also Morley, *Home Territories*, pp. 149–50.

15. A. Giddens, *The Consequences of Modernity* (Cambridge: Polity Press, 1990), p. 141.

16. Arjun Appadurai, 'Disjuncture and Difference in the Global Cultural Economy', in Mike Featherstone (ed.), *Global Culture: Nationalism, Globalization and Modernity* (London: Sage, 1990), pp. 295–310; Jame Lull, *Media, Communication, Culture: A Global Approach* (Cambridge: Polity Press, 2000), pp. 239–41.

17. Karim (ed.), *The Media of Diaspora*.

18. Kaarle Nordenstreng and Herbert I. Schiller, *National Sovereignty and International Communication* (Norwood, NJ: Ablex, 1979), passim.

19. Ralph Negrine, 'Introduction', in Ralph Negrine (ed.), *Satellite Broadcasting: The Politics and Implications of the New Media* (London: Routledge,

1988), p. 1. See also Herbert Schiller, 'Electronic Information Flows: New Basis for Global Domination?', in Phillip Drummond and Richard Paterson (eds), *Television in Transition* (London: BFI, 1986), pp. 11–20, and Armand Mattelart, *Multinational Corporations and the Control of Culture: The Ideological Apparatuses of Imperialism* (Brighton: Harvester Press, 1979).

20. See also Asu Aksoy and Kevin Robins, 'Thinking Across Spaces: Transnational Television from Turkey', *European Journal of Cultural Studies*, 3(3) (2000), pp. 343–65; Asu Aksoy and Kevin Robins, 'Banal Transnationalism: The Difference that Telelevision Makes', in Karim (ed.), *The Media of Diaspora*, pp. 89–104.

21. Aksoy and Robins, 'Banal Transnationalism', p. 101.

22. Ulrich Beck, 'The Cosmopolitan Society and Its Enemies', *Theory, Culture and Society*, 19(1–2) (2002), p. 18.

23. Ulrich Beck, 'The Cosmopolitan Perspective: Sociology of the Second Age of Modernity', *British Journal of Sociology*, 51(1) (2000), p. 87.

24. Ibid.

CHAPTER 2

Whoever Looks Always Finds: Transnational Viewing and Knowledge-Experience

Kevin Robins and Asu Aksoy

§ IN the discussion that follows, we are concerned with trans-nationalization in contemporary media cultures, and specifically with the question of how media audiences are now negotiating positions between national and transnational spaces. We are interested in how people – audiences – talk about their experiences of the media and think about their strategies of cultural positioning. Our discussion develops out of research that we have been conducting in London over the last three years among what are now called the 'Turkish-speaking communities' (a category that includes Turks, Kurds and Turkish Cypriots). The work that we have done has focused, to a large extent, on the media use of these populations, and particularly on the significance for Turkish-speaking migrants of transnational satellite channels (there are around a dozen now available), which seem to have made an important social and cultural difference.

The findings of our research resonate strongly with those of migration researchers who have identified the formation of new 'transnational communities'.[1] Transnational communities are made up of the 'growing number of persons who live dual lives, speaking two languages, having homes in two countries, and making a living through continuous regular contact across national borders'.[2] These migrants – transmigrants – are involved in new kinds of transnational mobility and networking, developing what we might call transcultural dispositions that confound old (national) models of minority integration or assimilation. We have found the same kind of dispositions among members of the Turkish-speaking communities in London. Focusing, as we did, on cultural practices, we became aware of an emerging transnational sensibility – transnational experiences were often associated with new kinds of mental and imaginative spaces, and with the capacity to function and think across cultural domains.[3]

Our discussion will also draw on a second project, one that had a more specific focus. It was undertaken in the context of a larger project investigating audience responses to the media coverage of the events of 11 September 2001. We were concerned with the responses and attitudes of the Turkish-speaking 'minority' in London, and were particularly interested in their transnational perspective. And we may say that, in the aftermath of the 11 September events, their sense of transnational positioning was heightened and, at the same time, ironically complicated.[4] As Turks, they were aware that they were being perceived as members of 'the Muslim world', and yet many of them had no cultural affinity with Islam and prided themselves on their secularism. And yet, at the same time, they could easily identify with Muslims elsewhere (Palestinians, for example) for *political* reasons (supporting them as victims and underdogs). And, while Turks generally identified with Western culture and the Western way of life, they also had particularly strong and heartfelt anti-American sentiments (often as a consequence of left-wing and Third Worldist political trajectories). The events of 11 September were critical, then; after them Turkish-speaking migrants found themselves situated in an even more complex field of transnational identifications and dis-identifications, alignments and disalignments.[5]

Transnational audiences are involved in a complex process of negotiating a position between familiar national moorings and new transnational connections. And what sense we make of these negoti-ations will depend on where we, as researchers, stand with respect to the known world of national media and the new, let us call them counter-national, possibilities of transnational connection and associ-ation. Our own position is very much concerned with these latter possibilities, and focuses on what might be new in the experiences of transnational viewers. We are interested in developments and pos-sibilities that move us beyond the national frame. We would situate our research agenda in the context of the cosmopolitan project addressed by Ulrich Beck.[6] Like Beck, we seek to valorize the cosmopolitan per-spective and its 'dialogic imagination', which – in sharp contrast to the monologic imagination of the national perspective – involves 'the coexistence of rival ways of life in the individual experience, which makes it a matter of fate to compare, reflect, criticise, understand, combine contradictory certainties'.[7] And, like Beck, we recognize that, in social research, the shift away from methodological national-ism will require us radically to scrutinize the naturalized categories of modern social science, which has been very much *national* social science – categories that now exist as 'zombie categories'.[8] For if one sees and thinks through a national grid, then one is always likely to see national things – and we will argue that a great deal of research on transnational phenomena does precisely this. A key issue, then, in the following discussion, will concern the kind of concepts and categories that might be used in order to perceive the cosmopolitan possibilities that are present – we believe – in the strategies of cultural negotiation being elaborated by Turkish-speaking migrants.

A cosmopolitan sociology now must be a sociology with a gerun-dive imagination, in the sense that Osip Mandelstam once evoked:

> What tense do you want to live in?
> 'I want to live in the imperative of the future passive participle, in the "what ought to be".'
> That's the way I'd like to breathe. That's what pleases me. There is such a thing as mounted, bandit-band, equestrian honour. That is why I like the splendid Latin 'gerundive' – the verb on horseback.[9]

Indeed, the gerundive is, for Mandelstam, even more than this: 'not merely "that which ought to be", but "that which ought to be praised" – *laudatura est* – that which pleases ... ' What we are interested in is what might be pleasing and praiseworthy in the transnational per-spective of Turkish-speaking migrants. Our discussion is centrally concerned with what might actually be learned from their cultural and political negotiations – concerned, that is to say, with the banal cosmopolitanism that might exist in their by now banal transnational practices.

National Logics and Transnational Prospects

The socio-spatial frame within which media cultures have generally been considered has been the national frame. Much has been written about the way in which media figured historically in the institution of 'imagined communities' – about how they have contributed to the creation of the common culture and shared public space of nation states. And, of course, media policy has been predominantly nation-centric. Over the last half century, the order of national broadcasting spaces came to seem a self-evidently good order – an almost natural form of cultural and political ordering.

Recently, we have seen a growing awareness that this idea of a unitary, national sphere can no longer be taken as a given. Todd Gitlin draws our attention to new dynamics of social and cultural segmentation, and to the consequent need to take account of the emergence of what he calls new 'public sphericules', centred on the particular interests of different social and cultural groups. The question now, he says, is whether the pluralization of publics is a good thing, or whether we should be concerned with how these diverse publics fit into the bigger public and the overall collective interest: 'A public sphere or separate public sphericules? Does the proliferation of the latter, the comfort in which they can be cultivated, damage the prospect for the former?'[10] Developments in media industries have made us more aware of what was being taken for granted in old models of cultural space – though perhaps no more than aware, and thereby in a constant state of alert about fragmentation and secession in the national culture. We may say that the national imagination persists in media cultures, albeit in a disconcerted mode.

Our argument is that the national framework still prevails in media policy, to the extent that the possibilities and potential of new transnational media practices cannot easily be discerned. When it comes to transnational migrant audiences, it seems to us that the explanatory framework that is generally mobilized is a national one. For some commentators transnational viewing is understood in terms of migrants' relation to their country of origin – in terms of diasporic connections, that is to say. For other commentators, their media practices have to be considered within the framework of the 'host' society – in terms of their status as 'ethnic minority' audiences, or as members of cultural sphericules, to use Gitlin's more catchy and contemporary terminology. The tendency is to put migrant viewers into one or the other national frame, rather than address the difference and distinctiveness of their transnational positioning. Media policy has been a resolutely national affair. And to such an extent has this been the case, we would argue, that the question of transnational audiences and viewing cannot be meaningfully taken on board as an issue. Transnational broadcasting of the kind we are looking at is something of a policy blindspot.

And what is striking, in the context of contemporary developments working against the grain of the national configuration of media cultures, is the resilience of the national imaginary and the national policy frame. In a recent volume on *Media and Globalization*, the editors introduce us to the challenges of global and transnational media, in order, it seems, then to persuade us of the virtues of state-based media systems. Silvio Waisbord and Nancy Morris argue that 'a reevaluation of the notion that globalization erodes state power is necessary in studies of media globalization', and they claim that 'it is premature to suggest that the state is withering away'.[11] They believe:

> It would be premature to announce that states have become irrelevant either as sites for political activity or as hubs for cultural solidarity. Collective identity is still fundamentally tied to the state as both a power container and an identity container. State control over citizenship not only as the organization of persons within and crossing borders but also as a primary category of self-definition remains a powerful tool that has not succumbed to globalization.[12]

James Curran and Myung-Jin Park put forward a similar argument against what they regard as the hyperbole of 'globalization theory' – against the assumption, and acceptance, that nation states and national cultures are being weakened as a consequence of transnational media flows. Communications systems are 'still in significant respects national', they argue, and we can still rely on 'the continuing power of national political authority to regulate media systems ... '[13] These intended reassurances concerning the robustness of national media systems are framed within the broader (and normative) context of belief in 'the continuing importance of the nation' ('the nation is still a very important marker of difference').[14] These defences of national media cultures mobilize the rhetoric of political pragmatism and realism, intending to convey the idea that the old national model still 'works' – and aiming to rule out the possibility that there could be any meaningful potential in new transnational or global media developments.

What we see here is a reassertion, then, of the nation state as central to media cultures and policy. The nation state is presented as the abode of order in a world now increasingly threatened by global turbulence. What is being perpetuated is the image of the nation state as container, and of the correlation of national cohesion and social order within the state's containing boundaries.[15] And what is at issue is not just a contemporary response to the perceived threats of global change, but the force of the national logic, and an inability to think beyond the national frame. In the context, here, of social science research and policy, what we have to address is the logic of what Peter Taylor calls 'embedded statism',[16] whereby the nation state has become the ontological basis upon which social research and policy have been grounded. The root issue, as Andreas Wimmer and Nina Glick Schiller observe, is that the social sciences have been 'captured by the apparent naturalness and givenness of a world divided into societies along the lines of nation-states': they are deeply informed by a principle of methodological nationalism that 'tak[es] national discourses, agendas, loyalties and histories for granted, without problematising them or making them an object of an analysis in its own right'.[17] The consequence, with respect to contemporary media developments, is an insistence on the national model – what Wimmer and Glick Schiller call the 'container model',[18] in which societies are imagined in terms of an isomorphism of culture, polity, economy, territory and a bounded social group. So powerful is it as a way of imagining the social world that, in the European context, it has become the 'natural' ontology for media futures – for a possible Europe of the regions or for a pan-European audiovisual space.[19] And so powerful, too, that no alternative configuration can be envisaged, particularly with respect to the kinds of transnational developments we are concerned with in this article. Within the national mentality, migrants can be regarded only as anomalous presences. For migrants are the ones who come and destroy the isomorphism between people, polity and nation. 'Immigrants are perceived as foreigners to the community of shared loyalty towards the state and shared rights guaranteed by the state. Transnational migrants presumably remain loyal to another state whose citizens they are and to whose sovereign they belong.'[20] Transnational developments promise only to confound the established order of cultures, societies and media.

We should qualify our argument at this point. Let us say that the question of migrancy and media has not figured significantly in mainstream debates on media cultures and policy. It has, however, been taken up by scholars and policy-makers concerned more centrally with issues of migration and of multiculturalism. But, at the same time as we qualify our argument, we want also to put more forcefully our point concerning the significance of methodological nationalism. What we want to emphasize here is the deeply embedded nature of the national imaginary, the degree to which it permeates social and cultural thought and analysis. Thus, within the field of media studies, a small sub-area of research has begun to develop around the theme of 'diasporic media'. The general assumption in this work is that migrants want to connect back to some 'homeland' – it is precisely the idea that migrants remain loyal to another state whose citizens they really are – and that new communications technologies now make such long-distance 'bonding' realizable. The belief seems to be that their ethnic identity is central to their lives, and that the consumption of transnational media is ethnically motivated (that it is about the affirmation of ethnic belonging). The point that we are making is that 'diaspora' is a category (*par excellence*) of the national imaginary, a category that subordinates the social world to the national logic. It is no surprise that the 'diasporic imagination' is isomorphic with the 'national imagination', we would say, for the ideal of 'imagined community' has been used as the basic template for capturing migrant experience and aspirations. Stuart Cunningham draws on Todd Gitlin's concept of public 'sphericules' in order to say something about the nature of 'diasporic communities'. Such communities are described as 'ethno-specific diasporic sphericules', and the argument is made that such 'ethno-specific global mediatised communities display in microcosm elements we would expect to find in "the" public sphere'.[21] Minoritarian public spheres are seen, very positively, as being 'vibrant, globalised but very specific places of self- and community-making and identity'.[22] Now the problem, as we see it, is that while he is trying to understand new kinds of global and transnational media developments, Cunningham is caught up in a conceptual grid formatted according to the national imaginary. His interest is in the processes of mediated community building and identity strengthening, in the context of the same kinds of unitary public spheres developed by nation states.[23] Much of what is new – by which we also mean what might be unforeseen – in transnational media cultures is lost as a consequence of Cunningham's a priori commitment to the diaspora template – and the all too familiar tropes of 'imagined community' – as a key to explaining the use of transnational media by global migrants.

The nation state and its logic of 'imagined community' clearly remains an imaginary institution of great power and resonance, and we should not underestimate the hold that it continues to have on hearts and minds. More particularly, in the domain of media, we can accept that it is still the case, as James Curran argues, that the national frame continues to prevail – to be the fundamental organizing principle for the cultural and political experience of most people, and in such a way as to inhibit other social, cultural and political possibilities. As to whether the nation state should continue into the future to be the central organizing principle for meditated social and cultural life, however, that is where we depart from Curran. Media industries and cultures have been changing dramatically, bringing to the world all kinds of new transnational connections, encounters and confrontations. Monroe Price points to a vast 'remapping' of media spaces, involving 'the increasing tendency toward the incapacity of the state to maintain control over the shape and mix of images', with the consequence that 'the cultural bonds and loyalties that seemed once to be within the control of the state are now less so'.[24] For those who now regularly watch MBC, Sony Asia, Zee TV, TRT-INT, TV Ahmadiyya, Al-Jazeera or the Kurdish Medya TV, we may say that a significant difference has been made with respect to cultural attachments and allegiances. These transnational channels are responding to more complex forms of cultural experience and demand that can no longer be contained within the national frame, and we regard their proliferation as potentially productive – though by no means necessarily or inevitably so. The key issue in this respect, it seems to us, is whether we can find new ways of thinking about media spaces and cultures – by which we mean ways that work against the gravity field of the national imaginary. A different kind of media order – a transnational or transcultural order – cannot come into existence automatically. We will have to think it into existence, thinking counter-nationally, thinking against the grain of the national mentality.

How might it be possible, then, to think about media cultures in a counter-national way? And how, in the particular case of Turkish-speaking migrants living in London, might we conceptualize their cultural practices and experiences so as to take into account their transnational context and aspirations? What is absolutely crucial here is how we think of the people – the individuals – with whom we are concerned. One possibility – the one pursued in cultural studies and in the 'diasporic communities' agenda – would be to consider Turkish migrants in the context of changing identities and identity politics. This is a possibility we refuse. In part, this is because such collective identities have essentially served as the ordering devices of nations and states. 'For what *is* Turkishness,' asks Marisca Milikowski, 'other than an administrative category?'[25] Identities are abstract national inventions. But more fundamentally (and not at all unrelatedly, actually), 'identity' is a category that makes no place for human consciousness, awareness, reflexivity and thoughtfulness, as Anthony Cohen has persuasively argued.[26] Where collective identity assumes some kind of homology between the individual and the group (the nation), critical research must regard the relation between individual and group as problematic, and in need of analysis.[27] There must be a thinking self beyond identity. A second possibility for how we might conceptualize our transnational social actors would be in terms of the rational and deliberative citizen, as posited in the Habermasian model of the public sphere. Again, this is not a possibility that we want to pursue. For here, too, there have been very national assumptions at work: the public sphere coincides with the imagined community; and rational communication and deliberation are intended to sustain political participation and involvement in a national frame. Also problematical in this 'public sphere' model of the social actor is its excessive rationalism (what John Peters refers to as its underlying 'Apollonian' assumption – its positing of a world of 'unity, light, clarity, sunshine, reason').[28] As such, it is again (like 'identity') a rather abstract category, remote from the complexities of actual consciousness, or consciousnesses, from the ways actual minds and thoughts operate in situated contexts, from the ways in which they go about making sense, making demands, making choices, making decisions, and all the other makings that people do.

We choose to work in a different conceptual space, and the core category that we have found most productive is that of 'experience' and the 'experiencing subject'. 'Experience' is a term that has had a marginal presence in social science research, though one can trace a slender line of development from the pragmatist social philosophy of John Dewey to more recent work in cultural anthropology, associated particularly with Victor Turner.[29] Drawing on Dewey particularly, let us briefly suggest the value of the category of 'experience' for addressing the issues with which we are here concerned. Experience starts from what people 'live through', from the multiplicity of their implications in, and engagements and interactions with, the social world. Most basically, then, it is concerned with the texture and the movement of living and of lives that are lived. 'For life is no uninterrupted march or flow,' says Dewey.[30] 'It is a thing of histories, each with its own plot, its own inception and movement towards its close, each having its own particular rhythmic movement … '[31] What is conveyed is the possibility, perhaps the inevitability or even the necessity, of discontinuities, shifts and divagations (rather than the continuity of reified 'identity'). But, of course, something has to be done with the raw materials of primary experiences; they have to be processed and organized in some way by our sense-making capacities. We are brought, that is to say, to the processes of thinking – and, at the same time, of course, to the possibility of non-thinking. Thinking is more than the abstract and general rationality predicated in the 'public sphere' model. Here it should be regarded in terms of a broader cognitive-emotional repertoire including thinking, feeling, willing and desiring,[32] and also as embedded or situated in particular social contexts, circumstances and dynamics. In reality, of course, thinking is consecutive upon experience, but inhabits it – the course of experience is constantly monitored and shaped by reflexivity. Experience is actually both 'living through' and 'thinking through'. Following Dewey,[33] we might best refer to it as 'knowledge-experience'.

Importantly, Dewey sees experiencing-thinking in terms of a temporal relation between past and present. The constant task of thought, he says,

> is to establish working connections between old and new subject matters. We cannot lay hold of the new, we cannot even keep it before our minds, much less understand it, save by the use of ideas and knowledge we already possess. But just because the new *is* new it is not a mere repetition of something already had and mastered. The old takes on new colour and meaning in being employed to grasp and interpret the new.[34]

Or, as Victor Turner puts it, experience involves us in at once 'living through', 'thinking back' and 'willing or wishing forward'.[35] Through reflective and reflexive experiencing, we are constantly involved in processes of reworking, retelling, redescribing and revisioning. There is a continuous negotiation between ascribed or acquired realities (roles, identities, ideas, thoughts) and new cognitive and imaginative possibilities. The outcome, the success or not, of these negotiations is of course contingent upon particular lived realities and circumstances. But what is clear for Dewey is the constancy of the potential for opening up new possibilities and truths. And also the belief that the creation of new insights, new understandings and new stories is an important and valuable goal in itself. In this respect, Dewey's pragmatist philosophy is strongly normative. It is predicated on respect for 'concrete human experience and its potentialities'.[36] And by 'its potentialities', Dewey means the 'enlargement and enrichment of meaning' – this is the fundamental principle at the heart of Dewey's own social demands.[37] 'Mind in its individual aspect is shown', says Dewey, 'to be the method of change and progress in the significance and values attached to things.'[38] As Dewey insisted, 'Every thinker puts some portion of an apparently stable world in peril and no one can wholly predict what will emerge in its place.'[39]

Transnational Viewing and Knowledge-Experience

We are mindful of the philosophical pitch of Dewey's discourse, and aware of the need to think his ideas through in a more sociological context. This we will now endeavour to do, to some extent at least, in the context of the experience of Turkish-speaking migrants living in London. Through the process of migration, these groups find themselves in a new space for experience. They are removed from the habitual space – the habitual national space – of their country of origin. Their relocation puts them into a more international frame of reference. And, perhaps above all, they find themselves in the new metropolitan context of London.[40] In this changed space of migration, new social and cultural possibilities are made available; there is potential space for a certain degree, at least, of social and cultural renegotiation. Of course, the fact of migration does not of itself make change inevitable – there are many migrants who are unwilling or unable to open themselves to change. We can say only that there is a new possibility space in which to articulate demands.

In focusing on experience, we are concerned with what we consider to be the crucial space of engagement between old and new: between ascribed identities and obligations (of which migrants are very conscious) and new realities encountered. Out of experience come decisions about what to retain or revitalize or revise or reject from the old; and about what to incorporate or refuse from the new. It is here that we need to be attentive to processes of thinking (and also, of course, to processes of non-thinking, for thought can be painful, and its avoidance may often seem preferable). 'Thinking goes on in trains of ideas ...' says Dewey.⁴¹ It is a simple but suggestive metaphor. Trains come in connected and consecutive sequences of carriages. They run along rails (but can also be derailed). But they take you places. And when they come to points, then they can be switched on to alternative routes. And you can change trains. This is a metaphor that allows for the momentum and inertia of the past in thought, while also allowing for the possibility of new and alternative directions and destinations. Experience and thought negotiate between known and potential trajectories, between established cultural frames and new horizons and expectations

With Dewey, we share a normative leaning. We are concerned with possibilities for the enlargement and enrichment of meaning. We are, of course, aware that many Turkish migrants may be drawn into, or opt for, monocultural, national identifications and attachments – we do not underestimate the appeal of what Michael Herzfeld calls the 'presumption of sameness', associated with myths of cultural homogeneity.⁴² But our interests are in where we might find more complex perspectives, ones that might serve to extend and diversify cultural repertoires, what we might call transnational retellings. Indeed, we consider our own work as contributing to this retelling project, seeking to draw out and put into circulation other-than-national kinds of cultural narrative from the discourses of our respondents and interviewees.

We turn now to consider how Turkish-speaking migrants talk about their relation to the media, and also, through this, their relation to the wider social and cultural contexts in which their lives are lived out. The material that we draw on here comes from focus groups conducted between 1999 and 2002; in the earlier groups the discussions are general, while the 2002 groups centre more specifically on reactions to the coverage of the events of 11 September 2001.⁴³ We will organize the material according to three broad categories: first, issues pertaining to identity; second, issues pertaining to mediated knowledge and public debate; and, finally, and more generally, issues pertaining to what we will call the relation to society and sociality.

The Relation to Identity The first agenda concerns identity, then – or, more precisely, we would say that it concerns the relation of Turkish-speaking migrants to the issue of identity. In academic discussions, the question of identity is commonly seen in terms of how migrants adjust or adapt their identities to the new context of migrant settlement. They are said to have various options: they might hold on to their Turkishness (the 'diaspora' scenario); they can take on the identity of the 'host' society (the 'integration' agenda); or they have the possibility of developing some kind of composite or hybrid identity. We are going to suggest that, for many migrants at least, something else is actually taking place. What is happening is not to do with which identity of those on offer they will opt for. It is, rather, to do with a renegotiation of their relation to both Turkishness and Britishness, and of the (national) cultural logic that positions them uncomfortably 'between cultures', as if they ought to make a choice between one or the other. The social experience here concerns a renegotiation of their relation to identity as such.

Turkish-speaking migrants now demand transnational connectivity. They expect to have Turkish, Kurdish and/or Turkish-Cypriot culture as part of their everyday lives in Britain. Access to Turkish television, particularly, is a crucial aspect of people's social and cultural lives. This is apparent in all kinds of ordinary, banal observations. Thus, one middle-aged Kurdish woman, who had recently arrived in Britain to join her husband, describes her need to be able to watch the Turkish and Kurdish channels.

> Our families are all in Turkey, our mothers, fathers, our brothers and sisters. You get curious, you wonder what is happening there. You want to know what is happening on a day-to-day basis. We try never to miss the news because we're very curious. We generally watch the news every hour. It's just as if you are in Turkey, you are curious about the daily things. (Focus Group 5)

Another participant in the same focus group – she had been in London for twelve years – confirmed this need and expectation, giving it a more general relevance beyond transnational connection to the immediate family, however:

For the last two years, Turkey's situation has been really terrible. I mean, there is a civil war going on there. People's lives are terrible, there's constant oppression ... Many people lost their relatives in the earthquake, their livelihood, everything. People are having a really tough time. Life is in a crisis. I mean, I don't watch Turkish television because I have relatives there. I watch it because I am curious about everybody there, because, however much oppression I experience there, it is still my country. However much I am here [in London], my heart is there. I mean, I will never forget there because I was brought up there. I lived there and everything that is happening there has an effect on me here. However much I lead a different life here, in my brain I live there. And it's very good that we can now watch Turkish television and Kurdish television here. (Focus Group 5)

There is considerable appreciation, then, of the fact that trans-national media can now bring Turkish actualities into the cultural space of Britain (and elsewhere in Europe, too, of course). There is clearly a strong desire for access to Turkish television culture, as well as to other cultural products and services from Turkey.

But what is this desire all about? Let us immediately say that we do not think that it is about buying into identity. It is not about Turkish media providing a means to sustain 'homeland' identities. (Keith Negus and Patria Román-Velázquez are rightly critical of the strange but common notion that 'the piece of land you are born on defines your identity and your culture, and that you carry this identity with you and take it somewhere else').[44] Watching Turkish television channels is not about reinforcing identities. What people are expressing is actually something else. If one is attentive to what is being said, then the agenda in fact turns out to be about something quite different. What the women we have just been quoting from are saying is that they simply want to continue being in touch with the everyday Turkish communicative space that has, over the years, become familiar to them. Why should they be expected to become disconnected from it simply because they happen, for now at least, to be living somewhere else?

The issue is not one of identity, then, not a matter of retreating into a Turkish 'sphericule'. Indeed, we would argue that it is actually about the *weakening* of identity. Before the coming of Turkish and Kurdish satellite TV, people felt themselves to be much more out of touch with, disconnected from, Turkish realities and affairs. And this tended to lead to the formation of fixed and frozen images and ideas of the Turkey that had been left behind. We may say that, under these earlier conditions of migrancy, identities flourished more easily – identities reflected and stood for the lack of connection to Turkish actuality. However, once satellite TV arrived, it brought with it the everyday Turkish realities. Even a young woman who migrated from Turkey when she was quite young, and who is therefore not really very familiar with the country, conveys this sense of the positive value of mediated access to Turkish actuality. She thinks that it is very good to be able to watch satellite television, 'because you too can see what's been going on in Turkey, the news ... I used to think that Turkey was a different kind of place [*başka bir yer*]. It's bringing it [Turkey] closer [*yakınlaştırıyor*]' (Focus Group 1). She is drawing attention to the demythologizing capacity of satellite TV, which counters abstract images and gives back to Turkish culture a sense of palpable reality.

The point, then, is that Turkish culture is demystified, rendered ordinary again – such that the defence of identity no longer seems the fundamental issue that it once might have. Migrants are relieved of the feeling of having to hang on defensively to a culture and identity that might be lost. Access to the Turkish media brings with it a new experience of cultural freedom. They feel free to continue to be like ordinary human beings again, getting on with their lives, as they did back in Turkey. They can take Turkish culture for granted, and so they are free to get on with other things. Once migrants no longer feel disconnected from, or deprived of, Turkish culture, they can regain a sense of ease. Satellite television affords them the chance once again to make meaningful cultural and informational choices, and to feel that they are themselves in control of the choices they make.

The Relation to Knowledge Turkish migrants want access to Turkish culture, or cultures, then, as part of their daily lives in London – to have Turkish media, that is to say, as part of the ordinary, everyday cultural repertoire available in Britain. A further aspiration, which is again an ordinary one, is to have as much information as possible about the events going on in the world that are of concern to them. This is captured by a young man who had been in Britain for eleven years, since the age of six. 'For me,' he says, it's important to know what's going on in the world, and Turkey is part of the world. [When you watch Turkish television] you know what's going on in Turkey, and you know what's going on around the world. If you just watch English television – because there are a lot of things which they don't tell you about abroad – they do, but they tell you the main stories, but they hardly ever occur in Turkey … I find it interesting [to watch Turkish television] because you know what is going on in Turkey, and you get informed about stuff that is going on abroad. (Focus Group 6)

In another focus group, one of the participants, a Turkish-Cypriot man, who had been in Britain for a very long time, emphasized the importance also of the diversity of information sources. Having access to a variety of different sources allowed him, he said, to move across channels for news that he found interesting. 'First we watch the English news,' he went on, 'then we listen to the news about our homeland, and then, when we are bored with them, we switch over to the French or German stations, or to CNN' (Focus Group 2). The ability to range transnationally across channels and programmes means being able to find information that might not be available on British television, information that may be more thorough, and which also reflects different perspectives on international events. In a group discussion that took place during the war in Kosovo, another Turkish-Cypriot man makes the following observation: 'For instance, this morning our Turkish journalists went to Albania [the Albanian part of Kosovo]. We saw this happening live, the [Turkish] soldiers came, it was nine o'clock in the morning. That's a good thing. The commander spoke, the Albanian leader gave a speech. They translated it into Turkish' (Focus Group 2).

The demand for more and varied information becomes especially significant in times of international tension and crisis, such as in the period after 11 September. This is because, during such times, there is an increased desire for more, and more diverse, sources of information – and yet we may say that this desire is complicated by a simultaneous scepticism about the reliability of these different sources. One participant – the owner, at the time, of a broken-down satellite dish – expressed this mixture of need and ambivalence thus:

When there's a news item about a world event, we always look at British television as well. We compare them both [British and Turkish].

If our satellite dish were working, we would have done the same. We would have watched the news on both, to see who says what; a bit of curiosity, a desire to catch a bit more detail about something. We think that they all report in a biased way. Maybe we're mistaken, maybe what they're reporting is correct, but we're not satisfied ... That's why we change channels, move across different channels, to have more knowledge, to be reassured, to be better informed ... As long as I'm not satisfied, I look at other channels, to see what this one is saying, what that one is saying ... It's a kind of a small-scale research on our part. (Focus Group 8)

Through this mobility across channels, these transnational viewers seek out and select different elements from the various bodies of mediated evidence, as it were, in order to build up a more coherent overall picture than any single channel puts on offer. In a discussion of the 11 September events, a Kurdish participant emphasizes the need for critical comparative research on the part of viewers:

Of course there is difference [between different television stations]. Medya TV [the main Kurdish station] concentrated on the implications of these events for the Kurds. If you wanted to see things live, then you had to watch the English media, because they are more technologically advanced. They can show things at the same time as they are happening, and they could show things from different sides. This is true for channels like CNN. If you are interested in the implications of all this for us, for Turks and Kurds, then you watch Medya TV. (Focus Group 9)

In the aftermath of 11 September, different stations and channels were constantly being compared. Transnational viewers sifted through the information available to them, constantly making evaluations of the different channels they watched, assessing news coverage in terms of a variety of criteria – factual information, direct coverage, historical perspective, political point of view, bias, censorship and so on.

This comparative positioning that migrant audiences find themselves in with respect to the media makes them particularly aware, then, of the limits of media in terms of being objective mediators of information. As a consequence of their experience of Turkish state media, Turks and Kurds are particularly sensitive to bias and manipulation in the media. 'In general, when you look at the news, they are literally propagating views,' said a Kurdish woman. 'In Turkey the media are extremely controlled. This is so clear. Maybe it's because we are looking at it from afar, from the outside. I sometimes feel I am going to explode from frustration. They [Turkish media] manipulate things' (Focus Group 9). Another participant in the same group then added that 'English media do it more professionally, more unnoticed, in ways we don't understand. In fact we are influenced by it, but we don't realize … Very smooth. The Turkish ones are more blatant' (Focus Group 9). The point, then, is that there is a generalized scepticism and caution with respect to all media – they are all seen as in some way politically biased. And because they feel that they cannot trust any television channel, they become aware that they have to do the thinking for themselves. 'When we watch [television] … we don't just accept what they're telling us,' said a politically engaged young Kurdish woman. 'The news that we get, we evaluate in our own heads. We don't think in the way things are presented to us' (Focus Group 9). And a devout Muslim man put the point to us even more forcefully (with particular reference to Turkish media): 'I ask you to take this message, write this down. There are many people who think like us. When they broadcast, they shouldn't insult us. They shouldn't try to direct us or influence us when they are presenting the news. We will decide ourselves' (Focus Group 7). These transnational migrants want to be in a position – because they feel they now have to be in a position – to make their own interpretations and form their own judgements about news events.

What we are saying, then, is that Turkish and Kurdish migrants are in a process of changing their relation to knowledge. In the transnational context in which they now live, they no longer take the national community – the British or the Turkish – as their natural frame of reference. Sonia Livingstone draws attention to the way in which the relation between social knowledge and audiences has been conceptualized in terms of an 'interpretative community'.[45] According to this model, the media are conceived as 'a resource by which, almost irrespective of their institutional purposes, meanings are circulated and reproduced according to the contextualised interests of the public. Public knowledge … becomes the *habitus*, the shared representations, the lived understandings of the community.' Livingstone recognizes that mediated knowledge is not just about recognition of the familiar and known, but also about the discovery of the new. But, even with respect to the new and unfamiliar, the point is that 'we also need a ritual model to understand such knowledge in terms of local meanings and shared assumptions'.[46] What we are saying with respect to the transnational migrants we have been looking at, is that they no longer 'belong' to such a 'interpretative community' – which is essentially conceived as a national knowledge community. The idea of 'the public' and 'the community' can no longer be taken for granted, that is to say. For them – and for those trying to understand their experiences – the container model of the public sphere no longer works. They are not buying into – and do not want to buy into – the 'set of assumptions and understandings of everyday life' that characterize national knowledge communities.[47]

Turkish-speaking migrants cannot so easily relate to a singular and consensual knowledge space. The trains of thought that they ride travel across frontiers, and pass through different cultural and value spaces. Their condition is one in which they are bound to be making comparisons between the different cultural systems to which they have access. And, in so far as they are making comparisons, they are, necessarily almost, aware of the constructedness, arbitrariness and provisionality of those systems. They are more aware of the rhetorics, the ideologies and the biases that characterize different media systems. These transnational viewers do not relate to knowledge, then, as they once might have. There is no longer the basis for the sense of trust that was grounded in the seemingly natural – and absolute – consensuality that national communities have always sought to institute. In so far as they become alienated from the world of national common sense, we may say that transnational viewers find themselves in an ironic stance to cultures, an outsider stance. If irony is, as James Fernandez and Mary Taylor Huber argue, to do with the 'questioning of established categories of inclusion and exclusion',[48] then we may say that our Turkish-speaking viewers are prone to ironic apprehension. The way in which they become distanced from both British and Turkish knowledge communities may amount to a productive kind of alienation. It can produce thinking that challenges the assumptions of imagined communities, and, more profoundly, of the container metaphor in terms of which the self-imagination of such communities is ultimately grounded and legitimated.

The Relation to Society Turkish-speaking migrants are, in different ways and to different extents, negotiating their position with reference to British culture and the British public sphere. And what we are saying is that they are not readily acceding to the two fundamental regulatory mechanisms of the nation state: that of the identity of 'the community' ('the imagined community'); and that of knowledge-ability in the restricted frame of 'the public' (the national public). In this final section of this part of our discussion, then, we want to consider what this means with respect to their relation to society and to sociality. What we will suggest is that these transnational migrants now seem to be developing a different kind of involvement with society – which could mean involvement on a different basis, or, alternatively and more radically, involvement in a different kind of social space.

To understand the position of Turkish-speaking migrants, we first need to take account of the broader historical context for the negotiations they are now making. Like all immigrant groups in Britain, Turkish-speaking populations have tried out a range of strategies to position themselves in the 'host' community. There has been a readiness, at certain junctures, to adapt to British society. This was particularly the case with the Turkish Cypriots, who arrived in Britain through the 1960s and 1970s, the high point of integrationist ideology, and who sought to 'get on' in the colonial 'motherland'. But the Turks who came as political refugees in the 1970s and 1980s were also appreciative of what they considered to be the modern/Western 'secular' values of Britain. And compared to other countries – Germany notably – they were able to get citizenship and passports relatively easy, and consequently became relatively well integrated into the British way of life.

Integration was fine for many Turkish-speaking migrants, but it was not the only coping strategy. Many Turkish-speaking migrants were also, at the same time, working hard to create their own social and cultural space. In the parts of London in which they live, they have succeeded in building a flourishing consumer culture (shops, supermarkets, cafés, hairdressers, restaurants). There is a local Turkish radio station and many (free) local Turkish newspapers. There are mosques and other institutions for those who are religious,[49] and numerous clubs and associations for those who want to be involved in anything from football to political debate. Satellite television began to arrive in the mid-1990s, and singers and performers from Turkey began to make European cities part of their circuit. Increasingly, then, it became possible to live an almost completely *'allaturca'* lifestyle in London.

In the early days of migration into Britain, things were not at all easy for the new arrivals. As Aydın Mehmet Ali says, the Turkish Cypriots struggled to 'adapt' to their new migrant context,[50] and they paid a high price for their efforts, with the younger generation failing to benefit from the British education system, and, at the same time, losing their Turkish language and their access to Cypriot culture. She refers to it in terms of a dreadful experience of 'exclusion, invisibility and silencing', which she attributes to the unfortunate combination of the Cypriots' own eagerness to become part of British society and 'the racist structures and attitudes in British society'. The institutions and attitudes of the 'host' culture did not make integration an easy matter for Turkish-speaking migrants. We may say that 'British society' expected migrants to integrate, but at the same time there was the sense that 'they' could never really become like 'us'. As one long-settled Turkish-Cypriot man put it to us, 'it doesn't matter how much your ways are close to the English ways, at a certain stage you are reminded that you are not English'; migrants are always 'reminded that they will never be English or British in the true sense' (Interview, Haringey, 26 May 2000). The fundamental problem was with the 'either/or' nature of the integrationist logic (you are either British, or Turkish). A whole discourse and practice of social work developed around the 'support and stress of states of mind' of immigrants, where states of mind included 'questions of identity, self-image, world-view and value systems'.[51] A frequent trope, right up to the 1980s, was that of 'living between cultures' – of being 'caught between' conflicting cultural worlds, and of not being able to properly 'fit' in either.[52] We may say that the logic of national integration projected impossible demands on immigrant populations, creating a damaging and disabling cultural environment.

By the 1990s, through the course of long accumulated experience, the situation of many Turkish migrants improved in significant ways. This was in part a consequence of much broader shifts in the way in which culture and ethnicity were being debated. Actually, Turkish-speaking migrants were able to benefit from the cultural-political struggles of black and Asian activists in Britain, who had considerably undermined the hegemony of integrationist discourses. Even the elderly Turkish-Cypriot man we quoted earlier was tuned in to the new discourses of multiculturalism. 'There are Chinese groups,' he says, 'Greeks, Indians and Bangladeshis, and they are trying to keep their identity. I think we can only do that by respecting each other ... We can only get along with each other by respecting that, our views and ways, and live as a multicultural community' (Interview, Haringey, 26 May 2000). New possibilities have developed for how Turkish-speaking migrants can relate to British society. When asked how much she felt part of British society, a Turkish-Cypriot woman in her forties, born in London, speaking in English, and able to speak only a little Turkish answers clearly: 'I don't feel part of it at all. It's funny because you live in it, but at work I sort of mix more with black colleagues. I have a few English friends, but again I would identify with them more politically – so we would think along the same political lines, rather than over the things I do too. I don't have that many friends from outside, that is from English culture' (Focus Group 4). There is a possibility now for her to distance herself somewhat from Englishness – 'we don't associate ourselves with the English community, we are not English, and I think it is an alienation from what we perceive as being British, the Empire and all that' – to connect with different (i.e. post-colonial) kinds of British people, and also to reassert her Cypriot affiliations. By the 1990s, the language of 'in-betweenness' can be used in a more positive, and even joking, way. 'We are going to coin a term like English Turks,' says one young woman, 'and try to walk in between. There will be a new kind of society of English Turks, there will be English and Turkish in us. That is how we will be able to express ourselves' (Focus Group 3). Elsewhere, a young Turkish man refers to himself as a 'London Turk' (*Londralı Türk*) (Focus Group 6). Through the 1990s, then, the language of multiculturalism and cultural hybridity made it easier for Turkish migrants to renegotiate their relation to British society.

The discourse of multiculturalism and hybridity was, in certain respects, productive, but it was a limited discourse.[53] It retained a nation-centric framework, and still positioned Turkish-speaking (and other) migrants in a 'minority' context. What we want to argue is that, from the late 1990s, a further transformation has begun to occur, beyond the hybridity paradigm. A new relation to society has begun to develop as a consequence of both the embeddedness now of Turks in London and the possibilities inherent in new transnational connectivity. Turkish-speaking migrants feel that they are grounded and involved in British society. Many work in local authorities, the health service, advocacy groups, social work and so on, and feel socially committed. Among Turkish-speaking migrants, we would say that there is a considerable level of engagement, in both local and national political issues (these are people with political pasts – many of them had to leave Turkey as a consequence of political involvement). As one man involved in a community association put it, 'Where we live is England, London, and everybody is involved in something, according to their capacities' (Focus Group 2). London is where they have chosen to make their lives. At the same time, transnational connections have massively proliferated. Turkish-speaking migrants find it easy to travel to Turkey, and they are also in touch with friends and relatives in other European countries (there are now Turks and Kurds living in all European countries). Many Turkish, Cypriot and Kurdish businesses are also transnational in their operations (the import of consumer goods from Turkey, the export of textiles manufactured in London sweatshops, travel agencies and tourism). And, of course, the availability of satellite television, cheap international phone calls, and Internet connections have also made transnational connections relatively easy. All of this means that Turkey and Europe figure to a great extent in the lives of Turkish-speaking migrants. As well as becoming embedded in London, then, they are also extending their horizons of experience and involvement.

And this combined development is, we think, producing a new kind of relation to society. Put simply, their thinking is now moving beyond the frame of national society, beyond the agenda according to which 'minority' affairs have hitherto been conducted, beyond the logic of social integration, that is to say. As Ulrich Beck has observed, people increasingly 'live and think transnationally, that is combine multiple loyalties and identities in their lives', with the consequence that 'the paradigm of societies organised within the framework of the nation-state inevitably loses contact with reality'.[54] Turkish-speaking migrants provide a particular example of what the changed reality may be turning out to be. We should consider carefully how Turks are reformulating their sociality. We would say that there are two aspects to what is happening. First, they insist on being involved in British society – they have chosen to live in Britain – and they want, moreover, to be involved now on revised terms. What they are putting forward is a complex demand that argues for the acceptance of their difference, but then immediately insists on the release of difference from the discourse of identity. Their difference, that is to say, is not a reflection of their nationality or identity (of some essential 'Turkishness'), but should be considered in terms of their particular social and political experiences, expectations and ideas. And, second, Turkish-speaking migrants want it to become the case that 'the social' should no longer be confined to British society. They are invoking what we might call a transnational imagination of the social and of sociality. James Anderson has noted how transnational developments have increasingly 'upset the familiar dichotomy between "foreign" and "domestic" affairs'.[55] This is precisely the experience of Turkish-speaking migrants. The society they see themselves living in does not stop at Dover or Heathrow. What is 'outside' is also part of their everyday experiential world. They are insisting, that is to say, on the continuum between the British space and the space beyond. The demand is for a social paradigm in line with the reality of those who now 'live and think transnationally'. Turkish-speaking migrants are now, at the beginning of the twenty-first century, seeking to renegotiate their relation to society. It is a radical and interesting situation. And we would argue that it shows how much the thinking of transnational migrants is ahead of that of their more sedentary British national neighbours.

Conclusion: Towards the Enlargement of Meaning

What we have been arguing in this chapter is that there is something important to be learned from the experiences of transnational migrants. We have consciously distanced ourselves from the culturalist discourses that consider migrant experiences in terms of 'diasporic communities' and 'ethnic identities'. As a starting point for thinking about what Turkish-speaking migrants think and want, we have chosen to use the category of 'experience', rejecting the categories of 'identity' and of the 'rational individual'. We propose that 'experience' is the most productive point of departure. We have been concerned with how their experiences provoke these migrants to *think* – concerned, that is to say, with their knowledge-experience. Following Dewey, what we have taken as the primary assumption is the 'mind' or 'intelligence' that is central to all human experience (migrants included). This intelligence, as Dewey maintains, is what provides the 'funding of meanings and significance, a funding which is both a product of past inquiries and knowings and the means of enriching and controlling the subject-matters of subsequent experiences'.[56]

In listening to what Turkish-speaking migrants have to say, we have wanted particularly to be attentive to what might be new or innovative in their transnational experience. Our concern, again following Dewey, has been with what they might contribute to the enlargement and enrichment of meaning – for all of us. Jacques Rancière – in his book about the 'ignorant schoolmaster', Joseph Jacotet – points to something simple, but very important, about the way in which minds and intelligences work. 'Whoever looks always finds,' he and Jacotet observe. 'He doesn't necessarily find what he was looking for, and even less what he was supposed to find. But he finds something new to relate to the thing that he already knows.'[57] We would say that this looking and finding process is precisely what can happen in the process of transnational viewing. What seems to us to be significant in the knowledge-experience of our Turkish-speaking migrants is precisely this relating of something new to what is already known – what emerges through experiences of comparison.

Ulrich Beck has referred to Nietzsche's characterization of the modern era as 'the Age of Comparison' – an era in which 'the various cultures of the world were beginning to interpenetrate each other', and involving a logic according to which 'ideas of every culture would be side by side, in combination, comparison, contradiction and competition in every place and all the time'.[58] This principle of comparison provides the grounding principle for what Ulrich Beck calls the 'dialogic imagination', characteristic of the cosmopolitan perspective. In contrast to the monologic national perspective, it represents 'an alternative imagination, an imagination of alternative ways of life and rationalities, which include the otherness of the other. It puts the negotiation of contradictory cultural experiences into the centre of activities …'[59] It is precisely this kind of negotiation that is to be found in the reflections of our transnational migrants. What can be discerned, we would say, is the dialogical imagination in a banal, everyday articulation.

Notes

1. Alejandro Portes, Luis E. Guarnizo and Patricia Landolt (eds), 'Transnational Communities', special issue of *Ethnic and Racial Studies*, 22(2) (1999); Alejandro Portes (ed.), 'New Research and Theory on Immigrant Transnationalism', special issue of *Global Networks*, 1(3) (2001).

2. Portes et al., 'Transnational Communities', p. 217.

3. Asu Aksoy and Kevin Robins, 'Thinking Across Spaces: Transnational Television from Turkey', *European Journal of Cultural Studies*, 3(3) (2000), pp. 343–65; Kevin Robins, 'Au-delà de la communauté imaginée? Les médias transnationaux et les migrants turcs en Europe', *Réseaux*, 107 (2001), pp. 19–39; Kevin Robins and Asu Aksoy, 'From Spaces of Identity to Mental Spaces: Lessons from Turkish-Cypriot Cultural Experience in London', *Journal of Ethnic and Migration Studies*, 27(4) (2001), pp. 685–711; Kevin Robins and Asu Aksoy, '"Abschied von Phantomen": Transnationalismus am Beispiel des türkischen Fernsehens', in Brigitta Busch, Brigitte Hipfl and Kevin Robins (eds), *Bewegte Identitäten: Medien in transkulturellen Kontexten* (Klagenfurt: Drava Verlag, 2001), pp. 71–110; Asu Aksoy and Kevin Robins, 'Banal Transnationalism: The Difference that Television Makes', in Karim H. Karim (ed.), *The Media of Diaspora: Mapping the Global* (London: Routledge, 2003), pp. 89–104.

4. Asu Aksoy, 'Some "Muslims" within: Watching Television in Britain after September 11', in Peter van der Veer and Shoma Munshi (eds), *Media, War and Terrorism: Responses from the Middle East and Asia* (London: Routledge Curzon, 2004).

5. The first project to which we refer was conducted within the ESRC Transnational Communities Programme – Award L214252040, 'Negotiating Spaces: Media and Cultural Practices in the Turkish Diaspora in Britain, France and Germany'. The second was a multi-agency project, 'After September 11: TV News and Transnational Audiences', directed by Marie Gillespie, and funded by the Economic and Social Research Council, the Independent Television Commission, the Broadcasting Standards Commission, the Open University and the British Film Institute.

6. Ulrich Beck, 'The Cosmopolitan Perspective: Sociology in the Second Age of Modernity', in Steven Vertovec and Robin Cohen (eds), *Conceiving Cosmopolitanism: Theory, Context, and Practice* (Oxford: Oxford University Press, 2002), pp. 61–85; Ulrich Beck, 'The Cosmopolitan Society and Its Enemies', *Theory, Culture and Society*, 19(1–2) (2002), pp. 17–44.

7. Beck, 'The Cosmopolitan Society and Its Enemies', p. 18.

8. Ibid., p. 24.

9. Osip Mandelstam, 'Journey to Armenia', in *Osip Mandelstam: Selected Essays* (Austin: University of Texas Press, 1977), p. 204.

10. Todd Gitlin, 'Public Sphere or Public Sphericules?', in Tamar Liebes and James Curran (eds), *Media, Ritual and Identity* (London: Routledge, 1998), p. 173.

11. Nancy Morris and Silvio Waisbord, 'Introduction: Rethinking Media Globalization and State Power', in Nancy Morris and Silvio Waisbord (eds), *Media and Globalization: Why the State Matters* (Lanham, MD: Rowman and Littlefield, 2001), p. ix.

12. Ibid., pp. xv–xvi.

13. James Curran and Myung-Jin Park, 'Beyond Globalization Theory', in James Curran and Myung-Jin Park (eds), *De-Westernizing Media Studies* (London: Routledge, 2000), pp. 11, 14.

14. Ibid., pp. 15, 12.

15. See R. E. Pahl, 'The Search for Social Cohesion: From Durkheim to the European Commission', *Archives Européennes de Sociologie*, 32(2) (1991), pp. 345–60.

16. Peter J. Taylor, 'Embedded Statism and the Social Sciences: Opening up to New Spaces', *Environment and Planning A*, 28(11) (1996), pp. 1917–28.

17. Andreas Wimmer and Nina Glick Schiller, 'Methodological Nationalism and Beyond: Nation-State Building, Migration and the Social Sciences', *Global Networks*, 2(4) (2002), p. 304.

18. Ibid., p. 307.

19. Kevin Robins, 'Imagined Community and Cultural Identity in Europe: Television and the European Cultural Space', in Karin Liebhart, Elisabeth Menasse and Heinz Steinert (eds), *Fremdbilder – Feindbilder – Zerrbilder: Zur Wahrnehmung und diskursiven Konstruktion des Fremden* (Klagenfurt: Drava Verlag, 2002), pp. 255–67.

20. Wimmer and Glick Schiller, 'Methodological Nationalism and Beyond', p. 309.

21. Stuart Cunningham, 'Popular Media as Public "Sphericules" for Diasporic Communities', *International Journal of Cultural Studies*, 4(2) (2001), p. 134.

22. Ibid., p. 133.

23. Gitlin himself alerts us to the dangers of the 'unity image' in what is, after all, the metaphor of the 'public sphere'. Gitlin, 'Public Sphere', p. 168.

24. Monroe E. Price, *Media and Sovereignty: The Global Information Revolution and Its Challenge to State Power* (Cambridge, MA: MIT Press, 2002), p. 26.

25. Marisca Milikowski, 'Learning about Turkishness by Satellite: Private Satisfactions and Public Benefits', in Karen Ross and Peter Playden (eds), *Black Marks: Minority Ethnic Audiences and Media* (Aldershot: Ashgate, 2001), p. 126.

26. Anthony P. Cohen, *Self-Consciousness: An Alternative Anthropology of Identity* (London: Routledge, 1994).

27. Ibid., p. 119.

28. John Durham Peters, 'Distrust of Representation: Habermas on the Public Sphere', *Media, Culture and Society*, 15(4) (1993), p. 563.

29. John Dewey, *Experience and Nature* (New York: Dover, 1958/1929); John Dewey, *Art as Experience* (New York: Perigee, 1980/1934); Victor W. Turner and Edward M. Bruner (eds), *The Anthropology of Experience* (Urbana: University of Illinois Press, 1986).

30. Dewey, *Art as Experience*, pp. 35–6.

31. Ibid.

32. Victor W. Turner (1986) 'Dewey, Dilthey, and Drama: An Essay in the Anthropology of Experience', in Turner and Bruner, *The Anthropology of Experience*, p. 35.

33. John Dewey, 'Experience, Knowledge and Value', in Paul Arthur Schilpp (ed.), *The Philosophy of John Dewey*, second edition (La Salle, IL: Open Court, 1951), p. 564.

34. Dewey, *Experience and Nature*, pp. viii–ix.

35. Victor W. Turner, *From Ritual to Theatre: The Human Seriousness of Play* (New York: Performing Arts Journal Publications, 1982), p. 18.

36. Dewey, *Experience and Nature*, p. 39.

37. Ibid., p. 6.

38. Ibid., p. xiv.

39. Ibid., p. 222.

40. On the significance of the urban frame, see Kevin Robins, 'Becoming Anybody: Thinking against the Nation and through the City', *City*, 5(1) (2001), pp. 77–90.

41. Dewey, *Art as Experience*, p. 37.

42. Michael Herzfeld, *Cultural Intimacy: Social Poetics in the Nation-State* (New York: Routledge, 1997), pp. 59, 60.

43. The composition, location and date of Focus Groups are as follows: Focus Group 1: Islington, 29 March 1999 – held at a youth project office with Turkish and Kurdish teenagers; Focus Group 2: Enfield, 18 May 1999 – held at a local Turkish-Cypriot Association. The participants were all middle-aged men who had been living in London for many years; Focus Group 3: Hackney, 3 November 1999 – held at a primary school in Hackney. The participants were all young Turkish, Kurdish and Turkish-Cypriot men and women, who are part of a drama project; Focus Group 4: Haringey, 22 November 1999 – held at a local Turkish Cypriot Women's Association. The participants were all Turkish-Cypriot women in their late thirties and early forties who had either been born in Britain or came quite early in their lives; Focus Group 5: Tottenham, 1 December 1999 – held at a Kurdish Community Centre. The participants were Kurdish men and women who had arrived in Britain relatively recently; Focus Group 6: Hackney, 11 December 1999 – held at a community centre known for its left-wing politics. The participants were all young Turkish and Kurdish men and women; Focus Group 7: Hackney, 16 December 1999 – held at a Turkish mosque. The participants were all men, and of different ages; Focus Group 8: Islington, 5 February 2002 – held in a family home. The participants were Turkish Alevis, with left-wing affiliations;

Focus Group 9: Hackney, 15 March 2002 – held at a Kurdish Community Centre, known for its political engagement. The participants were young Kurdish men and women.

44. Keith Negus and Patria Román-Velázquez, 'Belonging and Detachment: Musical Experience and the Limits of Identity', *Poetics*, 30 (2002), p. 138.

45. Sonia Livingstone, 'Mediated Knowledge: Recognition of the Familiar, Discovery of the New', in Jostein Gripsrud (ed.), *Television and Common Knowledge* (London: Routledge, 1999), p. 96.

46. Ibid., p. 97.

47. Ibid.

48. James W. Fernandez and Mary Taylor Huber, 'The Anthropology of Irony', in James W. Fernandez and Mary Taylor Huber (eds), *Irony in Action: Anthropology, Practice, and the Moral Imagination* (Chicago, IL: University of Chicago Press, 2001), p. 9.

49. Talip Küçükcan, *Politics of Ethnicity, Identity and Religion: Turkish Muslims in Britain* (Aldershot: Ashgate, 1999).

50. Aydın Mehmet Ali, *Turkish Speaking Communities and Education – No Delight* (London: FATAL Publications, 2001), p. 10.

51. Verity Saifullah Kahn, 'Introduction', in Verity Saifullah Kahn (ed.), *Minority Families in Britain: Support and Stress* (London: Macmillan, 1979), pp. 1–11.

52. James L. Watson (ed.), *Between Two Cultures: Migrants and Minorities in Britain* (Oxford: Basil Blackwell, 1977).

53. Floya Anthias, 'New Hybridities, Old Concepts: The Limits of "Culture"', *Ethnic and Racial Studies*, 24(4) (2001), pp. 619–41.

54. Beck, 'The Cosmopolitan Perspective', p. 62.

55. James Anderson, 'Questions of Democracy, Territoriality and Globalisation', in James Anderson (ed.), *Transnational Democracy: Political Spaces and Border Crossings* (London: Routledge, 2002), p. 7.

56. Dewey, 'Experience, Knowledge and Value', p. 520.

57. Jacques Rancière, *The Ignorant Schoolmaster: Five Lessons in Intellectual Emancipation* (Stanford, CA: Stanford University Press, 1991), p. 33.

58. Beck, 'The Cosmopolitan Society and Its Enemies', p. 18.

59. Ibid.

CHAPTER 3

The Quiet Invention of a New Medium: Twenty Years of Transnational Television in Europe

Jean K. Chalaby

§ TRANSNATIONAL television has attracted less attention in Europe than almost anywhere else in the world. In South Asia, the development of networks such as Star TV and Zee TV has accompanied a revolution in broadcasting and sweeping cultural changes (Chapters 6 and 7). In the Middle East, satellite channels such as MBC (now Al-Arabiya) have raised the standards of news reporting and the independent voice of Al-Jazeera has unsettled governments (see Chapter 4). In Europe, cross-border channels have yet to make such an impact on culture and the media. After twenty years of satellite television, the European TV market remains fragmented and dominated by national broadcasters. Until the 1990s, the outlook of transnational channels was bleak and few observers believed they would survive much longer.

This chapter retraces the history of trans-border channels since the beginning of satellite television in Europe in 1982. This history can be divided into two periods, starting with the pioneering years that stretch throughout the 1980s. The early international TV channels faced seemingly insurmountable technological, economic and programming difficulties. The satellite technology was in its infancy, too few households subscribed to cable networks and those that did had access to international programming that was unadapted to their tastes. The decade witnessed many casualties and most ventures had a short life span. Channels were taken off air or sold to new investors, sometimes to re-emerge in a new format or under a different name.

The prospects of the industry improved in the mid-1990s. The fast increase of homes having access and subscribing to satellite and cable television services expanded the reception universe of transnational channels, alongside the collapse of communism in Central and Eastern Europe, which opened out new markets eastwards. Communication satellites became more powerful, capable of carrying many more channels and delivering them directly to viewers, heralding the era of direct-to-home broadcasting. The digitization of cable and satellite platforms opened up space for cross-border channels that were frequently kept out by cable operators. The European directive Television without Frontiers removed the lingering national barriers to the international transmission of TV signals. In addition, the broadcasters who survived the early years had acquired experience and knew better how to deal with a multinational audience. They began to adapt their international feeds to European cultural diversity, leading to the emergence of practices of localization ranging from multilingual services to local programming inserts.

This chapter reviews these developments and argues that transnational TV channels will have a growing impact in Europe. International broadcasters' latest strategy, the setting up of international TV networks, is innovative and particularly apt at dealing with the local and the global. Slowly but surely, they have been inventing a new medium that might one day have the potential to dominate European broadcasting.

The Pioneering Years

From the early 1980s to the early 1990s, the emergent international broadcasters found the shift from a national to an international context more difficult than they had foreseen. The fledgling industry was in the grip of a series of problems that included poor satellite transmissions, expensive home reception equipment, governments reluctant to grant access to their market, and a reception universe that was too small to attract advertisers and cover costs. It was also searching for a workable model of international broadcasting and a suitable way of addressing a multinational audience. It was struggling with issues regarding programme production, scheduling, marketing, presentation and a whole range of linguistic problems from translation to multilingual television services.[1] Facing such difficulties, many of the early cross-border channels were ventures of short duration, either disappearing altogether or relaunched in a new format by a new proprietor.

The first satellite channel was launched in April 1982 and operated under the name of Satellite Television, after the company that launched it. It transmitted from the OTS, the first communications satellite launched by Eutelsat, the inter-governmental satellite operator founded five years earlier. The channel was taken up by cable operators only in the few countries where commercial television had been authorized. By the summer of 1983, the company was bought by Rupert Murdoch, who was keen to take his press empire in new directions.[2] He renamed it Sky Channel and in order to increase viewing on the continent he promptly developed an international programme schedule including shows from Germany, Belgium and the Netherlands. By 1987, more than half of Sky's programming was of European origin.[3] Despite reaching a record 15 million homes across Europe the following year, the channel was accumulating debts and the media mogul was forced to consider scaling down his European ambitions. In June, he announced that he was pulling back from Europe and retracted Sky to the British market.[4]

As Murdoch was about to leave the European market, the ITV franchise holders (with the exception of Thames Television), and Richard Branson, the British entrepreneur, launched Super Channel to European audiences on 30 January 1987. The channel, intended to be a showcase for ITV programming, soon ran into trouble when it became clear that English-language programmes were not as popular as expected with European audiences.[5] The channel modified its plans and introduced German and Dutch programmes, only to confuse viewers further. Constant meddling with the schedule prevented Super Channel from building an audience, attracting advertisers and turning a profit.[6] In March 1988, the ITV companies pulled out of the channel, which was progressively phased out by successive owners.

Among the cross-border channels launched in the 1980s and early 1990s, approximately fifteen did not last more than a few years.[7] The satellite technology attracted newcomers such as British Telecom and WH Smith (the UK newsagent) who treated international television as their entry ticket into the broadcasting industry. Their channels, which included WH Smith's Lifestyle and British Telecom's Star Channel, never found an audience and closed down following heavy losses.

Among the other ill-fated ventures were TEN – The Entertainment Network (1984–85), Robert Maxwell's Mirror Vision and Premiere (1986–89), and the Arts Channel (1988).[8]

The development of satellite television was a mixed blessing for public service broadcasters. In the 1980s, they were adjusting to the recent emergence of commercial rivals following the break-up of state broadcasting monopolies in several European countries. On the one hand, satellite technology was being recognized as an exciting new medium that would provide an opportunity to disseminate the 'best' of European television to the 'widest possible European audience'.[9] It was also perceived as a fresh threat to their position; they feared, in particular, that the technology would allow commercial broadcasters to rewrite industry standards.[10] Thus the early interest of public service broadcasters in satellite technology was prompted by their enthusiasm for a new technology as well as their concerns about competition from the commercial sector.

The current doyen of transnational TV channels in Europe is the francophone TV5, launched in 1984 by five public television channels from France, Belgium and Switzerland. SAT3 quickly followed, launched by three public broadcasters from Germany (ZDF), Austria (ORF) and German-speaking Switzerland (SRG) in December of that year.[11] These channels did not develop new programming but scheduled recycled material from their backers.

Public broadcasters' most ambitious projects were organized under the auspices of the European Broadcasting Union (EBU). Eurikon, their first project, was an experiment carried out on a broadcaster-to-broadcaster basis for five non-consecutive weeks in 1982.[12] Each of five EBU members, the IBA (UK), RAI (Italy), ORF (Austria), NOS (Netherlands) and ARD (then West Germany) transmitted to fifteen countries in turn for a week. They tested the pan-European appeal of their programmes, tried to identify a 'pan-national editorial viewpoint' for their news services, and experimented with different methods of communicating simultaneously with a multilingual audience.[13]

Following the success of the experiment, six EBU members set up a fund and feasibility study and the Dutch government and several European institutions offered support.[14] After lengthy negotiations and deliberations at the EBU, five broadcasters from the Netherlands (NOS), Germany (ARD), Italy (RAI), Ireland (RTE) and Portugal (RTP) launched Europa on 5 October 1985.

Europa (based at the NOS studios in Hilversum), started with a handicap since most of the heavyweight EBU members refused to get involved. The French Antenne 2 and FR3 and the German ZDF feared that it would jeopardize their own TV5 and SAT3. Likewise, the BBC stayed away because it was not convinced of the quality of the project, it was involved with ITV's Super Channel and had plans of its own.[15] The absence of a British broadcaster was a major draw-back in the channel's attempt to reach a European audience. To make matters worse, Europa was moulded in the public broadcasting ethos of its backers, it did not pay enough attention to audience tastes and broadcast too many highbrow programmes. The running costs were high (vast sums were spent on translation), the channel reached too few homes and failed to attract any significant advertising revenue. The Dutch broadcaster, unwilling to carry on assuming the financial costs, put its colleagues out of their misery and switched off the signal on 27 November 1986, thirteen months after its launch.[16]

Europa had specific difficulties but the débâcle was symptomatic of a difficult period for satellite television. At the root of the problem was the size of the reception universe that international TV channels tried to reach. Only 18 million European households were connected to cable in 1989, too small a figure to build a viable audience for advertisers.[17] During the 1980s, the record distribution was reached by Sky Channel, with 15 million connections, closely followed by Super Channel (13.5 million homes), but the other channels never broke the 5 million mark.[18]

Another difficulty for cross-border channels was gaining access to foreign markets. Since the implementation of the Television with-out Frontiers directive in 1991, channels can broadcast throughout Europe holding a single licence, because European Union member states are no longer allowed to stop international TV transmissions from other member states.[19] Before this ground-breaking piece of legislation, international TV channels needed to go through a lengthy process of authorization with local authorities. Government officials rarely knew how to deal with these requests and passed them on from one ministry to another. Once the appropriate department had been pinned down and assuaged, the consent of the local Post, Telegraph and Telephony was also needed to downlink the signal.[20] The next task was to find cable operators and secure access on their networks. The cable industry was fragmented and several partners were necessary to cover the main areas of a territory. Furthermore, the capacity of analogue networks was limited and cable providers were in the position of cherry-picking channels they wished to carry. Foreign-language channels were often dropped because they were seen as least relevant to their audience.[21]

The problems of cross-border TV channels were compounded by the limits of the pan-European advertising market. Satellite television lacked a sizeable – and measurable – audience that would have tempted advertisers to transfer some of their budget to transnational television. The small number of multinationals that might have been interested in running international campaigns usually devolved marketing to their local affiliates, which passed on the advertising budget to a local agency.[22] Thus the pool of advertisers was limited to a few brands sold uniformly across the continent that could benefit from a regional advertising campaign. Industry experts openly questioned the viability of the transnational television industry on the grounds that pan-European advertising was 'never more than a chimera'.[23]

By the early 1990s, the pan-European TV industry seemed to be doomed. Cross-border channels lacked an audience, did not attract nearly enough advertising revenue and struggled to put together a coherent schedule. The favoured business model for satellite TV operators was shifting from international feeds to national channels, and the two industry leaders were clearly heading in this direction. Once Sky retreated to the UK, success quickly followed and the company was turning a profit by March 1992.[24] Canal Plus dominated the pay-TV market in France and was expanding in Europe by establishing local channels with ad hoc partners in selected markets. The most hyped transnational channel of the time, MTV, was assailed by emerging local competitors such as France's MCM, Germany's VIVA and Italy's Videomusic.[25] Industry analysts agreed that transnational satellite television had little prospect on the continent. They were openly sceptical when a group of EBU members launched Euronews on 1 January 1993 and continued to predict the death of transnational television as late as 1998.[26] Despite the obituaries, cross-border TV channels managed to survive – and eventually prosper – in the competitive European market.

The Coming of Age of Satellite Television in Europe

By the mid-1990s, the pan-European TV industry had matured and consolidated. Newcomers who had tried to enter the television industry via the pan-European route had left the market. The well-established broadcasters who had underestimated the difficulties of international television had either retreated to their home markets or learned from their mistakes and redesigned their channels. The players who survived the early years acquired expertise in transnational broadcasting and were more confident about the future. These included CNN, which had arrived in Europe in September 1985, and MTV, which followed suit two years later. Sky News, one of the four British channels Murdoch launched in 1988, was made freely available in Europe the same year. In 1989, News International launched Eurosport in partnership with sixteen members of the EBU as the American documentary network, Discovery, crossed the Atlantic.

Public service broadcasters continued to launch international channels, adding to TV5 and SAT3. Arte, a cultural channel, went on air in 1991 following a Franco-German treaty. Two years later, Euronews was started by eleven members of the EBU in answer to CNN's dominance of international news during the first Gulf War. In 1995, the BBC replaced BBC TV Europe (launched in June 1987) with BBC Prime, a subscription-based entertainment channel, and BBC World, a news channel supported by advertising.

Despite the efforts of European public broadcasters, the 1990s were characterized by the arrival of American commercial broadcasters. Cartoon Network, operated by Turner Broadcasting System (a Time Warner subsidiary), arrived in Europe in 1994. Two years later, CNBC (Dow Jones and NBC) and Bloomberg started two European financial and business news channels. Fox Kids, controlled by Disney since 2001, and VH1 (Viacom's second music television network with MTV) also began in 1996. National Geographic started in 1997, and the following year Universal Television Network introduced Studio Universal and 13th Street in the largest markets in Europe.

These channels have had considerably more success than their predecessors. After years of deficit, most of them are showing reasonable returns on investment. The key factor was that the number of households connected to cable and satellite finally became large enough to provide a viable market for cross-border TV channels.

In 2001, the number of households connected to cable and satellite reached 75.7 million homes in the European Union, representing 51.7 per cent of all TV households.[27] The collapse of communist regimes in Central and Eastern Europe in the late 1980s brought an additional 31.3 million connected households by 2001.[28] The total 2001 figure of 107 million homes represents a fourfold increase compared with the 1991 figure of 25.1 million cabled homes.[29]

Cross-border TV channels have also benefited from the development of a new technology in the 1990s: direct-to-home (DTH) satellite broadcasting. The Astra 1A, launched in December 1988, was the first satellite powerful enough to allow reception with small dishes and low-cost equipment. DTH has opened whole new markets for satellite channels in countries that were poorly cabled, notably in Southern and Central/Eastern Europe. It has also given access to many more channels to viewers in cabled areas, adding the choice of satellite platforms to existing cable networks. DTH has grown faster than cable since 1988, to represent 39 per cent of all connections in 2001, up from 35 per cent of all connections in 1999.[30]

The distribution of satellite channels further accelerated with the digitization of cable and satellite networks in the late 1990s. Signal compression freed up much needed space on these networks, which were able to offer a far greater variety of channels to subscribers. As a result, cable and satellite operators no longer squeezed transnational channels out of their platforms. An added advantage of signal compression is that many more channels can fit into the transponders of communications satellites, lowering the cost of international transmission by a factor of six.

The present over-capacity in the satellite industry has brought costs even lower. There are approximately forty communications satellites with their footprint covering a part of Europe, more than is needed by the television industry and telecom companies. The two industry leaders, SES Global, which operates the Astra fleet, and Eutelsat, have respectively fourteen and twenty spacecraft in service. Increased transponder capacity gives them the space to broadcast in excess of a thousand television channels each.[31]

The current size of the reception universe is significant for two reasons. It has enabled the leading cross-border TV channels to develop their reach across Europe. Over recent years, their distribution has grown from an average of 33.3 million to 47.8 million TV households, and the two leading pan-European channels, Eurosport and MTV, currently stand just below the threshold of 100 million households (see Table 3.1).

TABLE 3.1 Full-time distribution of the leading sixteen pan-European television channels, 1997–2002 (in million of TV households)

	1997	1998	1999	2000	2001	2002
Arte	–	78.9	61.9	61.9	65.0	65.0
BBC Prime	–	–	–	8.2	10.5	10.8
BBC World	25.1	33.1	39.3	45.5	49.4	56.4
Bloomberg	–	27.7	10.3	24.6	30.1	37.6
Cartoon Network	–	–	–	21.0	28.6	26.9
CNBC Europe	12.6	21.0	26.7	32.9	40.2	41.9
CNN International	58.9	67.8	68.8	73.2	81.0	84.7
Discovery	7.0	16.3	20.4	26.7	31.4	32.9
Euronews	30.4	34.3	34.9	34.0	44.0	48.9
Eurosport	71.9	75.6	80.6	88.3	93.0	95.3
Fox Kids	–	–	15.4	23.1	25.0	31.0
MTV	44.0	58.8	79.1	83.6	94.2	92.8
National Geographic	4.0	14.9	15.3	19.2	22.9	26.9
Sky News	–	–	38.9	18.6	22.7	24.0
TV5	45.5	55.7	57.6	66.1	68.0	71.4
VH1	–	–	20.3	23.1	19.1	18.5
Average distribution	33.3	44.0	40.7	39.1	45.3	47.8

Sources: Media and Marketing Europe Guide: Pan-European Television, 1998 to 2002.

In addition, the reception universe is now large enough to sustain the development of smaller transnational channels that specialize in sub-genres, such as those that concentrate on a specific music style or type of documentary. Channels with a focused proposition and a narrow subscription base in terms of demographics need a European-wide distribution to leverage costs over more than one market and create economies of scale. This applies to all cross-border channels but particularly to the newer 'super-niche' channels such as E! Entertainment (celebrity news and entertainment) and Reality TV.

Financial health was also brought by the growth in advertising revenues. Between 1988 and 2001, the value of the pan-European advertising market has increased from €31 million (approximately US$36 million) to €628 million (approximately US$728.5 million).[32] The number of advertisers on pan-European TV grew from an estimated 200 in the late 1980s to more than 600 in 2002.[33] There has been a surge of products and services sold on a multinational basis. Banks, such as UBS and HSBC, and insurance companies (for instance AXA and Allianz) frequently advertise on international television, reflecting the trans-border scope of their activities. Computing and IT companies also figure prominently among pan-European advertisers. Their products are sold worldwide and need little adaptation from one market to another. Furthermore, multinationals that used to deal exclusively with local advertising agencies are increasingly committed to pan-European advertising campaigns. Cross-border advertising enables them to develop international brands homogeneously across a region and achieve consistent brand image and positioning.[34] Nike and Levi's have both run European campaigns to make general statements about their brand.[35]

Above all, transnational television has successfully attracted advertising for the elites. The leading cross-border TV channels, especially in the news sector, deliberately target affluent audiences.[36] The pan-European TV industry commissions an annual audience survey conducted by IPSOS in sixteen European countries. The survey universe is restricted to individuals with a personal annual income of at least €45,000 (approximately US$52,000)[37] and who either travel at least six times a year or hold the post of company director. The resulting sample's average respondent has an annual income of €78,000 (approximately US$90,500) and holds investments worth €318,000 (approximately US$369,000). Twenty per cent of them own three cars or more and 12 per cent possess their own art collection.[38] Seventy per cent of the respondents watch a pan-European TV channel at least once a month and 57 per cent at least once a week.[39] CNN International is the channel most frequently watched, followed by Eurosport, MTV, Euronews, BBC World, Discovery and CNBC.[40] These blue chip demographics are much sought after by advertisers, and particularly by those who prefer 'talking to the people who count' than 'counting the people they talk to'.[41] These include manufacturers of luxury goods, high-tech products and service providers to a transnational corporate elite.

Pan-European TV channels, with the exception of BBC World and Euronews, have also introduced local advertising windows, enabling them to insert commercials for a specific territory or group of territories (for instance German-speaking countries). Bloomberg has introduced separate ad windows for Britain, France, Germany, Spain and Italy, and TV5 has windows for French- and non-French-speaking countries.[42] Advertisers can buy a local campaign and advertise in one country, opt for an international campaign and select a group of territories, or buy a whole pan-European campaign. This flexibility has allowed cross-border channels to compete for local advertising budgets, which represent more than half the advertising revenue of channels such as MTV and Discovery.

Thus, several factors have combined to sustain the development of transnational television in the course of the 1990s. The expansion of the reception universe has enabled cross-border channels to increase coverage and leverage costs over many more markets, direct-to-home broadcasting has facilitated reception, digitization has increased network capacity and viewers' choice, the growth of supply on communications satellites has lowered transmission costs, and the money spent on international advertising has increased twentyfold in less than fifteen years. On top of this, the transnational TV industry itself has learned to operate in a multinational environment. After years of trial and error and changes in strategy, cross-border channels have finally developed successful ways of adapting to local cultures.

Struggling for Local Relevance: The Practices of Localization

In the early days of satellite television it was widely believed in corporate circles that the boundaries between cultures were fast disappearing and a global culture was emerging.[43] It led corporate players to overlook the formidable linguistic and cultural differences among European nations. It was assumed that English was understood and spoken everywhere and that cultural tastes, albeit still different, were converging.[44]

In the 1990s, it progressively dawned on international broadcasters that Europe was too competitive a market for television services that might be seen as foreign and irrelevant to viewers. Although the number of cable and satellite homes in Europe was growing, a fast increasing number of national channels were competing for this audience. Between 1991 and 2000, the number of cable and satellite channels grew from 145 to 1,013, thus saturating niche markets such as children's, movies and sport.[45] National news and music television channels began eating into the audience share of CNN and MTV. The distribution of pan-European TV channels was progressing, but ratings remained stagnant. To carry on in business, cross-border channels had to address the issue of local relevance and begin to adapt to local tastes.

There exist different ways of localizing a cross-border signal. The most basic technique is to introduce a local language, which can be achieved through translation or multilingual service. Translation involves either dubbing or subtitling, depending on the broadcaster's resources and the audience. Territories where English is a strong second language, such as Scandinavia or the Netherlands, get more subtitles than do the French or Portuguese. Discovery subtitles its documentaries in twenty-two languages while Cartoon Network dubs its cartoons in nine languages. Multilingual service consists of covering the same video track with different commentaries (thus disposing of the notion of original language) and is predominantly employed for live programming. Both Euronews and Eurosport cover their main feed with seven and eighteen languages respectively. The francophone TV5 has introduced subtitles in seven languages, including Dutch and Portuguese, to help French learners. Using one method or another, the leading sixteen pan-European TV channels broadcast on average in eight languages.[46] BBC World, Sky News and VH1 are the only channels to broadcast solely in English.

Transnational TV channels can also split their video signal and introduce local programming windows for specific territories lasting from a few minutes to several hours. National Geographic has introduced devolved programming in eight European countries and CNN International broadcast three fifteen-minute news bulletins in Germany. An extension of this principle is the local opt-out, which involves isolating an important market from the transnational feed and creating an ad hoc channel to service it. Eurosport launched devolved channels in France in 1998 (Eurosport France) and Britain the following year (British Eurosport). Both markets were important for advertisers, but presented Eurosport with difficulties because of divergence in audience interests. Taste in sport varies from one market to another, and even though a sport such as football is popular across Europe, team following remains domestic.[47] VH1 met with similar difficulties in music markets, and while it covers Europe with a single feed (VH1 European), it runs a specific channel for the UK.[48]

Localization procedures might help cross-border channels remain relevant in a multicultural environment, but cannot on their own iron out all difficulties associated with transnational television. Cross-border feeds are notoriously complex to schedule because of the different lifestyles and viewing habits across Europe. The peak viewing time in Scandinavia is earlier (7 p.m.) than in France (8 p.m.) or Spain (10 p.m.). Holidays and school days vary from country to country, presenting children's channels with an acute problem. Multilingual tracks address the language issue but prevent commentaries from being read on-camera by a presenter. Euronews's and Eurosport's main feeds are faceless and have therefore experienced difficulty in building an identity. Tastes and interests differ greatly throughout Europe. Eurosport's retransmissions of, for example, ski jumping and Nordic skiing competitions are of little interest to Southern European audiences. As MTV found out in the early 1990s, Europeans' tastes in music are far too eclectic to be covered by a single feed.

In addition, different market conditions prevail in each country, as determined by broadcasting legislation and policy, the shape of the distribution platforms and the weight of public service broadcasting. For instance, the French government has reinforced the quota requirements outlined by the European directive Television without Frontiers, requesting that television schedules contain at least 60 per cent of programming of European origin. Local regulatory regimes regarding decency, swearing and nudity remain different across Europe, requiring channels to be cautious about some of the material they broadcast. All these factors have led international broadcasters to conclude that their expansion goals will be met only by a responsive approach to local realities. European diversity has thus forced them to adopt a more radical expansion strategy.

The Emergence of Pan-European TV Networks

The limits of localization, which remains a centralized approach to local adaptation, have prompted many broadcasters to review the way they operate across borders. Since the mid-1990s, many have begun shifting to a practice of international networking, which can be defined as *the creation of a network of local channels around a core broadcasting philosophy*. Local channels share a concept, brand, part of their programming and library titles, resources and infrastructures, and teamwork, but develop according to their respective environment. They employ local staff, register with local regulatory bodies, and set up their own schedule mixing shared network content with their own material. Local teams have the advantage of being able to exchange ideas, knowledge and experience with other teams. While they benefit from the network's global expertise, the network takes advantage of their local knowledge. Thus the local ceases to 'interfere' with the global but complements it, becoming a source of growth and creativity. Networks break down the opposition between the local and the global to make each term an 'extension' of the other.[49]

The existing networks in Europe cover the continent with an average of 8.5 channels, using a mix of country- and region-specific channels (see Table 3.2). Some broadcasters privilege region-specific feeds, like Discovery, while Bloomberg concentrates its efforts on country-specific operations.

MTV, Cartoon Network, Discovery and Turner Classic Movies have progressively regionalized their pan-European feeds, while Bloomberg and Fox Kids have started with local channels and gradually increased their reach across Europe. Some of these networks run pan-European feeds in parallel to their local channels, either as a complement to existing channels (Bloomberg) or to fill the gaps (sometimes momentarily) between their country/region-specific channels (Cartoon Network and MTV). Cartoon Network broadcast slightly localized versions of its pan-European feed in Central Europe to test whether the markets can sustain a local channel.[50] It launched its first country-specific channel in the UK in 1994, quickly followed by MTV in Italy. Bloomberg started its European operations in France in 1995, and Fox Kids launched in Britain the following year.

Europe's most extensive network is that of MTV, with five country-specific and four region-specific channels spanning the continent.

Soon after MTV had launched a devolved service in Italy, it split its pan-European feed into MTV North, covering most of Europe, and MTV Central, servicing the German-speaking countries. In 1997, MTV UK and Ireland and MTV Nordic were launched. A second wave of local channels appeared in Poland, the Netherlands, Spain and France in 2000, and most recently in Romania. MTV has made considerable investments in its network, opening large production centres in places like Milan and Munich, each employing around 100 staff.[51]

Networks constitute the most elaborate answer to the difficulties of operating TV channels across frontiers, allowing broadcasters to combine local adaptability with global leverage. Within a network, channels have many ways of differentiating themselves. While sharing programming, they can set their own schedule in order to adapt to

TABLE 3.2 Pan-European television networks

	Country-specific channels	Region-specific channels
Bloomberg	France, Italy, Spain, UK	Germany +[1]
Cartoon Network	France, Spain, Italy, the Netherlands, Poland	Central & Eastern Europe, Scandinavia, UK +[2]
Discovery	Denmark, Italy, Poland	Benelux, Central Europe Eastern Europe, German +, Scandinavia, Spain & Portugal, UK +
Fox Kids	France, Greece, Italy, Poland, Spain, the Netherlands	Central & Eastern Europe, Germany +, Hungary and Czech Republic, Scandinavia, UK +
MTV	France, Italy, the Netherlands, Poland, Romania, Spain	Germany +, Scandinavia, UK +
Turner Classic Movies	France, Spain, Italy, the Netherlands, Poland	Central & Eastern Europe Scandinavia, UK +

Notes: 1. Includes Austria and German-speaking Switzerland. 2. Includes Ireland.
Sources: interviews (see notes), company literature.

local viewing habits. The Turner Classic Movies channels schedule the same prime-time movie when best suited for their audience, thus starting earlier in Scandinavia than in Spain.[52]

Channels can acquire and produce material locally, including promos, interstices and shows, and expand local programming as advertising revenue and audiences grow. A network can also be prompted to invest in local content because of regulatory constraints. In France, Fox Kids was perceived as an American company and experienced difficulties getting distribution from local cable operators. It could expand only by taking a licence from the French regulatory body (the CSA) and respecting the quotas regulation, which requests that 60 per cent of the schedule be of European origin. In order to reach this target, the channel has increased its own production and acquisition of European material. As a result, half the schedule of Fox Kids France comes from the network's library, a quarter is bought from third parties for the European network and the last quarter is bought specifically for the French market.[53]

The variations among the MTV channels are set to increase as its management aims to make them '100 per cent different'.[54] The channels have their own schedule and produce an increasing number of shows fronted by their own veejays and presenters. The playlists, which can incorporate up to 70 per cent of local acts, closely match local preferences.[55]

Networks can vary the positioning of their channels from one territory to another according to local variables ranging from audience tastes to the competition. Fox Kids is more edgy in France and Britain than in Scandinavia, where parents display zero tolerance for violent content.[56] MTV UK has remained close to its initial remit of music television but MTV Italy has transformed itself into a youth channel that schedules lifestyle programmes such as *Loveline*, a talk-show, and *Stylissimo*, a fashion show. The competition is different in Britain, where MTV's main competitors are Emap's stable of music television channels, from that found in Italy, where they include youth channel Canal Jimmy.

While channels evolve according to their environment, they share attributes and resources at the network level. First, they have a common broadcasting philosophy. The foundation of all current transnational TV networks that specialize in niche markets is a well-defined television concept and the selling of a clear proposition to the audience. These concepts range from breaking international news (CNN), real-time financial information and analysis (Bloomberg) to classic music video hits for twenty-five to thirty-five-year olds (VH1). Network channels also share a brand that is often translated into a common visual identity. The five European Bloomberg TV channels are scheduled independently and broadcast in their own language but 'look and feel' similar and share a common style and layout. They benefit from the signature multiscreen format simultaneously delivering global news, market data, financial market updates, breaking news headlines and weather.

Branding plays an increasingly significant role in the current television environment. Channels need to be quickly identified by viewers flicking through the categories of their electronic programming guide. The consolidation of distribution platforms, which started in the early 2000s, has reinforced this trend. Now that cable and satellite operators are in a dominant position in a national market they can afford to force channels to renegotiate their carriage fees. The only leverage of such channels is a distinct content and a strong identity.[57] Thus media executives spend an increasing amount of money and energy on the marketing of their channels. Network channels hold the distinct advantage over local competitors of being able to tap into the expertise and financial resources of the group.

Another great benefit of networks is their capacity to recycle content and share channel programming. The Turner Classic Movies network is built around the MGM library, which holds the worldwide rights to classics such as *Casablanca* and *Gone with the Wind*. The Cartoon Network's and Fox Kids' schedules are based respectively on the extensive Warner Bros (Batman, Tom and Jerry, etc.) and Saban libraries. Networks offer exceptional flexibility in the international distribution of content. They can exclude items they think are inappropriate for their public, buy content specific for their market or share material with one or two other channels in the network.

Occasionally, channels come together to create a 'network moment'. The MTV channels broadcast the European MTV Awards show, which is held in a different city each year. The Fox Kids network invites local teams to its own children's European football cup every June. The Bloomberg channels simultaneously broadcast interviews with CEOs and personalities whose comments are likely to have an immediate impact on the stock market. These events create a sense of occasion and help channels generate a 'regional feel' for the audience.

Channels can share resources and infrastructures, allowing networks to generate greater economies of scale. Transnational TV channels target audiences with such specific demographics that many would not survive more than six months were they unable to leverage costs over more than one market. Several networks have set up pan-regional production facilities and television studios. MTV offers American artists doing promotional tours in Europe the opportunity to give interviews to as many MTV channels as they wish without ever leaving London. The company flies its presenters to studios in Camden Town, North London, and artists spend fifteen minutes with each, covering the continent's key territories in a couple of hours.[58] The Bloomberg channels benefit from the company's worldwide newsgathering facilities. It employs 7,000 people across the world, including 1,000 journalists who feed the financial data services, news wires and television channels.[59]

Networks frequently centralize departments that deal with acquisitions, legal affairs and copyright agreements, distribution and research. Most of them direct their European operations from London, which has become a regional hub of international TV players. Centralization brings several advantages, notably when negotiating with third parties. For instance, it is easier for networks to exert leverage during negotiations for the acquisition of programming at a regional level. Likewise, content rights holders would rather sell them to a region as a whole than on a country-by-country basis.

Networks organize creative sharing as local teams are encouraged to exchange ideas, knowledge and experience. Every Friday morning, staff from all corners of Europe meet at the MTV's headquarters in London where they come with folders and videos containing intros, trailers, title sequences and plans for marketing campaigns. Material such as promos can be shared by two territories or adopted across the board.[60] The MTV European network has adopted the Italian *MTV Kitchen*, a show that involves artists chatting about music while cooking. Fox Kids France originated several ideas that can now be seen across the children's network, such as Roger and Melissa, the rubber glove puppets that appear during programme links.[61]

Pan-European TV networks constitute today's most sophisticated answer to the dilemmas faced by transnational broadcasters. Networks allow management teams to articulate the local and the global in a unique way by combining global leverage with sensitivity to local specificity. Network channels can adapt to a local environment and develop their own schedule, positioning and programming. At the same time, they benefit from the network, sharing with other channels a broadcasting philosophy, style, brand, programming, resources and infrastructures. Networks are interactive places where the flow of communication is not only vertical – from head office to local teams and vice-versa – but also horizontal among channels exchanging ideas and experience. They have the unique ability of making the local and the global coexist as knowledge of both dimensions is generated and information cross-bred between them.

Conclusion: Bright Prospects Despite a Chequered Past

The first twenty years have been difficult for cross-border TV channels. The numerous obstacles met, as outlined in this chapter, explain why many did not survive the 1980s and why analysts were so disparaging of them late into the 1990s. It is only recently that those that persevered have found an audience and advertising clients, and turned a profit. Will this reversal of fortune continue?

All the environmental factors that have contributed to their recent success remain positive. Increasingly sophisticated communications satellites will continue to bring down costs of international transmission and offer greater flexibility. The number of European households connected to cable and satellite (the reception universe of transnational channels), is forecast to continue expanding, albeit at a slower pace.[62] The growth of direct-to-home reception should also bring in a new public, especially in Central and Eastern Europe.

Provided the current trends continue, rising viewing figures will allow leading cross-border TV networks to increase advertising rate cards and local advertising inserts will enable them to make further inroads into the market shares of national channels. Their client base will continue to see steady growth as a rising number of brands are developed internationally and advertisers realize the advantages of pan-regional marketing campaigns.

Continuing political integration of the continent under the aegis of the European Union is a positive development for cross-border TV channels. Legislative frameworks will further conform to the

European Commission's aim of creating a single audiovisual market. The ten new entrants, including Hungary, Poland and the Czech Republic, will be brought into line with European legislation and thus contribute to the expansion of an already large market of consumers. From a content perspective, the development of transnational democracy in Europe validates the cosmopolitan editorial viewpoint of the news channels (BBC World, CNN and Euronews in particular), in the same way that the business news channels (Bloomberg and CNBC Europe) have benefited from the introduction of the European currency.

The field has become dominated by corporate players, both public and private, with the resources, expertise and determination to play the international game. In the 1990s, global media companies have either upped investment in cross-border channels or entered into the industry. Examples include Viacom, which added VH1 to MTV, and Turner Broadcasting System, which now operates Cartoon Network and Turner Classic Movies in addition to CNN. New arrivals include Disney (Fox Kids), Dow Jones and NBC (CNBC), Bloomberg and Universal Television Network. Companies such as these join public service broadcasters (the BBC, TV5, etc.), which have a long tradition of international broadcasting.

These corporate players have devised successful strategies to operate in a multicultural environment. In the 1980s, they were unsure how to transmit across boundaries and were at first oblivious to local culture and market conditions. They had overestimated audience appetite for foreign programming and launched general entertainment channels in direct competition with established national broadcasters. To remedy this, they have progressively focused on niche markets and begun adapting their feed to local tastes. In the mid-1990s, the emergence of networks demonstrated how corporate players had acquired a much better understanding of the relationship between the local and the global, and learned how to articulate the two polarities while benefiting from both.

Europe still presents many challenges for broadcasters operating across frontiers. Audiences differ in terms of viewing habits, lifestyle, language and cultural dispositions. Market conditions continue to vary from country to country, depending on broadcasting history, the local regulatory framework, the weight of public broadcasting and the penetration of distribution platforms. Nevertheless, everything indicates that cross-border TV channels will continue to prosper and affirm their presence in European broadcasting.

Notes

The author wishes to thank the interviewees for their time and co-operation.

1. Charles Barrand, 'Europa Television – The Transponder's Eye View', *EBU Review. Programmes, Administration, Law*, 37(2) (1986), p. 11.

2. Malcolm Tallantire, 'The Beginnings of Empire', *Cable and Satellite Europe*, January 1994, p. 32.

3. Richard Collins, *Satellite Television in Western Europe – Revised Edition* (London: John Libbey, 1992), p. 83.

4. Malcolm Tallantire, 'Falling from Sky', *Cable and Satellite Europe*, July 1989, pp. 29–31.

5. 'Super Side up', *Cable and Satellite Europe*, June 1988, p. 63.

6. Collins, *Satellite Television*, pp. 86–8.

7. 'Brief Encounters', *Cable and Satellite Europe*, January 1994, p. 40.

8. 'Rest in Peace', *Cable and Satellite Europe*, January 1990, p. 18.

9. Neville Clarke, 'Pan-European TV?', *Irish Broadcasting Review*, 14 (Summer 1982), p. 44.

10. Barrand, 'Europa Television', p. 11.

11. '3SAT Makes Its Bid', *Cable and Satellite Europe*, December 1984, p. 45.

12. Neville Clarke, 'Eurikon Promises a New Programme Concept', *Intermedia*, 11(3) (1983), p. 29.

13. Neville Clarke, 'The Birth of the Infant Eurikon', *Intermedia*, 12(2) (1984), p. 50.

14. Ibid., p. 51.

15. Stylianos Papathanassopoulos, 'Towards European Television: The Case of Europa-TV', *Media Information Australia*, 56 (May 1990), p. 60.

16. Vanessa O'Connor, 'Climbing a Euro-mountain', *Cable and Satellite Europe*, July 1986, p. 54; Richard Collins, *From Satellite to Single Market: New Communication Technology and European Public Service Television* (London: Routledge, 1998), pp. 143–9.

17. Chris Woodman, '15 Years of Intelligence', *Cable and Satellite Europe*, May 1999, p. 32.

18. Nick Snow, 'Europa: End of a Dream', *Cable and Satellite Europe*, January 1987, p. 22; Glyndwr Matthias, 'Many Happy Connections', *Cable and Satellite Europe*, November 1987, p. 27; Tallantire, 'Falling from Sky'.

19. Channels need to respect certain conditions. Notably, Article 6 of the directive stipulates that at least 50 per cent of TV schedules must be of European origin.

20. Matthias, 'Many Happy Connections', p. 27.

21. Cynthia Ritchie, 'Crunch Time for Cable', *Cable and Satellite Europe*, May 1994, p. 18.

22. Toby Syfret, 'A Recall for the Euro-ad?', *Cable and Satellite Europe*, April 1989, p. 55.

23. Toby Syfret, 'The Ad-man's Dream', *Cable and Satellite Europe*, January 1994, p. 42. See also Collins, *Satellite Television*, p. 44.

24. Paul Barker, 'From Pariah to Paragon', *Cable and Satellite Europe*, June 1992, p. 16.

25. Julian Clover, 'Playing it by Ear', *Cable and Satellite Europe*, February 1993, pp. 18–24.

26. Paul Barker, 'Nouvelles Cuisine', *Cable and Satellite Europe*, February 1993, p. 32; Tania Alonzi, 'Growing Up is Hard to Do', *Media and Marketing Europe Guide: Pan-European Television*, 1998, pp. 18–19.

27. European Audiovisual Observatory, *Yearbook Volume 2: Household Audiovisual Equipment – Transmission – Television Audience* (Strasbourg: European Audiovisual Observatory, 2002), pp. 38–9.

28. Ibid.

29. Woodman, '15 Years of Intelligence', p. 32.

30. European Audiovisual Observatory, *Yearbook Volume 2*, pp. 38–9.

31. <Http://www.ses-astra.com and http://www.eutelsat.com>. Consulted June 2003.

32. Collins, *Satellite Television*, p. 44; *Media and Marketing Europe Guide*, 2002, p. 16.

33. Toby Syfret, 'Commercial Breaks', *Cable and Satellite Europe*, January 1987, p. 34; Sonia Marguin, marketing researcher, Euronews, interview, 23 October 2003.

34. Malcom Hanlon, media group director, Zenith Media, interview, 20 September 2002.

35. Marie-Catherine Dupuy, 'What's the Big Idea?', *Media and Marketing Europe Guide: Pan-European Television*, 2002, p. 15.

36. Chris Cramer, president, CNN International, telephone interview, 9 July 2002.

37. As of 30 September 2003.

38. Ipsos-IRL, *Europe 2002: A Survey of Decision Makers and Leading Consumers* (Harrow, 2002), p. 10.

39. Ibid., p. 13.

40. Ibid., p. 14.

41. Errol Pretorius, director of advertising sales, National Geographic, interview, 14 August 2001.

42. *Media and Marketing Europe Guide: Pan-European Television*, 2002, pp. 22–3.

43. David Morley and Kevin Robins, *Spaces of Identity: Global Media, Electronic Landscapes and Cultural Boundaries* (London: Routledge, 1995), p. 15.

44. An analyst for Saatchi and Saatchi, the London advertising agency, ascertained in 1984: 'The most advanced manufacturers are recognising that there are probably more social differences between midtown Manhattan and the Bronx [...] than between midtown Manhattan and the 7th arrondissement of Paris.' In Simon Baker, 'Will Euro-sell Help Euro Channels?', *Cable and Satellite Europe*, February 1984, p. 22.

45. *Screen Digest*, March 2001, p. 87.

46. *Media and Marketing Europe Guide: Pan-European Television*, 2002, pp. 22–3.

47. Jean Chalaby, 'Transnational Television in Europe: The Role of Pan-European Channels', *European Journal of Communication*, 17(2) (2002), pp. 194–5.

48. Tanja Flintoff, head of programming and production, VH1, interview, 2 July 2002.

49. Jocelyn Cullity, 'The Global *Desi*: Cultural Nationalism on MTV India', *Journal of Communication Inquiry*, 26(4) (2002), p. 414.

50. Peter Flamman, director of business development for corporate networks and entertainment, Turner Broadcasting System Europe, interview, 16 May 2002.

51. Jamie Caring, head of talent and artist relations, MTV Networks UK, interview, 3 July 2002.

52. Fritha Sutherland, 'Night after Night at the Movies', *Cable and Satellite Europe*, December 1999, p. 17.

53. Ronan Lunven, president-directeur general, Fox Kids France, interview, 20 June 2002.

54. Ibid.

55. Keith Roe and Gust De Meyer, 'Music Television: MTV-Europe', in Jan Wieten, Graham Murdock and Peter Dahlgren (eds), *Television across Europe: A Comparative Introduction* (London: Sage, 2000), pp. 141–57.

56. Rick Plata, director of advertising sales, Fox Kids, interview, 19 April 2002.

57. Sarah Marsh, 'Survival of the Fittest', *Cable and Satellite Europe*, March 2003, p. 23.

58. Jamie Caring, interview, 3 July 2002.

59. Bronwyn Curtis, editor in chief, Bloomberg Television, interview, 25 April 2002.

60. Richard Godfrey, senior vice-president, MTV Networks Europe, interview, 17 April 2001.

61. Ronan Lunven, interview, 20 June 2002.

62. Zenith Media, *Television in Europe to 2010* (London, 2002).

CHAPTER 4

. . . .

Maverick or Model? Al-Jazeera's Impact on Arab Satellite Television

Naomi Sakr

§ IN February 2003, as US and British troops massed on Iraq's borders and spectacular anti-war protests erupted around the world, an Arab-owned satellite television channel became the subject of unprecedented news coverage in the Western press.[1] For once the player in question was not the high-profile Qatari broadcaster, Al-Jazeera Satellite Channel, already by then almost an international household name. Instead, the focus of attention on this occasion was a new venture, a rolling news operation called Al-Arabiya, established with the express intention of luring away Al-Jazeera's large and loyal audience. With Al-Arabiya's arrival, another milestone was reached in the short history of transnational television in Arabic. A phenomenon born in the aftermath of Iraq's 1990 invasion of Kuwait, Arab satellite television was dominated during the first half of the 1990s by broadcasters so closely allied to governments that they had far more interest in shaping public opinion than in reflecting it.[2] Initially, therefore, the new transnational medium's power to liberate viewers from tight government censorship was not realized. So when Al-Jazeera emerged on to the scene during the second half of the decade, its appetite for airing controversy and reporting dissent shocked most Arab governments and rocked the hitherto steady broadcasting boat. An Egyptian journalist, looking back some years later, said it was like 'a stone being thrown into still waters'.[3] As millions of viewers equipped themselves to receive Al-Jazeera's programmes, a new generation of other broadcasting hopefuls elbowed their way into an increasingly crowded satellite television arena, eager to benefit in one way or another from the chance to transmit to Arabic-speaking audiences inside and outside the Arab world. Yet it was only with the entry of Al-Arabiya that Al-Jazeera finally faced a self-proclaimed competitor that was also amply resourced. So how was it that Al-Jazeera remained 'one of a kind' between its launch at the end of 1996 and the birth of Al-Arabiya just over six years later? Did Al-Arabiya's start-up signify that Al-Jazeera, viewed for so long as a maverick, had finally been acknowledged (albeit tacitly) as a model? This chapter explores changes in the Arab satellite media landscape during the six years in question. In doing so it also aims to assess Al-Jazeera's impact on that landscape.

Exploring change in the television sector requires an approach that takes account of trends in ownership and management control as well as changes in programme content. Helpfully, the critical political economy approach perceives an interplay between these two aspects. In the words of Peter Golding and Graham Murdock, the critical political economy approach can show how 'different ways of financing and organizing cultural production have traceable consequences for the range of discourses and representations in the public domain and for audiences' access to them'.[4] These consequences are clearly visible in the case of Al-Jazeera itself. Its controversial talkshows, although not wholly unprecedented in the Arab pay-TV sector,[5] were nevertheless highly unusual by regional standards and completely new on Arabic-language free-to-air TV. Yet explanations for this departure from the norm are readily available in policy choices made at the highest levels of the Qatari government. These included the ruler's decision to launch the channel with a five-year loan large enough to enable it to make an impact, thereby boosting Qatar's profile in regional politics,[6] but small enough to encourage its staff to aim for financial independence by achieving viewing figures high enough to attract lucrative advertising. At the same time the loan arrangement enabled the government formally to distance itself from Al-Jazeera's editorial content, since this provoked outrage from Arab regimes criticized by Al-Jazeera's interviewees and talkshow guests. When those regimes used their leverage to divert advertising budgets away from Al-Jazeera, the ruler of Qatar refrained from calling in his loan at the end of 2001. It had become clear by then that he valued the non-financial returns on his investment.[7] A prominent Al-Jazeera presenter, when asked about the nature of these returns, remarked that the station was to the Qatari government 'what nuclear weapons are to Israel'.[8] In the tightly controlled and highly censored media environment of the Middle East, the unelected leadership of the very small, very rich Gulf state of Qatar,[9] with apparently little to lose from allowing free speech, had decided to adopt freedom of expression as a foreign policy tool.

Bearing in mind the extent to which funding and organization are seen to have had traceable consequences for Al-Jazeera's output, corresponding patterns of causality may well be observable in relation to the Arab satellite channels that followed it. Tracing patterns, however, does not automatically produce evidence of change. For that task, certain criteria need to be established by which change can be measured. Existing studies of change in media environments, conducted from a political economy perspective, offer various axes of measurement. One possibility is to monitor the entry of private or foreign capital. Manjunath Pendakur and Jyotsna Kapur discuss the privatization of Indian television in terms of a 'continuum' that starts with allowing privately produced TV serials on the state broadcaster and proceeds to full private ownership and private production.[10] Another possible axis, discussed by Karel Jakubowicz in relation to Poland, is one that tracks changes in the degree to which specific media outlets enjoy structural freedom from 'inhibiting forms of economic, political or other dependency'.[11] This has the advantage of acknowledging that the market can censor as well as the state. A third option is to focus on styles of management and the status of journalists. Louise Bourgault, analysing broadcasting changes in African countries, finds extremes of patronage and deference at one end of a hypothetical spectrum, at the other end of which are trained and engaged individuals alert to the needs of all sectors of society.[12]

All three sets of criteria highlight relevant areas of investigation probed in the present study. At the same time, however, the study also seeks to clarify the direction of change in Arab satellite television from a normative viewpoint, in terms of benefits to society. To that end it adopts indicators suggested by Colin Sparks as an alternative to what he calls the 'sterile debate' about distinctions between state and market, or bureaucrat and entrepreneur.[13] Sparks advises looking for change in the way media outlets relate to their audiences, and in the way power is distributed inside individual media organizations.[14] Both these lines of inquiry link content with ownership and organization. The question of how owners, directors and producers of Arab satellite channels regard their audience is at the centre of debates about programmes screened on this medium. Similarly, there would seem to be a correlation between levels of creativity and individual initiative within channels or networks and the latter's willingness or ability to meet the challenges of stiffer competition for viewers. In order to do the groundwork for examining these issues in some detail, the next step is to scrutinize the successive waves of channel start-ups that occurred between 1996 and 2003.

Market Entrants: Policies, Resources and Content

Strenuous activity in the setting up of Arab satellite channels during the first half of the 1990s was not matched by major breakthroughs in programme content. The few modest advances achieved qualified as such only by comparison with the censored, mostly second-hand fare available up to that point on government-monopolized terrestrial television. Middle East Broadcasting Centre (MBC), the second Arab satellite channel to be launched, differed from the first, the state-owned Egyptian Space Channel (ESC), in describing itself as privately owned, even though copious start-up funds were supplied from within the Saudi ruling family via the brother-in-law of King Fahd. MBC started up just in time to provide first-hand coverage of the multilateral Arab–Israeli peace talks in Madrid in the autumn of 1991. Since any Arab media coverage of politically sensitive events was a novelty at that stage, MBC's presence in Madrid and its bureau in Jerusalem indicated that its backers were serious in at least some respects about providing an Arab alternative to CNN. They were prompted to do so because CNN had captivated Arab audiences by its coverage from Baghdad of the 1991 Gulf War. Over the next four years, the precedents set by MBC paved the way for other channels. Two multi-channel pay-TV networks, Arab Radio and Television (ART) and Orbit, were created by private Saudi business associates of Saudi Arabia's ruling elite.[15] Meanwhile the governments of Dubai, Jordan, Morocco, Syria and a number of other Arab countries emulated ESC's policy in deploying existing television production facilities to provide material aimed at nationals overseas. By the time these transnational channels came on the scene, large-scale labour migration had created clusters of Arab expatriate communities in Gulf states, Europe and the USA. As may be deduced from the origins of the material being transmitted by satellite, traditions of extreme editorial caution, or even heavy-handed censorship, prevailed in transnational channels as they had in domestic ones.[16] The strength of such constraints was exposed when the ART network was kept devoid of any news programming and when Orbit's Arabic-language news channel, run on contract by the BBC, was taken off the air altogether in April 1996 because of objections to BBC reporting on Saudi Arabian current affairs.

It was into this tightly controlled environment that three new satellite channels entered in 1996. One was Al-Jazeera. To many viewers it seemed as though Al-Jazeera Satellite Channel had resurrected the BBC Arabic news service that Orbit had killed off. Sheikh Hamad bin Khalifa al-Thani, who ousted his father and took over as ruler of Qatar in mid-1995, had reportedly watched the BBC service along with his entourage, and liked what he saw. Staff made redundant when the BBC operation folded were given jobs with Al-Jazeera in time for its start-up in November the same year. The other two arrivals at this time were predominantly, but not purely, Lebanese. Lebanon's fifteen-year civil war, brought to an end in 1990, had resulted in the mushrooming of dozens of sectarian television channels, the numbers of which the post-war government sought to reduce. An Audiovisual Law passed in 1994 made Lebanon the first Arab state to authorize locally based private broadcasting. It resulted in the allocation of broadcasting licences to representatives of the country's biggest confessional groups. A separate law allowed licence holders to transmit by satellite but gave government ministers the right to decide whether or not satellite programming could include news and political reports.[17] Thus LBC-Sat (part-owned by Saudi Arabia's ART) and Future TV (part-owned by Lebanon's prime minister, Rafiq Hariri, holder of dual Lebanese and Saudi nationality) burst on to the satellite television screens with flair and flamboyance but without guarantees of freedom of speech. Hariri, as head of government, channel owner and leading Lebanese entrepreneur, responded to Gulf governments' alleged unease about satellite television content by invoking the power to ban news and political coverage on both Future and LBC-Sat. The ban, imposed at the start of 1998, remained in force for most of that year.

As indicated by the ban, Arab governments appeared rattled by content appearing on satellite television, material which Arab ministries of information would never allow to be aired on terrestrial channels. Their nervousness stemmed first and foremost from Al-Jazeera. Launched in November 1996, it finally became more widely available to viewers across the Arab world after technical changes to its transmission in November 1997. From then on its disregard for the sensitivities of authoritarian Arab governments induced a growing number of households across the region to gain satellite access. Between 1995/96 and 2000/01 the proportion of homes able to receive satellite television programmes increased by a factor of eleven in Lebanon, seven in Egypt and three and a half in Jordan and Kuwait.[18] As satellite reception spread, the incentives increased for other broadcasters to join the transnational competition for viewers. Few, however, aspired to emulating Al-Jazeera. Arab News Network (ANN), devoted to news and current affairs and launched only months after Al-Jazeera, displayed a fairly typical set of constraints. ANN was set up in London in mid-1997 as the latest in a series of privately funded attempts to carve a media presence for a disaffected branch of Syria's ruling Assad family.[19] ANN's management announced that they planned to talk freely not only about politics but also neglected social issues, such as family relations, marital problems, housing and education.[20] Managers were philosophical about competing with existing channels. They pointed out that viewers in the Arab world rarely sit patiently through whole programmes or news bulletins, preferring instead to zap through several channels to sample the range of offerings – a practice that would benefit ANN if it timed its schedules correctly.[21]

In the event, ANN lost viewers because its political agenda and associated financial difficulties affected its output. Rifaat al-Assad, father of ANN's youthful chairman, Sawmar al-Assad, was stripped of his position as Syria's vice-president in early 1998 and his private port in Latakia was reportedly demolished.[22] When Hafez al-Assad, president of Syria and brother of Rifaat, died in 2000, ANN repeatedly broadcast a statement on Rifaat's behalf, saying that he had been denied entry to Syria to attend the funeral. The statement also questioned the choice of Hafez's son Bashar as the new president.[23] This was by no means the first time that Sawmar and Rifaat al-Assad had used the channel as a personal noticeboard and photograph album,[24] thereby replicating the very same kind of 'leadership news' that had supposedly been discredited by the arrival of transnational TV. A subsequent decision to save money by switching to cheaper digital transmission meant that ANN became unavailable to viewers without the necessary receiver. At the same time major staffing cuts took the channel's flagship talkshows off the air from time to time.[25]

After ANN's appearance in 1997, the next arrival to the Arab satellite scene was no more geared to modelling itself on Al-Jazeera than ANN had been. Nile News was launched in June 1998 as one of a digital bouquet of Nile Thematic Channels beamed from the first Egyptian-owned satellite, Nilesat 101. Since satellite penetration was still below 10 per cent of Egyptian households at that stage, and digital reception lower still, the Nile Thematic Channels provided an opportunity within the vast state-owned and government-run Egyptian Radio and Television Union (ERTU) for a certain amount of experimentation with content and editorial procedures. Given the limited audience, such experimentation was regarded by the country's political leadership as relatively risk-free. Hassan Hamed, a former journalist with US and Japanese radio stations, was made executive director of the Nile Thematic Channels. He had apparently originally hoped that the new bouquet could be kept organizationally separate from the ERTU.[26] Separation might have freed it from having to comply with the ERTU's strict code of ethics, which prohibits criticism of officers of the state, the leadership, religious figures or the army.[27] In the event, a separate existence was not allowed, although the channels were added to the ERTU as a new department instead of being integrated into the existing Satellite Department that housed ESC and its affiliated channel, Nile TV. The implications of this arrangement were mixed. It meant that the existing, tightly controlled ERTU Production Department would supply the vast majority of dramas, films and series for the digital entertainment and variety channels. Nile News, in contrast, rather than relying on the ERTU's existing News Department, would build up its own newsgathering network. But Hassan Hamed rejected comparisons between Nile News and either Al-Jazeera or ANN. 'Ours is still official news,' he said. 'We have to weigh things very carefully and not go for sensationalism.'[28]

During the next two years three more entrants joined the fray, each different from the next but none combining the key attributes – secure funds, live uncensored programming and free-to-air, analogue, twenty-four-hour transmission – enjoyed by Al-Jazeera. February 1999 saw the launch in London of Al-Mustaqillah, run by a Tunisian expatriate, Mohammed El-Hachimi Hamdi, who had founded his own newspaper, also named *Al-Mustaqillah*, in 1993. Through the newspaper, and then through his television venture, Hamdi gave airtime to London-based Arab and Islamist opposition groups. Starting with just one hour every Thursday, Al-Mustaqillah gradually increased its programming, using satellite broadcasts to overcome jurisdictional barriers to the circulation of opposition newspapers like *Al-Mustaqillah* and to redress what Hamdi saw as the excessive orientation of most existing Arab media outlets towards the Gulf. But Al-Mustaqillah's funds were limited. As one member of its staff noted, the new channel was the first to be unconnected with an Arab government or ruling family. Some of its content could be compared with that of Al-Jazeera, he said, but its technical capabilities could not.[29]

A much bigger impact was made by Abu Dhabi Satellite TV after its relaunch in early 2000. Strictly speaking it was not a newcomer, although it behaved as such. Created by the government of Abu Dhabi (the richest of the seven emirates that make up the United Arab Emirates – UAE), the satellite channel was revamped after all Abu Dhabi's radio, television and publishing outlets were formally grouped together in 1999. They became part of Emirates Media Incorporated, a new conglomerate headed by Sheikh Abdullah bin Zayed al-Nahayan, the UAE's minister of information and son of the ruler of Abu Dhabi, who is also president of the UAE. The choice of names for Abu Dhabi TV and its parent company emblazoned their national affiliation in a way avoided by the Qatari authorities and Al-Jazeera. Nor did the Abu Dhabi channel position itself as an all-news venture. It offered entertainment as well as news, plus a few panel discussions in English that provided further differentiation. Nevertheless, Abu Dhabi's news component was well funded and highly ambitious, taking over from entertainment during times of crisis in the region. This was made possible not only by the emirate's oil wealth but also by its leadership's widely publicized conviction that the best way to respond to the challenge of incoming global media is to ensure that local media are robust enough to compete.[30]

As the second Palestinian *intifada* (uprising) exploded in late 2000, and Israeli military might was unleashed, the Abu Dhabi channel soon faced the challenge of providing credible coverage of an issue that, judging from phone-ins to Al-Jazeera, was further deepening gargantuan rifts between rulers and ruled in the Arab world. Managers of Abu Dhabi TV proved they were not afraid to expose dissent, fuelled as it was by the dependence of unpopular Arab governments on Israel's principal backer, the USA. A spokesman for the channel declared after Israeli attacks on Palestinian towns in 2002 that it was his channel's job to air local criticism of Arab leaders. Freedom to express these views had a salutary impact on both leaders and people, he said.[31] Even so, as a top presenter for the Abu Dhabi channel discovered in semi-private exchanges with one of his most fiery Al-Jazeera counterparts, the latter seemed to enjoy considerably more editorial latitude than the former.[32]

If the Palestinian *intifada* was a baptism of fire for the Abu Dhabi channel, it provided a fresh *raison d'être* for the satellite arm of Al-Manar, the television outlet of the Lebanese Shia Muslim resistance movement, Hizbollah. Hizbollah, backed by the governments of Syria and Iran, was founded to resist the Israeli occupation of Lebanon in 1982. It started terrestrial broadcasting in Lebanon in 1991 and, in recognition of its resistance activities, was allowed to continue operating despite being denied a licence when the country's Audiovisual Media Law was first implemented in 1996. The licence it eventually obtained in 1997, for Al-Manar and its affiliated radio station, Al-Nur, contradicted the published recommendation of Lebanon's National Audiovisual Council, charged with adjudicating broadcasting licence applications.[33] In March 2000, Hizbollah applied for permission to broadcast by satellite so as to spread 'resistance news' across the Arab world and beyond.[34] Far from altering this aim, Israel's troop withdrawal from southern Lebanon in May 2000 was seen as testimony to Hizbollah's achievements, giving a boost to Al-Manar. When Palestinians rose up against Israeli occupation in September that year, Al-Manar responded by increasing its daily satellite transmission time from four to eighteen hours. But Al-Jazeera was in no way a model for Al-Manar. For one thing its schedules included entertainment programming, such as family-friendly soap operas and political quiz shows. More importantly, its anti-occupation agenda dictated an altogether different approach from Al-Jazeera's declared commitment to 'opinion and counter-opinion'. Far from respecting objectivity or neutrality, Al-Manar was conceived as a weapon of psychological warfare against the Israeli enemy. It was intended to reawaken the 'spirit of struggle in the Arab nation' by documenting the exploits of the resistance forces.[35] In pursuit of this aim, Al-Manar copied Al-Jazeera in one respect. It smartened its studio sets and presentation techniques.[36]

After the reconfigurations described above, the next significant rearrangement of the Arab satellite television landscape came with the entry of a small group of privately owned Egyptian channels in 2001–02. They were noteworthy in apparently signalling a chink in the Egyptian government's monopoly of locally incorporated broadcasting. For, although the ERTU had by this time learned to collaborate with private local production companies in order to fill the additional broadcasting capacity afforded by Nilesat, the authorities in Cairo had hitherto resisted giving private Egyptian ventures direct access to that capacity. So it was seen as something of a breakthrough when Egypt's information minister, Safwat al-Sharif, announced in January 2000 that non-government broadcasters would be allowed to operate from a designated media 'free zone' near Cairo, provided they did so by satellite. As concessions go, however, this one went only part of the way to satisfying would-be channel owners. Their business plans specifically required that Egyptian advertisers and Egyptian audiences be brought together. With satellite penetration still limited in Egypt at that point, the audience that could be reached by satellite transmission was widely regarded as too small to attract the kind of advertising that would make new television channels viable.[37] Nevertheless, a few local entrepreneurs were ready to take a chance. One was Ahmad Bahgat, head of a group of companies making a wide range of consumer goods, including televisions and video recorders, and owner of the ambitious Dreamland theme park and leisure complex near Cairo.[38] Bahgat established Dream TV with an initial investment reported at just E£30 million (US$4.8m), this being roughly equivalent to the amount he would otherwise have spent to advertise his wares on other channels.[39] Dream TV began in November 2001, setting out to build up gradually to three digital channels offering entertainment and talkshows aimed primarily at young people. The company made a virtue of focusing on music and movie stars, alongside analysis of political, economic and sports events. But it was not free to broadcast news or act independently of the ERTU. For, in order to be allowed to operate in the Media Production City free zone and transmit via Nilesat, Bahgat agreed to have the ERTU as a minority shareholder in Dream TV.[40] The pitfalls of this arrangement soon became apparent. Surviving in a crowded television market requires more publicity than a few video clips and film reviews will provide. Dream TV sought to make an impact by hiring a prominent Egyptian presenter, Hala Sirhan, who had made her name hosting talkshows on the Saudi-owned pay-TV network, ART. Sirhan twice sparked controversy on Dream TV in late 2002. On one occasion she interviewed the veteran Egyptian political analyst, Mohammed Hassanein Heikal. He used the interview to offer the politically risky opinion that the Egyptian president, Hosni Mubarak, should not expect to be succeeded as president by his son. In another incident, Sirhan opened a discussion on female masturbation, a subject widely regarded in the region as utterly taboo. This provoked an instant threat from the authorities that Dream TV's broadcasting licence would be withdrawn.[41]

Some Egyptians believed the threat of closure had more to do with Heikal's views on the presidency than sensitivities about sex. Either way, the furore demonstrated the risks of courting publicity by stepping out of line. Al-Jazeera, which established facilities in the Media Production City free zone, was also warned that its Egyptian operations could be jeopardized if its programmes caused offence. 'Unless Al-Jazeera stops attacking Egypt,' Safwat al-Sharif had warned in October 2000, 'I will be forced to take measures against it [including] forbidding it from having studios and correspondents in Egypt or broadcasting by satellite from Egypt.'[42] The constraints imposed on Dream TV also applied to other channels based in the so-called 'free' zone or uplinking from there to Nilesat. For some the constraints made little difference. Concerns about controversy hardly applied to operators such as the Lebanese fashion and cooking channel Heya (She), the Bahraini children's channel Space Toon, the Tiba channel of Dubai's ruling family, or the Egyptian home shopping channel Tamima. In contrast, Al-Mehwar, launched in February 2002 by a consortium of Egyptian investors, set itself up as the 'voice of civil society', offering a mix of entertainment and current affairs. On one hand Al-Mehwar faced restrictions imposed via the ERTU, which took a minority shareholding in Al-Mehwar as it did in Dream TV. On the other it could reach only homes equipped to receive digital transmissions from Nilesat. And all the time the number of competitor channels was increasing. For example, this period saw the emergence in London of two channels run by Rafiq Abdel-Moneim Khalifa, head of Algeria's Khalifa Group, which also incorporated a bank and an airline. The group, Algeria's biggest private company, collapsed in 2003 amid reports of financial irregularities and in August that year an international arrest warrant was issued for Mr Khalifa.[43]

Against this background of proliferating but often unstable channels, the creation of Al-Arabiya in February 2003 might seem unremarkable. But those Western reporters who drew attention to its arrival knew why it was newsworthy. Al-Arabiya, backed with initial capital of US$300 million and created from the news division of Saudi-owned MBC, was the project of a rich, influential and determined group of media investors who had made their aversion to Al-Jazeera very plain. Saudi Arabia recalled its ambassador to Qatar in September 2002 in protest at coverage on Al-Jazeera of a Saudi Arabian plan for Middle East peace. Saudi officials then boycotted regional meetings in the Qatari capital and denied visas to Al-Jazeera crews seeking to report on the annual pilgrimage to Muslim holy places in Saudi Arabia.[44] A similar ban prevented Al-Jazeera from covering meetings in Jeddah of Gulf Co-operation Council defence and foreign ministers, despite the heightened public interest in such meetings as US pressure mounted for war on Iraq. Depriving Al-Jazeera of access could work only to the advantage of Al-Arabiya and its backers.

These backers' identity was partially obscured by an arrangement that put Al-Arabiya under the ownership of a new Dubai-based company called Middle East News. Ownership of Middle East News, however, lay with the ARA group that owns MBC and with MBC's business ally, Future TV.[45] Collaboration over Middle East News appeared to reinforce a recently agreed alliance between MBC and Future TV in newsgathering and selling advertising space.[46] The editorial agenda for Al-Arabiya reflected the MBC connection and a concern to avoid any material deemed provocative. Ali al-Hedeithy, head of Middle East News, declared that the new channel would offer a 'wise and balanced alternative to Al-Jazeera'.[47] The man appointed as director of Al-Arabiya, Saleh Qallab, was a former information minister of Jordan, whose government had twice closed the offices of Al-Jazeera in protest at views expressed by talkshow guests – once in 1998 and again in 2002.[48] Confirmation of an initial Kuwaiti shareholding in Middle East News[49] expanded the representation of countries with governments hostile to Al-Jazeera. Kuwait ordered Al-Jazeera to close its Kuwaiti office in November 2002 for allegedly taking a 'hostile stand' against the country.[50]

What emerges from this narrative of Arab satellite station start-ups is that Al-Jazeera remained unusual, even after the launch of its rival, Al-Arabiya. Indeed, promotion for the latter stressed basic policy differences, pledging that Al-Arabiya would avoid what it described as 'deliberate provocation' on Al-Jazeera's part.[51] Further distinctions were also apparent. While most other satellite broadcasters began as offshoots of an existing cross-media operation or had guarantees of advertising revenue, Al-Jazeera was a stand-alone venture in which advertising deals could be clinched only for a single television channel (plus website, from 2001). This characteristic, combined with its controversial output, put Al-Jazeera more at risk of losing advertising income and made it more dependent in turn on state subventions from Qatar. But another conclusion to be drawn from the present study so far is that the nature of Arab satellite channels' editorial content is not necessarily determined by whether their funding comes from government or private sources. Indeed, the channels that spoke most openly of criticizing Arab governments (namely Al-Jazeera and Abu Dhabi TV) were themselves funded by governments, whereas the supposedly private backers of Al-Arabiya made it clear that they regarded such criticism as provocation. Having shown that dichotomies between state and market are not helpful in gauging levels of censorship or editorial autonomy in the Arab satellite media, it is time to look more closely for changes in output that might reflect greater responsiveness to audiences and greater scope for the initiative and creativity of editorial personnel.

Regard for Audience Appreciation

Arab populations across the Middle East and North Africa share a language and culture with each other and with Arab expatriate communities in Europe and America. Transnational television can bring them all together in a geolinguistic community configured by the footprints of communications satellites.[52] The size of this community, at around 310 million,[53] is sufficient to make it a readily viable market for film and television productions in Arabic, in the same way that the size of the US domestic market has long been a major factor in the economic success of the US television and film industry.[54] Where returns on investment are boosted by the sheer volume of sales, the profits from hit productions can be sufficient to cover the losses incurred by flops. The advent of Arab satellite television coincided with the rise of weighty Arab television companies owned by private businesses. Yet, as explained above, most had motives other than making financial profit directly from programme schedules. If audience satisfaction is not regarded as a prerequisite for survival, this undermines the commercial imperative of maximizing hits and minimizing flops. It may even suppress the science of discovering which programmes are most popular and why. Precise viewer ratings for channels and programmes would anyway have been out of keeping with a long tradition of Arab government resistance to public opinion polls.[55] Moreover, serious soundings of audience responses might have uncovered some unwelcome results. The two main research bodies in the region, the Pan-Arab Research Centre (PARC) and Stat-Ipsos, supplied clients with indications of channel 'reach' and approximate levels of advertising revenue, divided by channel. But detailed comparisons of viewer figures for specific programmes were either not publicly available or not trusted. Advertising executives regularly warned that, in the absence of metering systems and organized viewer panels, no company advertising on an Arab satellite channel could be completely sure what they were purchasing. In September 2002 the publisher of the Beirut-based monthly *ArabAd* found reason to bemoan once again the disconnection between satellite broadcasters' motives on one hand and viewer satisfaction on the other. He urged the Arab satellite stations to turn themselves into 'viable and transparent institutions that answer only to the viewer, take the dynamics of the market into consideration and feel the pulse of the [Arab] nation through professional research'.[56]

If the satellite stations were perceived as not answering 'only to the viewer' at this stage in their development, how far had they moved towards answering to the viewer at all? And to what extent was this an outcome of the simple fact that transnational television allowed viewers a level of choice they had not enjoyed hitherto, thereby creating de facto competition among broadcasters? Given this more competitive environment, could Al-Jazeera take credit for a shift towards responsiveness to viewers? In the absence of credible comparative audience studies, any evidence of a reorientation towards viewer appreciation has to be collected at the production end of the cycle, in the form of changes in programme format and content. Here the most notable change can be summed up in the notion of interactivity, in the sense of interactivity with viewers but also with sources. Moves in this direction could be seen in the evolving style of Arab satellite broadcasters' news bulletins and in the ever-growing phenomenon of the live phone-in talkshow. Importantly, Al-Jazeera, while emphasizing both genres, was not the first to invoke inter-activity. MBC and Orbit had already set precedents on both counts. MBC, as the first channel on the scene after ESC, distinguished itself from ESC by means of noticeably greater use of spot reports from its own correspondents in world capitals, who in turn gained access to a much greater range of sources. As Muhammad Ayish has noted, newscasts used to consist of either 'very long items dealing with leadership news or very short items dealing with regional and international developments',[57] presented with voice-overs that ignored the visual potential of television, treating it more or less like radio. MBC broke with this 'reactive' style. Its proactive and technically adept approach was deemed to be 'far more appreciated' by viewers, even though careful content analysis proved that MBC was avoiding a host of relevant and critical social and political issues, apparently for fear of their 'potentially alienating' effects.[58]

MBC also pioneered the transnational talkshow on Arab television when, in 1995, it introduced *Dialogue with the West* in partnership with Voice of America. The programme, which clocked up eighty episodes before running into US objections in late 1997,[59] enabled Arab and US representatives to talk to each other and to members of the public in the Arab world. Despite its name, therefore, it was also a mild form of inter-Arab dialogue and consequently judged to be popular with Arab viewers, who previously lacked opportunities for open debate.[60] Orbit, keen to attract subscribers to its expensive pay-TV bouquet, carried the experiment forward. In January 1996 it launched *On the Air* as what its chief executive said was the region's first show in the style of CNN's *Larry King Live*.[61] The format, involving interviews with high-profile political personalities, encouraged viewers to phone the programme to ask questions, which they could do without having to give their real name.

Thus the live phone-in talkshow was alive on Arab satellite tele-vision before Al-Jazeera. But it was not exactly kicking. Al-Jazeera's contribution was to stage debates guaranteed to cause controversy. The titles of its best-known shows – *The Opposite Direction* and *More than One Opinion* – illustrate this intent. The channel's director at that time, Mohammed Jassem al-Ali, told an interviewer in 1999: 'Debate on our channel is always controversial' because 'that is what makes for interesting television'.[62] The presenters of phone-in programmes on Al-Jazeera made history by inviting guests with diametrically opposed views to confront each other over acrimonious inter-Arab disputes. Too numerous to list, disputes discussed on screen included Kuwaiti support for UN sanctions on Iraq and Syrian objections to Jordan's 1994 peace treaty with Israel. Other Arab media organs might refer to these, but generally only from a single viewpoint, not as a matter of debate. At first, Arab viewers witnessing televised rows on such topics could hardly believe their eyes and ears. When the Egyptian novelist, Ahdaf Soueif, first stumbled on Al-Jazeera, she thought she was watching a play or a hoax. Here was a channel speaking in Arabic, but in a way she had only ever heard people speak in private, out of earshot of the feared and ubiquitous intelligence services.[63] The debate she watched was

> between two Algerians: one a dissident (and exiled) journalist, the other a representative of the government. It was ferocious. They were naming names, citing incidents, quoting figures. It was live – and alive. Then, wonder upon wonder, there was a phone-in. People called from all over the world to ask questions, express views [...] I phoned my mother, my brother: 'That's al-Jazeera,' they said. 'Isn't it amazing?'[64]

Officials criticized by talkshow guests on Al-Jazeera, or by interviewees on its news bulletins, accused the station of bias. Viewers disagreed. In 2002 a Gallup survey gauged responses to sixteen regional and international television channels, including BBC and CNN. At a time when the governments of Kuwait, Jordan and Saudi Arabia had imposed restrictions on Al-Jazeera in their territory, Kuwaiti, Jordanian and Saudi viewers with satellite access were found to be turning to Al-Jazeera first to catch up on the latest news before watching other channels. Fifty-four per cent of Kuwaiti residents questioned said they considered Al-Jazeera's news coverage objective, whereas only 19 per cent said the same of Kuwait Satellite TV.[65]

While Arab stations – both pan-Arab and terrestrial – sought to follow the format of Al-Jazeera's debates, they could not add the critical ingredient of editorial licence, either because they chose not to or because they were prevented. One account of attempts by Egyptian state television to follow Al-Jazeera's example summed them up as 'tepid glasnost'.[66] New programme titles, such as *Breakthrough*, *In-*

Depth, or *Without Censorship*, sounded adventurous. But closer inspection revealed that their content was manipulated to suit government agendas. Amr al-Leithy, presenter of *Breakthrough*, admitted that the Egyptian minister of information, Safwat al-Sharif, had to give his personal approval for political shows. A popular Egyptian programme, called *The Editor*, was billed by some as the state's answer to Al-Jazeera, boasting a presenter who rose to fame through pan-Arab satellite TV. Here again, however, the show was pre-recorded and sometimes clumsily cut.[67] As for live phone-ins on ESC, these typically allowed ample time for effusive salutations from callers to presenter and guest, but gave short shrift to thorny questions. This was in marked contrast to the strict rule of brevity imposed by the Al-Jazeera presenter, Faisal al-Qassem, on callers to *The Opposite Direction*. Although protracted greetings are customary in the Arab world, Qassem explained that this custom had to be set aside on *The Opposite Direction* in order to prevent each caller from 'taking time away from others'.[68] Meanwhile, broadcasters who tried to emulate Al-Jazeera in substance as well as form found themselves silenced. A Lebanese channel, New TV, advertised an episode of its talkshow *Without a Censor* with a line-up of pro-government and opposition figures from Saudi Arabia discussing gaps in the kingdom's budget, women's rights and tensions in relations with the USA. Immediately, the main owner of New TV, a long-time political opponent of the Lebanese prime minister, Rafiq Hariri, came under pressure to withdraw or alter the programme. As a last resort Hariri's government prevented it from being aired by cutting New TV's satellite link.[69] Officials later acknowledged that the programme had been censored to protect good relations between the Lebanese and Saudi governments. The episode was instructive to other satellite networks. Content that was barred to Lebanese channels would be equally unwelcome elsewhere.

Many pan-Arab channels paid Al-Jazeera the compliment of copying its programme titles. New TV's *Without a Censor* echoed Al-Jazeera's *Without Bounds*. Al-Jazeera's programme *Islamic Law and Life*, featuring an Egyptian cleric advising callers on matters of religion and personal conduct, inspired many copies. ART's religious affairs channel Iqra, Abu Dhabi TV and ESC were among those following the format, which provided a valuable opening for women callers to discuss treatment they had received in matters of marriage and divorce. In theory, perhaps, the programme with most scope for being reproduced in content as well as title was the daily, hour-long *Under Siege* slot, introduced to enable Palestinian callers to put on record their experience of Israeli attacks on West Bank towns and refugee camps in April 2002. In principle, accounts like this are not taboo on Arab television. Future TV's version of the programme was called *Above the Siege*, while the equivalent slots on Al-Manar had names like *Palestine Resists* and *Palestine is Steadfast*.

Expressing Palestinian anger is one thing and blaming those who failed to curb Israel or protect the Palestinians is another. Consisting entirely of live calls, e-mails and faxes from members of the public, *Under Siege* became a vehicle for outbursts as much against Arab leaders for their alleged impotence and inertia as against Israel or the USA.[70] Such protests were treated much more gingerly on other channels. And while Al-Jazeera, Abu Dhabi TV and Al-Manar showed worldwide demonstrations in solidarity with the Palestinians, most other Arab satellite channels were selective in which demonstrations they screened and which they overlooked. Nile News, for instance, had its own reporter interviewing demonstrators in Washington. On the Egyptian protests, in contrast, it was reduced to using official statistics and reports.[71] As world attention turned away from the Israeli–Palestinian conflict in the following months, callers pleaded with Al-Jazeera not to take *Under Siege* off the air. The channel's managers obliged by letting it run for six months and then renaming it *The Al-Jazeera Pulpit*. Under the slogan 'a platform for those without a platform', this was envisaged as a forum for public debate, in which callers would talk to each other over the airwaves, without having to direct their comments to a presenter and guest in the television studio. Public frustration with Arab governments was again evident before and during the US-led war on Iraq that began in March 2003. On 15 February 2003, a day of global protest against the war, satellite television images of a few hundred protesters in Cairo, ringed by rows of heavily armed riot police, contrasted starkly with images of millions marching in other capitals, including some in the Arab world. The Egyptian scenes were so widely seen on Al-Jazeera, Al-Manar and a few other channels that an embarrassed Egyptian government felt compelled to stage a more impressive anti-war rally in a stadium several days later.[72] But nor did Al-Jazeera save Qatar's blushes over its role in the US invasion of Iraq. In December 2002 it broadcast the signing ceremony at which the Qatari government gave permission for the USA to use Al-Udaid airbase as a command and control centre for the war.

For those channels unwilling or unable to air uncensored debates or screen footage of angry demonstrations on Arab streets, an alternative method was needed to woo viewers. LBC, one of the first to dub Mexican soap operas into Arabic and a conduit for many hours of American comedy and drama,[73] attracted male audiences with its culturally relaxed aerobics programme called *There's No-one for You but Haifa*. MBC and Future TV found suitable weapons when they bought the formats of two popular Western shows. MBC sought to replicate the success enjoyed by Western channels with *Who Wants to be a Millionnaire?*, while Future TV followed suit in late 2002 by launching auditions for an Arabic version of *Pop Idol*. In this way the gap left by an absence of risky or challenging home-grown productions was filled with safe imports. The imports chosen were also money-spinners, having the potential to earn revenues not only from advertising but from telephone calls by would-be contestants and, in the case of *Pop Idol*, by viewers voting for contestants.

Interest in these particular Western formats seems to confirm the trend towards interactivity as a dominant theme in the evolution of Arab satellite channels. But it also reinforces questions about whose interests interactivity ultimately serves. Whether in the delivery of current affairs or entertainment programming, interactivity sounds like evidence of a more balanced relationship between broadcaster and audience. Yet this study has revealed the reluctance of most broadcasters to allow their audiences to be freely and fully represented anywhere in their schedules and least of all in newscasts and talkshows. Any illusions about a new era of uncensored news coverage and free speech for all on satellite television were repeatedly shattered by events such as the closure of Al-Jazeera offices, the controls imposed on private Egyptian channels and the suspension of New TV's satellite link. Many argued that such illusions were anyway misplaced. 'What free media are we talking about?' a Saudi newspaper editor asked in 2001, rejecting the notion that an abundance of media outlets equates to media freedom.[74] A Bahraini businessman told a conference of Arab media professionals in 2002: 'The fact that we talk only about Al-Jazeera means it's the exception that proves the rule.'[75] It is true, conceded a veteran Jordanian columnist, that 'the fare on our Arab screens has changed'. But, he continued: 'the stark detachment between the Arab citizen who watches the new media and the realities of power in the contemporary Arab state means [...] the new Arab media are appendages of the ruling political and economic order in the Arab world, not challenges to it'.[76]

Al-Jazeera's particular brand of interactivity made viewers more acutely aware of the lack of uncensored public debate in their individual countries. But not even Al-Jazeera could be fully representative of its audience when officials from disapproving governments refused to take part in its debates. As for representing the interests of ordinary people to their local or national governments, Al-Jazeera, as a pan-Arab channel aimed at the widest possible transnational audience, could not be expected to plug the national gap.

Power Relations Inside Organizations

The final strand of investigation in this study concerns power relations between owners, managers and editorial staff inside the Arab organizations that broadcast by satellite. It was theorized in the Introduction,[77] and subsequently demonstrated, that dichotomies between state and private ownership of Arab satellite channels do not coincide with their willingness or otherwise to try to represent the public more effectively. It follows from this that the professional autonomy of media employees may not be linked intrinsically to whether they are employed by private companies or the state. Instead, in the context of Arab media, a more influential factor is likely to be the existence and enforcement of what are described locally as codes of ethics or 'honour' codes. The nature and content of these is key to understanding both the content of Arab satellite television and the company power structures that produce it. International norms, approved by bodies such as UNESCO and the International Federation of Journalists, see codes of journalistic practice as a matter to be decided not by administrators or law enforcement agencies but by journalists themselves.[78] This, as explained below, is not the way things work in the majority of Arab satellite channels. Nevertheless, during the six years under discussion, a process seemed to be under way whereby the most highly qualified media professionals across the sector increased their bargaining power *vis-à-vis* owners and managers, due in large part to a skills shortage and a training infrastructure that failed to keep pace with the rapid expansion of broadcasting capacity. Thus recruitment and promotion systems dependent on personal patronage were eroded. The question is whether this structural process was accompanied by an increase in editorial autonomy at the individual level and how widespread any such increase appeared to be.

A primary purpose of ethical standards in free media is to protect the rights of those who might be exposed to misrepresentation. It is also assumed that, in the age of instant live broadcasting, professionals may need ethical guidance on practical issues, such as handling scenes of violence or staged media events.[79] Both purposes imply that media workers have room for manoeuvre in making day-to-day editorial decisions. In the Arab media, however, live broadcasts (as shown above) generally remained carefully controlled well into the new millennium, while the question of misrepresentation continued to be seen primarily from the viewpoint not of ordinary citizens but of leaders and officials. The ERTU's Code of Ethics, for example, by prohibiting criticism of state officials, denied ERTU editors and journalists any real scope for initiative in probing official activities on behalf of the public at large. On the rare occasions when officials were held to account via the media, the process invariably resulted from government orchestration, not investigative journalism. Where terrestrial and satellite broadcasting is run by Arab governments, they, as employers, can enforce codes of conduct on employees. For those outside the government-owned media, vaguely worded penal codes and media laws give public figures and civil servants a higher level of protection from media scrutiny than ordinary individuals. 'In such a paradigm,' wrote Al-Jazeera's top investigative reporter Yosri Fouda, in 2001, 'the ruler becomes the chairman of the "journalistic" institution, the intelligence man the editor and the "journalist" the shadow.'[80]

It might be thought that transnational television would escape this paradigm. But transnational television companies, although transmitting through space, have their headquarters on the ground. By 2003, with MBC having moved from London to Dubai and Orbit moving from Rome to Bahrain, the majority of Arab satellite channels fell under Arab laws that interpret criticism of political leaders as defamation and make defamation a criminal offence. Some did not even need laws to encourage extreme caution and self-censorship. An MBC journalist who once did a report to camera on Israel's use of Apache helicopters against Palestinians was reprimanded afterwards for specifying that the Apaches were US-made.[81] Proof that formal re-strictions applied to transnational companies came when the Satellite Channels Co-ordinating Committee of the Arab States Broadcasting Union (ASBU), comprising both private and state channels, adopted a Code of Honour in 1998.[82] Although not published, this appeared to be aligned with the code adhered to by the Arab Federation of Journalists, itself replicating many elements of Arab countries' censor-ship laws. Following the ASBU decision, government ministers spoke of imposing a code of ethics on transnational companies operating in the various media 'free zones' set up around the Arab world.[83]

If a code of 'honour' also applied in Qatar, it was not obvious in Al-Jazeera's broadcasts. The Qatari ruler who came to power in 1995 abolished his country's ministry of information with the express intention of removing the very state institution that polices censor-ship in other Arab states.[84] Whatever Al-Jazeera's 'ethical' standards, its editorial norms rendered it ineligible for membership of the ASBU Satellite Channels Co-ordinating Committee.[85] The commit-tee sent many letters urging compliance but Al-Jazeera's executive director said his management would not accept the committee's terms.[86] Al-Jazeera's live broadcasts of 'vox pops' criticizing Arab government policies were clearly incompatible with observance of pro-establishment taboos. But the significant aspect of this incom-patibility from the point of view of internal power relations was that senior presenters on Al-Jazeera had to make instant decisions as individuals on how to handle politically sensitive material. They claimed to be left alone to make these decisions. Faisal al-Qassem, presenter of *The Opposite Direction*, once wrote: 'Al-Jazeera's editorial policy is so lax that I am hardly ever given orders regarding program content. My program is the most controversial show on the network, but no one interferes. I choose the subjects, and I choose the guests. [...] I tackle issues that I never even dreamed of covering during my service at the BBC.'[87] When a colleague from Abu Dhabi TV once suggested to Qassem that even the most adventurous presenters were effectively 'on a leash', Qassem strongly disagreed that this was the case in Al-Jazeera.[88] This was despite a recognition by all Al-Jazeera employees that, as Yosri Fouda put it, the channel's editorial freedom was the result not of structural economic and political independence, but of 'a grant from upstairs' – a grant that could be 'claimed back at any moment for whatever reason'.[89] Visitors to the Al-Jazeera studios, who watched *The Opposite Direction* being aired, confirmed that phone calls from viewers were not edited to remove insults or abuse.[90] Responsibility for handling contingencies was consequently in the hands of the presenter, increasing his celebrity status and bargaining power with his employer. When Qassem himself once referred to Arab leaders as 'bastards', he was taken off the air but brought back after four weeks.[91] Similar judgement calls about what should or should not be screened had likewise to be made in the heat of the moment by those reporting live events, without consultations with upper echelons of the hierarchy. Staff at Al-Jazeera during this period routinely identified their guiding principle as that of achieving balance, citing as evidence of their success the fact that they had been accused in almost equal measure of bias towards Osama Bin Laden and bias towards Israel and the USA. A senior representative of Abu Dhabi TV endorsed this indirectly in an interview, when he cited Al-Jazeera as a benchmark against which his own channel measured its professionalism.[92] Al-Arabiya paid the same compliment when it tried to poach fifteen Al-Jazeera staff, offering to double or treble their salaries.[93] It remained to be seen whether those leaving Al-Jazeera for other stations would take the ethos of Al-Jazeera with them, or whether their new employers would expect a more submissive approach. Al-Arabiya, for example, let it be known that its editorial policy would be decided by a 'council of wise men'.[94] In theory this was to protect the channel from the influence of shareholders. In practice it seemed more in keeping with Arab media traditions of deference to authority than a brave new future in which media professionals would be trusted to set standards of their own.

Conclusion

Al-Jazeera was one of a host of Arab newcomers entering the transnational television arena during the closing years of the twentieth century and the opening years of the twenty-first. By comparing Al-Jazeera's source of funding, its relationship with viewers, and its management style with those of other stations, this study aimed to assess the extent of change in Arab satellite television during this period and to discover whether, six years after its establishment, Al-Jazeera could be said to have provided a model that other channels followed. On all the criteria considered, critical distinctions emerged between Al-Jazeera and other channels. As a venture funded primarily by the ruler of a Gulf state, and thus able to ride out at least a temporary slump in advertising income, Al-Jazeera could be compared with other channels backed by ruling families. But that comparison was shown to break down with respect to day-to-day interference from owners and backers, which appears to have had much less direct effect on Al-Jazeera's content during the period under review than was the case for other channels. In its relationship with audiences, Al-Jazeera's emphasis on interactivity was not unique; it drew on experiments already conducted by existing networks and provided a stimulus for others to follow. But interactivity in format does not automatically bring interactivity in content. The evidence points to Al-Jazeera representing a noticeably wider range of opinion than its counterparts. Al-Jazeera's rejection of entrenched pan-Arab codes of journalistic submissiveness also distinguished it from other channels.

This comparative exercise also indicated the limits to change in Arab satellite television during the period reviewed. Al-Jazeera itself remained dependent on continuing financial support from Qatar's ruling family. The creation of Al-Arabiya, chronologically the last of the channels considered here, demonstrated that most Arab media investors were still motivated by the desire to get their own voice heard rather than by any interest in broadcasting the opinions and concerns of viewers. In other words, most ordinary citizens of Arab countries remained virtually voiceless despite the spread of transnational television, which may perhaps explain the angry street protests and extreme sentiments captured on camera by Al-Jazeera, Abu Dhabi TV and Al-Manar.

Notes

1. Examples of coverage monitored by this author include: *International Herald Tribune, Washington Post, Los Angeles Times, Financial Times*, BBC online and BBC Radio 4.

2. Naomi Sakr, 'Frontiers of Freedom: Diverse Responses to Satellite Television in the Middle East and North Africa', *Javnost/The Public*, 6(1) (1999), pp. 93–106.

3. Magda Maurice, deputy editor of *Al-Gumhuriya*, addressing the conference on New Media and Change in the Arab World (Amman, 27 February–1 March 2002).

4. Peter Golding and Graham Murdock, 'Culture, Communications and

Political Economy', in James Curran and Michael Gurevitch (eds), *Mass Media and Society* (London: Arnold, 2000), p. 70.

5. Naomi Sakr, *Satellite Realms: Transnational Television, Globalization and the Middle East* (London: I.B. Tauris, 2001), p. 87.

6. Sakr, *Satellite Realms*, p. 57.

7. Mohammed Jassem al-Ali, then executive director of Al-Jazeera, told the author in Amman on 1 March 2002: 'There is no pressure to pay [the loan] back in a given time frame because the Qatari government knows it will get the money back not as money but in intangible benefits.'

8. The presenter, Faisal al-Qassem, was speaking on the record to the author, in Cambridge, 3 November 2002.

9. Qatar's total population was 600,000 in 2000, with a total GDP that year of US$14.5bn, according to the United Nations Development Programme in its *Human Development Report 2002* (New York, 2002), pp. 163, 191.

10. Manjunath Pendakur and Jyotsna Kapur, 'Think Globally, Program Locally: Privatization of Indian National Television', in Mashoed Bailie and Dwayne Winseck (eds), *Democratizing Communication: Comparative Perspectives on Information and Power* (Cresskill, NJ: Hampton Press, 1997), p. 213.

11. Karel Jakubowicz, 'Media in Transition: The Case of Poland', in Monroe Price, Beata Rozumilowicz and Stefaan Verhulst (eds), *Media Reform: Democratizing the Media, Democratizing the State* (London: Routledge, 2002), pp. 203–4.

12. Louise Bourgault, *Mass Media in Sub-Saharan Africa* (Bloomington: Indiana University Press, 1995), p. 65.

13. Colin Sparks, 'Media Theory after the Fall of European Communism: Why the Old Models from East and West Won't Do Any More', in James Curran and Myung-Jin Park (eds), *De-Westernizing Media Studies* (London: Routledge, 2000), p. 47.

14. 'The attention of students of the media interested in finding ways in which they may be democratized would be better directed at the relationships between the media and their audiences, and the fault lines within media organizations between those who give orders and those who are forced to take them' (Sparks, 'Media Theory', p. 47).

15. Sakr, *Satellite Realms*, pp. 40–9.

16. Naomi Sakr, 'Al-Jazeera Satellite Channel: Global Newscasting in Arabic', in Annabelle Sreberny and Chris Paterson (eds), *News in the Twenty-First Century* (Luton: University of Luton Press, forthcoming).

17. Sakr, *Satellite Realms*, p. 51.

18. Jean-Marc Belchi, 'Evolution of TV Viewing in the Middle East 1996–2000'. Paper presented to the conference on New Media and Change in the Arab World (Amman, 27 February–1 March 2002).

19. Sakr, *Satellite Realms*, p. 59.

20. 'Rifaat Assad's Son to Launch "Bold" New Satellite Channel', *Mideast Mirror*, 28 May 1997, p. 9.

21. Author's interview with Paul Hitti, ANN executive director, London, 28 February 1998.

22. <Arabicnews.com>. Consulted November 1999.

23. Noha el-Hennawy, 'ANN: Satellite on a Shoestring', *Transnational Broadcasting Studies*, 9 (Autumn/Winter 2002), <http://www.tbsjournal.com/Archives/Fall02/ANN.html>. Consulted March 2003.

24. Sakr, *Satellite Realms*, p. 60.

25. Edmund Ghareeb, 'New Media and the Information Revolution in the Arab World: An Assessment', *Middle East Journal*, 54(3) (Summer 2000), p. 411.

26. Naomi Sakr, 'Contested Blueprints for Egypt's Satellite Channels', *Gazette*, 63(2–3) (May 2001), p. 163.

27. As summarized by Hussein Amin, professor of journalism and mass communication at the American University in Cairo. See Amil Khan, 'Al-Jazeera Inspires Citizens, Infuriates Government', *Middle East Times*, 11 October 2002.

28. Author's interview, Cairo, 15 August 1998.

29. Author's interview with Adel Hamdi, London, 18 July 2000.

30. Sheikh Abdullah bin Zayed al-Nahayan, the UAE minister of information, has regularly expressed such sentiments. See, for example, his speech printed in *ArabAd*, 8(4) (April 1998), pp. 36–7.

31. See Sarah Sullivan's interview with Mohamed Dourrachad, deputy director of Abu Dhabi Television, in *Transnational Broadcasting Studies*, 8 (Spring/Summer 2002), <http://www.tbsjournal.com/Archives/Spring02/dourrachad.html>. Consulted January 2003.

32. Panel debate on 'The Centrality of Live Talks' as part of a conference on 'Arab Satellite Channels in the Age of Globalization' (University of Cambridge, 2–3 November 2002).

33. Dima Dabbous-Sensenig, 'Ending the War?: The Lebanese Broadcasting Act of 1994', PhD thesis (Sheffield Hallam University, 2002), pp. 176, 185.

34. *Jordan Times*, 10 March 2000.

35. Hussein Humayed, Al-Manar, addressing the conference on 'New Media Change in the Arab World' (Amman, 27 February–1 March 2002).

36. Victoria Firmo-Fontan, 'Al-Manar's Narrative in a Post 9/11 Context'. Paper presented to the conference on 'Media Representation of Islamic Societies and War' (University of Sussex, 1 July 2002).

37. Heba Kandil, 'ERTU, Investors at Odds over Media Privatization',

Transnational Broadcasting Studies, 4 (Spring 2000), <http://www.tbsjournal.com/Archives/Spring00/Departments3/News/news.html>. Consulted February 2003.

38. David Butter, 'A Hint of Florida Comes to Cairo', *Middle East Economic Digest*, 2 April 1999, p. 8.

39. Naila Hamdy, 'A Dream TV Come True', *Transnational Broadcasting Studies*, 8 (Spring/Summer 2002), <http://www.tbsjournal.com/Archives/Spring02/sirhan.html>. Consulted February 2003.

40. The ERTU also owns 50 per cent of Media Production City and 40 per cent of Nilesat.

41. Middle East Online, 'Dream TV in Trouble over Program', *meo.tv*, 1 November 2002, <www.meo.tv/english/culture/?id=3-78=3078>. Consulted November 2002.

42. *Middle East Times*, 'Egypt Threatens to Pull Plug on Qatar-based TV Station', 26 October 2000.

43. *Middle East Economic Survey*, 'Interpol Issues Arrest Warrant for Head of Algeria's Khalifa Group', 25 August 2003.

44. *Jordan Times*, 'Al Jazeera TV Barred from Covering Hajj', 11 February 2003.

45. Ali al-Hedeithy, chief executive of Al-Arabiya, acknowledged the role of Future TV in an interview with Abdullah Schleifer published in *Transnational Broadcasting Studies*, 9 (Fall/Winter 2002), <http://www.tbsjournal.com/Archives/Fall02/Hedeithy.html>. Consulted March 2003.

46. May Farah, 'Together We are Stronger', *Gulf Marketing Review*, March 2002, p. 56.

47. *Arab News*, 'Al-Arabiya: A Balanced Alternative to Al-Jazeera?', 17 February 2003.

48. Sakr, *Satellite Realms*, p. 120; 'Jordan Carpets Qatar over TV', *BBC News Online*, 8 August 2002, <http://news.bbc.co.uk/1/hi/world/middle_east/2181647.stm>. Consulted August 2002.

49. Kuwaiti involvement was confirmed in the interview mentioned in Note 45. Kuwaiti investors, however, soon withdrew from Al-Arabiya because of differences over the channel's coverage of the US-led invasion of Iraq.

50. *Jordan Times*, 'Al-Jazeera Closed Down for "Hostile" Stand against Kuwait', 5 November 2002.

51. The word 'provocative' was used by Ali al-Hedeithy in his press interviews and by Saleh Qallab in his regular column in Jordan's official daily, *Al-Rai*. See Sana Abdullah, 'New News Channel "Calmer" than Al-Jazeera', *Middle East Times*, 28 February 2003.

52. John Sinclair, Elizabeth Jacka and Stuart Cunningham, 'Peripheral Vision', in John Sinclair, Elizabeth Jacka and Stuart Cunningham (eds), *New*

Patterns in Global Television: Peripheral Vision (Oxford: Oxford University Press, 1996), p. 26.

53. Arab inhabitants of the Middle East and North Africa numbered 281 million in 2000, according to the United Nations Development Progamme's *Arab Human Development Report 2002* (New York, 2002), p. 144. Annual growth rates implied in that report's population data would indicate an approximate total of 304 million in 2003. European and US residents of Arab origin may be assumed to raise this total to around 310 million, although the precise figure is uncertain. For example, the 2000 census in the USA listed 1.3 million Arab Americans, but some estimates were said to put the number three times that high. See *The Economist*, 'Arab-Americans: Under Suspicion', 29 March 2003, p. 53.

54. Colin Hoskins, Stuart McFadyen and Adam Finn, *Global Television and Film* (Oxford: Oxford University Press, 1997), pp. 38–9.

55. Mark Tessler, 'The Contribution of Public Opinion Research to an Understanding of the Information Revolution and Its Impact in North Africa and Beyond', in Emirates Center for Strategic Studies and Research (ed.), *The Information Revolution and the Arab World: Its Impact on State and Society* (Abu Dhabi: Emirates Center for Strategic Studies and Research, 1998), p. 79.

56. Walid Azzi, 'It's About Time … ', *ArabAd*, 12(8) (September 2002), p. 7.

57. Muhammad Ayish, 'American-style Journalism and Arab World Television: An Exploratory Study of News Selection at Six Arab World Satellite Television Channels', *Transnational Broadcasting Studies*, 6 (Spring/ Summer 2001), <http://www.tbsjournal.com/Archives/Spring01/Ayish.html>. Consulted February 2002.

58. Muhammad Ayish, 'Arab Television Goes Commercial', *Gazette*, 59(6) (December 1997), pp. 490–1.

59. Jon Alterman, *New Media, New Politics? From Satellite Television to the Internet in the Arab World* (Washington, DC: Washington Institute for Near East Policy, 1998), p. 21.

60. Najib Ghadbian, 'Contesting the State Media Monopoly: Syria on Al-Jazira Television', *Middle East Review of International Affairs*, 18 June 2001.

61. Orbit's chief executive at the time, Alexander Zilo, was interviewed by Rebecca Hawkes for *Middle East Broadcast and Satellite*, 5(3) (May 1997), p. 28.

62. Chris Forrester, 'Broadcast Censorship: It's a Question of Culture', *Middle East Broadcast and Satellite*, 6(7) (October 1999), p. 15.

63. Ahdaf Soueif, 'It Provides the One Window through Which We Can Breathe', *Guardian (G2)*, 9 October 2001.

64. Ibid.

65. *Gulf News*, 'Viewers Say Al-Jazeera Objective and Daring', 21 November 2002.

66. Andrew Hammond, 'Egyptian TV Fights Arab Rivals with Tepid Glasnost', *Middle East Times*, 8 June 2001.

67. Andrew Hammond, 'The Rise of Hamdi Kandil', *Middle East International*, 664, 7 December 2001, p. 23.

68. For instance, in his programme on 14 April 2002, Faisal al-Qassem reminded viewers he had two rules: 'no personal insults' and 'keep it short'.

69. Nagib Khazzaka, 'Row Grows in Lebanon over Government Bar on Saudi Programme', *Middle East Times*, 3 January 2003; Jim Quilty, 'The Politics of Television', *Middle East International*, 691, 10 January 2003, p. 18.

70. Sana Kamal, 'The Power of Satellite TV', *Middle East International*, 673, 19 April 2002.

71. Abbas El Tounsy, 'Reflections on the Arab Satellites, the Palestinian Intifada and the Israeli War', *Transnational Broadcasting Studies*, 8 (Spring/Summer 2002), <http://www.tbsjournal.com/Archives/Spring02/arab_satellites.html>. Consulted March 2003.

72. Steve Negus, 'State of Emergency', *Middle East International*, 695, 7 March 2003, p. 22. Despite organizing the rally, the government ordered harsh treatment of participants in subsequent anti-war protests, eliciting a strong protest from the Euro-Med Human Rights Network on 7 April 2003.

73. Edmund Ghareeb, 'New Media and the Information Revolution in the Arab World: An Assessment', *Middle East Journal*, 54(3) (Summer 2000), p. 403.

74. Abdel-Rahman al-Rashed, 'What Free Media are We Talking About?', *Arab News*, 26 August 2001.

75. Ubaydli Ubaydli of Al-Nadeem Technology, addressing the conference on 'New Media and Change in the Arab World' (Amman, 27 February–1 March 2002).

76. Rami Khouri, 'Arab Satellite Marriage – Ben Laden and Madonna', *Jordan Times*, 27 November 2002.

77. Based on Sparks, 'Media Theory', p. 47.

78. UNESCO's January 1996 Sanaa Declaration states: 'Guidelines for journalistic standards are the concern of the news media professionals. Any attempt to set down standards and guidelines should come from the journalists themselves' (United Nations Educational, Scientific and Cultural Organization, *Final Report of the Seminar on Promoting Independent and Pluralistic Arab Media*, Paris, 1996).

79. Nigel Harris, 'Codes of Conduct for Journalists', in Andrew Belsey and Ruth Chadwick (eds), *Ethical Issues in Journalism and the Media* (London: Routledge, 1992), p. 64.

80. Yosri Fouda, 'Here We Stand: We Cannot Do Otherwise', *Transnational Broadcasting Studies*, 6 (Spring/Summer 2001), <http://www.tbsjournal.com/Archives/Spring01/Jazeera.html>. Consulted January 2002.

81. Personal communication to the author, Amman, 2 March 2002. The reference to the helicopters' US origins was apparently deemed detrimental to Saudi Arabia's relations with the USA.

82. Sakr, *Satellite Realms*, p. 162.

83. For example, in April 2000, the ERTU's director, Abdel-Rahman Hafez, spoke of an 'Arab code of ethics' applying to organizations opening offices in the media free zone near Cairo. See Nadia Abou El-Magd, 'A Stone's Throw Away', *Al-Ahram Weekly*, 20–26 April 2000. For the application of similar codes in Jordan and Lebanon see Sakr, *Satellite Realms*, pp. 110–11.

84. Sheikh Hamad bin Thamer Al Thani, chair of Al-Jazeera, told an interviewer: 'Simply speaking, the ministry of information, in one way or another, is the ministry that controls the news media ... [W]e looked to the Western world which has very advanced media, and found that there are no ministries of information. We don't see that a ministry of information has any positive role to play in future media projects,' *Transnational Broadcasting Studies*, 7 (Fall/Winter 2001), p. 2, <http://www.tbsjournal.com/Archives/Fall01/Jazeera_chairman.html>. Consulted March 2003.

85. Sakr, *Satellite Realms*, p. 162.

86. Author's interview with Mohammed Jassem al-Ali, Amman, 1 March 2002.

87. Quoted in Mohammed El-Nawawy and Adel Iskandar, *Al-Jazeera: How the Free Arab News Network Scooped the World and Changed the Middle East* (Cambridge, MA: Westview Press, 2002), p. 97.

88. The exchange took place at the Cambridge conference on Arab satellite channels mentioned in Note 32.

89. Fouda, 'Here We Stand'.

90. Brian Whitaker, 'Battle Station', *Guardian*, 7 February 2003.

91. According to Qassem in remarks addressed to the conference on 'Arab Satellite Channels in the Age of Globalization' (University of Cambridge, 2 November 2002).

92. Mohammed Dourrachad, deputy director of Abu Dhabi Television, said in an interview with Sarah Sullivan: 'Abu Dhabi TV has one of the most professional groups of journalists in the Arab world, at the same level as Al-Jazeera if not more,' *Transnational Broadcasting Studies*, 8 (Spring/Summer 2002), p. 7, <http://www.tbsjournal.com/Archives/Spring02/dourrachad.html>. Consulted January 2003.

93. According to Al-Jazeera's then editor-in-chief, Ibrahim Hilal. See Anthony Shadid, 'Rivalry for Eyes of Arab World', *Washington Post*, 11 February 2003.

94. According to Ali al-Hedeithy, of Middle East News. See *Arab News*, 'Al-Arabiya: A Balanced Alternative to Al-Jazeera?', 17 February 2003.

CHAPTER 5

Transnational Television in Sub-Saharan Africa

Graham Mytton, Ruth Teer-Tomaselli
and André-Jean Tudesq

§ TELEVISION is less developed in Africa than in any other continent. Fewer people have a television set at home and there are fewer TV stations transmitting per head of population than on any other continent.[1] Television in sub-Saharan countries is characterized by the following features:

- the dominance of state-owned and -controlled broadcasting;
- broadcasting that is for the most part national, rather than local or regional;
- dominance of imported content, mainly from Europe and the United States;
- dominance of three European languages, French, English and Portuguese;
- under-investment and poverty of facilities leading to low levels of local production;
- low levels of inter-African co-operation in television production, exchange and marketing.

Each of these factors has also slowed or hindered the development of transnational television. The market is limited, the risks are high and the potential profit for commercial ventures is small. But at the start of the twenty-first century there are signs of change and of the beginnings of continent-wide activity that will begin to shape much of the future of African TV in a different way.

European influence continues to guide the development of African TV. This is not necessarily always something that comes direct from Europe; it happens because of the linguistic legacy that the colonial powers bequeathed the continent, for good or ill. As noted, European languages dominate African television, and chiefly this means English and French, with the less widespread addition of Portuguese. It means that these three languages define three broadly different television landscapes, certainly so far as transnational television activity is concerned.[2] US influence and input is now also of growing importance, mainly in anglophone countries. Similarly, Brazilian involvement and influence is beginning to be seen in lusophone countries.

Transnational Television in an African Context

In contrast to radio, which crossed national boundaries from its earliest days, depending as it does on areas of the electromagnetic spectrum that carry much further, television, for many years, was broadcast within the boundaries of a particular country. The exceptions to this rule were television channels that spilled over national boundaries. For instance, populations of the two capitals of the two Congos, on either side of the Congo River, have for several years been able to watch television services from the other country. People in northern areas of Tanzania could watch Kenyan TV in the 1960s, twenty-five years before TV eventually came to Tanzania. Similarly, people in Botswana and Lesotho could watch South African TV long before they had their own national TV stations. Aside from these, most services are contained within the boundaries of the nation state. Broadcasting frequency bands are pre-planned and internally co-ordinated through the International Telecommunication Union (ITU) to avoid mutually harmful interference between neighbouring countries. The current international frequency assignment plans for television are included in the regional agreements established by the ITU and adopted by signatory countries. Currently, the VHF and UHF bands for television are set between 174MHz and 470MHz to 854MHz, according to the Geneva Plan of 1989 for Africa and neighbouring countries. These regulations require that all medium- and high-power frequencies are co-ordinated with neighbouring countries so as not to cause intentional trans-border interference. Any new frequency or relation of a frequency or increase in transmitter power of a medium- or high-power transmitter situated within approximately 400km from any border of South Africa's neighbours (Namibia, Botswana, Zimbabwe, Swaziland, Lesotho or Mozambique), to take

just one important example, would require extensive bilateral negotiations. Although this planning and co-ordination takes place, in many
instances trans-border spillage is unavoidable.[3]

TV in Africa, with a few exceptions, was introduced after each
of the new states had achieved independence, and at a time when
government monopoly over the electronic media had been well established. Links with the former colonial powers were reflected to some
extent in the content and style of the output. This was especially
so in the former French colonies. The close links that the majority
of francophone states maintained with France led to a dependency
on programmes from France and on news images sent via satellite,
although the state-run national television stations exercised control
over their programming.[4]

Advances in television technology, together with a relative liberalization of the media and the phenomenon of globalization, led to the
growth of transnational television activity in Africa, starting during
the last decade of the twentieth century. The synergies between telecommunications, information technology and electronics all increased
the possibilities for satellite television business in Africa.

There were three main ways for transnational television to develop
at this stage in Africa's media development. One was to reach general
populations through existing terrestrial stations. For this to happen,
links needed to be made with these stations. The second way to go
was similar to the route taken by several entrepreneurs in Europe and
Asia – the direct-to-home satellite television service, as demonstrated
most successfully by BSkyB in the UK and Star TV in South Asia.
The third way was to use cable or MMDS – Multipoint Multichannel
Distribution Service – to bring satellite television services to households who paid a subscription for them to be provided without the
need for a satellite dish.[5]

For any of these three developments to occur, however, changes
in the political and cultural sphere were necessary. The more liberal atmosphere necessary for transnational television to grow was
slow to develop in many parts of Africa. To some extent it is still
to emerge in some countries. But in most of the forty-eight sub-
Saharan states, deregulation of some kind has lifted restrictions on
broadcasting activities, formerly a government monopoly in every
African country. This has facilitated not only the emergence of several
hundred private radio stations but also allowed the retransmission

of international short-wave services on local FM frequencies. This is how one can hear France's international radio service, RFI (Radio France International) as well as the BBC World Service on local FM frequencies in the capitals and major cities of many countries. The same liberalization that has allowed this development has also opened the market to the wider distribution of satellite TV services, both private and state-funded. It has also permitted the establishment of a growing number of private commercial stations.

Today, transnational television activities in Africa can be grouped into five categories:

1. terrestrial cross-border television – coming from a neighbouring country;
2. television received direct to the home from satellite. This can be further categorized or subdivided. There is direct reception by motorized satellite dish or, because of the high cost of these, by means of a less sophisticated fixed dish, which often may be home-made and relatively inexpensive. These are especially to be found in francophone countries such as Mali, Mauritania, Niger and Senegal, but are also seen increasingly in Nigeria, Kenya, Zambia and Angola;
3. television provided by national terrestrial television stations, both public and private, which relay foreign television programmes received via satellite at certain times;
4. terrestrially transmitted pay-TV services which broadcast mainly foreign programmes;
5. cable or MMDS television services, which transmit television channels received via satellite.

There is something of a gulf in sub-Saharan Africa between the number of television stations available on satellite and the number of channels actually seen by African audiences. In the former case, it was calculated that in July 2002, around 250 channels were transmitted by some twenty-two satellites over Africa, of which approximately one hundred were in English, eighty-six French, thirty Arabic, seven Portuguese, several in major Indian languages and the others in different non-African tongues. Only three were in sub-Saharan African languages – one in Amharic and two in Afrikaans. We concentrate in this study on those channels that are effectively received by viewers, either directly or indirectly by the above five methods.

Another major characteristic of transnational television in Africa is that, at present, little of its content is specifically designed for or created in the continent, another reflection of Africa's poverty. Aside from some South African productions that can be seen from services available from that country, there is at present not much else on offer that can be described as indigenous. Many of the present trans-national television services received in Africa are actually produced for domestic channels in Europe or North America – for example for TF1 or Canal Plus in France or for the BBC in the UK or NBC in the USA. Others are produced for international audiences in all parts of the world, such as much of the output of CFI, CNN and BBC World.

Although they are beyond the main focus of this study, terrestrial television stations represent the most common form of viewing of transnational television programmes. Some of the newer private channels broadcast mostly, or even entirely, imported programmes, as can be seen in Kenya with Nation TV. Many such stations have emerged in recent years and the trend can be expected to continue.

Transnational television in francophone Africa is better developed than elsewhere and reaches more audience numbers. For this reason the section on francophone activity will occupy more space here. While the different linguistic regions of Africa operate largely separately, this is not to say that there are no linkages. There is in fact a growing number of connections and further growth can be expected.

Francophone Africa

Television is unevenly established in sub-Saharan Africa. In some francophone countries, there is a wide gap between urban and rural areas. There are also some major differences between one country and another in levels of access to and development of the medium. Although it is widely available in Côte d'Ivoire, in Gabon and in Cameroon, and particularly well developed in the capital cities of Senegal and the two Congos, it is underdeveloped in the Central African Republic, Chad, Rwanda and Mali. State control is found everywhere. In the whole of francophone Africa, private television services are of significant importance only in the Congo (DRC). In the rest of francophone Africa, there are relatively few private tele-vision stations, and those that do exist are mostly the result of links with foreign partners.

The rapid and successful development of the more popular and successful francophone transnational television stations in Africa has resulted from France's own political and cultural approach, which among other things seeks to extend and strengthen co-operation between countries that have the French language in common. In effect francophone African countries have joined with France, Canada, Switzerland and Belgium in an international 'community' held together by the French language.[6] Interestingly, bilingual Canada appears to be the most active of these countries outside France. The policy of co-operation with state-owned African television services, which France has maintained since independence was gained by its former colonies, has been implemented thanks to good relations with these African states. France has extended its policy of co-operation to include those states that were former Belgian colonies.

Canal France International (CFI) is the outward audiovisual instru-ment of this aspect of international French policy. When it was set up in May 1989, CFI broadcast encrypted programmes via the Intelsat V satellite solely to African terrestrial television stations, combining the activities of AITV (Agence Internationale de Télévision) and those of FMI – France Media International. The AITV was set up in 1983 as part of RFO – Radio France Outre-mer – (taking over the transmis-sion of programmes previously sent daily by France's public channel, FR3), while FMI had exclusive rights over the export of programmes produced by French public television.

Some earlier ambiguity about this policy was due to another French collaboration with African states, devised by Hervé Bourges[7] in the context of Canal Plus Africa at the end of 1987 with the creation of Canal Horizons, the first pay-TV station aimed at fran-cophone Africa whereby a public company would be set up in every country where this service of encrypted programmes was received via satellite. Canal Horizons (supported by Canal Plus and SOFIRAD, the French state media enterprise) would be a shareholder in such a company and would market the channels, the first of which was established in Senegal in December 1991. Furthermore, in 1992, the francophone television station TV5, launched in Europe in 1984, created TV5 Afrique, pioneered by the Quebecois,[8] followed by the

Belgians and the Swiss, while the French joined in only later. At its inception, TV5 Afrique was simply a broadcast of TV5 Europe to Africa.

The domination of the English-speaking media at the beginnings of global television through satellite, as well as the dominance of US output in the field of internationally marketed programming, led to a reform of French media policy, as recommended by a report on France's 'international audiovisual policy', requested in 1987 by Jacques Chirac, then French prime minister. Developments followed quickly with increasing globalization and the extension of MMDS networks. CFI could now be received directly by the general public either through subscription services or through the terrestrial broadcasting of its programmes by African state television stations. Using the same satellite decoder, subscribers could also receive both TV5 and Canal Horizons in all parts of the continent.

Audiovisual broadcasts in French form one of the cornerstones of France's cultural policy and indeed the general policy in promoting France's interests and language. Alongside CFI (public), Canal Horizons (private) and TV5 Afrique (mixed), which is aimed particularly at sub-Saharan Africa, the interest in developing a French-language news channel benefited from the withdrawal of the British news production company, ITN, from the Euronews consortium in March 2003. ITN's departure has already facilitated a strengthening of the French presence in the news channel through an increase of France Télévisions' holdings.

French policy aimed to co-ordinate its international audiovisual programme more effectively and CFI was extended into lusophone and anglophone Africa. There was also the emergence of private, fee-charging networks. In January 1998 a digital platform was launched for francophone Africa, comprising eight channels: CFI-TV, TV5, Planète, Canal Plus, Arte, Euronews, MCM and RTL9. Later it added Canal Horizons and three others.

The main international francophone TV broadcaster is CFI. Since June 2000 one of its subsidiaries manages SAT (Satellite Africa Television) formerly Portinvest, created in 1997 by SOFIRAD, which sold its capital in June 2000 to CFI. Only CFI and TV5 are broadcast direct, while a subscription and a decoder are both necessary for the other French-language satellite channels. Since April 2002, however, SAT also broadcasts Arte, the Franco-German cultural TV channel, and France 2 and France 5, which can be received either by direct satellite reception or by MMDS in Mali, Niger, Senegal, Togo and Burkina Faso.

Since the launch of its first programmes on 17 May 1989, CFI has increased the duration of its programming. From 1995 it has been broadcasting twenty-four hours a day across five continents, especially to twenty-nine television stations in twenty-seven sub-Saharan African countries. The French Ministry for Co-operation has equipped the majority of these stations with the satellite receiving equipment needed.

Nowadays, there are two arms to CFI. The first is CFI Pro, which distributes 237 programme hours each month (of which 85 per cent are free), to forty-six African television stations in forty countries, mostly francophone but also some anglophone and lusophone, which are especially interested in receiving sports programmes (which make up 14.7 per cent of programmes broadcast by CFI Pro). These television stations receiving CFI services are then able to decide whether to retransmit entire programmes or parts of them in their schedules. CFI has also become accessible direct as a television channel, which can be received in its entirety from satellite, like other French digital programmes, and this is its second arm.

Canal Horizons has given rise to two companies in sub-Saharan Africa. Canal Horizons Senegal was set up in 1991 as a joint venture with Canal Horizons holding 15 per cent of the capital, together with the state broadcaster and private investors. Then in Côte d'Ivoire in December 1992, Canal Horizons won the tender to become a private television station and received its own frequency. The channel is broadcast by SEDACI, which was set up in 1994 by Canal Plus, together with SOFIRAD, and capital from Côte d'Ivoire. Danielle Boni-Claverie, former director of state broadcaster RTI and minister of communication in the Ivorian government, was its first president. Since April 1995, SEDACI also broadcasts TV5.[9]

In May 2002, Canal Horizons launched Canal Satellite Horizons in Côte d'Ivoire, a digital francophone bouquet of over twenty radio and television channels, which can be received direct via satellite with a 90cm dish. Broadcast from satellite NSSO7, the bouquet comprises channels for cinema (Cinecinéma, Action), sport (Pathé sport, Motor TV), youth (Cartoon Network), entertainment (AB1, 13ème Rue, RTL9, Paris Première), music (RFM TV), and general interest (CFI, France 2, TF1, TV5).

TV5 Afrique is one of the beacons of TV5's global network, the francophone channel whose shareholders are France Télévisions (47.38 per cent of shareholding), Arte France (12.5 per cent), SSR, the Swiss public television network (11.1 per cent) RTBF, the Belgian public broadcaster (11.1 per cent) Radio Canada (11.1 per cent), RFO (4 per cent), INA (2.61 per cent) plus three individual shareholders led by Serge Adda (0.6 per cent). The current managing director is Denise Epote Durand. TV5 is broadcast on satellite NSS7.

We are seeing the beginnings of local television enterprise in francophone Africa, marketing services that are available from trans-national sources. One example is Africable Network SA, launched in 2001 by cable operators in Bamako, Mali, and grouping together Multicanal (Bamako), Télé Plus (Cameroon), Mediastar (Niger), Linda Communication (Congo), TV Sat (Gabon), Delta 2000 (Senegal), APTV (Madagascar) and Neerwaya (Burkina Faso), with the intention of broadcasting private African television stations by operators of MMDS. The initial project seems to have been slightly altered following negotiations with Portinvest with a view to being broadcast on the francophone SAT, and also with francophone or anglophone public television stations (SABC, AIT of Nigeria, TV3 of Ghana).

There is a network of independent agents responsible for managing subscriptions and providing delivery services by MMDS or making direct satellite access possible in francophone countries as well as in some lusophone and anglophone countries. These companies have a variety of arrangements in place that differ from country to country and between cities and towns in the same country. MMDS services tend to be confined to major population centres while direct satellite services are available more widely. There are many different arrangements in place. For instance, in Senegal, Canal Horizons is distributed in Dakar by twenty-one distributors using MMDS, direct-to-home satellite service or by terrestrial transmission. In Rufisque and Thiès, terrestrial transmission is employed. For homes in Saint-Louis, Kaolack, Mbour, Tamba and Ziguinchor direct-to-home satellite is the main means of delivery. In Côte d'Ivoire, Canal Horizons is distributed in nine districts of Abidjan by MMDS, while direct satellite transmission is usual in most other parts of the country. In the second city, Bouaké, MMDS is employed.[10] In Cameroon, there are satellite distributors in Douala, Yaoundé and Garoua. Distribution is also provided by both direct satellite service and MMDS in

Cotonou, Benin, in Bujumbura in Burundi, in Conakry in Guinea, in N'djamena in Chad, in Bangui in the Central African Republic, in Nouakchott in Mauritania, and in Pointe Noire in Congo. Both means of reception are also found in Djibouti, Burkina Faso and Niger. In the Congo (DRC) both alternative services are available in Kinshasa and Lubumbashi. The same circumstances are found in Libreville and Port Gentil in Gabon, in Antananarivo in Madagascar and in Bamako in Mali.

Analysis of the content of francophone transnational services shows a high level of sport, news and cinema. Fifty per cent of Canal Horizons' programme output is accounted for by cinema (360 films per year), 25 per cent is sport, the remainder is comprised of music, documentaries and youth programmes. News is one of the genres especially sought by audiences, who look for the latest news and better news coverage (especially on Africa). In many cases, the television viewer expects the channel to overcome the blackout or restrictions imposed on news items broadcast by domestic or national media. TV5, for example, broadcasts a news bulletin every hour. In 2002, 13.3 per cent of CFI-TV's output was in news programmes from TF1 or France 2, as well as twelve minutes of a special daily pan-African news programme *Edition Afrique*. *Afrique Presse* is a forty-minute weekly programme on African current affairs, produced in conjunction with RFI, and *Boulevard du Midi* is a programme about social issues. In addition to news programmes, 13.4 per cent of output is devoted to magazine programmes and 4.2 per cent to features, adding up to around 30 per cent of the output that can be described as 'factual' content. Besides these two channels, SAT provides news from RTL9 and Euronews. Although not a news programme as such, but reflecting current affairs, *La Semaine des Guignols* (*Puppets' Week*), attracts a large audience in African capitals by poking fun at prominent figures in public life, mostly – it has to be said – non-African.

Entertainment programmes, as everywhere, constitute a substantial share of output. We have already noted Canal Horizons' high proportion of films. CFI-TV dedicated 27.5 per cent of its output in 2002 to fiction (films and serials), 4.6 per cent to other entertainment programmes and 21.5 per cent to music. Sport, which represented 6.3 per cent of CFI's content, can be linked both to information and entertainment. Finally 9.2 per cent is made up of programmes for the young. CFI broadcasts popular programmes that have met with huge success in France, notably variety shows such as *Sébastien c'est Show*, *Le Plus Grand Cabaret du Monde*, and *Stars Parade*. This channel also broadcasts African films as well as African music, such as the programme *Africa Musica* and musical clips featuring the likes of Manu Dibango. There are numerous cultural programmes on CFI, which usually come from Western television, such as *Histoire des Religions*, *De l'Actualité de l'Histoire*, *L'Aventure des Planètes*, *Les Géants du Siècle*. Some come from Africa, such as *Net d'Afrique*.

Canal Horizons is the most widely available transnational station in francophone countries. This is followed by CFI-TV and TV5, with other stations falling some way behind them. If we use the familiar market research concept of share, Canal Horizons' share of stations received is 31.5 per cent of households, CFI and TV5 each have a 17.7 per cent share, while the remaining 33.1 per cent is made up of all the rest.

We have information from audience research in some areas that tells us about the respective popularity of available television services and programmes. The importance of the role of transnational television stations in Africa is illustrated to some degree by size of the audiences watching the programmes. This can be fairly well evaluated from recent surveys, mainly conducted in urban areas. The assessment of the qualitative impact or importance of the broadcasts, however, is likely to be more difficult.

According to audience research, transnational television services have witnessed an increase in their audience in Africa since 1996. This is partly because the number of channels broadcast has increased. But it is also because less expensive means of delivery have been devised, other than the very large satellite dishes that have been required up till now. Free-to-air broadcasting for a few hours every day of otherwise subscription-based encrypted channels has also contributed to audience growth.

There is more than one way of describing the audience numbers for transnational channels. Those channels that rely on subscription give the numbers who subscribe. Thus Canal Horizons quoted 115,000 subscribers throughout Africa in 1995 and 150,000 at the end of 1999. Describing the situation in 2002 but referring only to sub-Saharan Africa, the figure of 75,000 was given. At the beginning of 2000 the French digital platform had 70,000 subscribers, 50,000 via MMDS and 20,000 by direct reception from satellite.

But the more interesting data are those that tell us about who actually watches and how many there are of them.[11] Côte d'Ivoire provides the best field of research for a study based on individual countries, partly because of the extent of television reception and partly because of the frequency of radio and television audience surveys there.[12] Two surveys in Côte d'Ivoire dating from 1995 and 2001 enable us to distinguish certain characteristics and developments. The first, in June 1995, was conducted in Abidjan, Bouaké and San Pedro, while the second, from June 2001, covered samples in the same three cities with the addition of Daloa and Korhogo. The tables that follow show the equipment used to access transnational television stations.

For the purposes of this study we have analysed the data by those demographic variables that are significantly correlated with access to the relevant equipment and actual viewing behaviour. These are especially knowledge of French, higher education and social and economic status.

TABLE 5.1 Percentage of households with direct access to transnational TV channels and video recorders, Abidjan, June 1995

	Satellite dish	MMDS	Subscribers to Canal Horizons	Video recorders
All	2.1	3.8	6.3	21.5
Affluent classes	17.4	24.3	52.7	75.6
Executives	13.3	5.7	22.3	41.8
With good command of French language	4.6	6.3	12.6	30.5
Higher education	21.1	11.9	44.7	59.3
Uneducated	*	1.7	3.8	11.9
Manual workers	*	4.4	2.2	16.8
Housewives	*	0.6	4.3	15.1
Basic command of French	0.9	2.6	2.6	17.3

*: nil or negligible

The data show that satellite TV access is much higher among elites. We see a similar pattern when we look at actual viewing behaviour.

TABLE 5.2 Consumption of transnational television, Abidjan, June 1995 (percentages)

| | Any TV | | Canal Horizons | | | | TV5 | | CFI | | Any international TV | |
| | | | Free-to-air | | encrypted | | | | | | | |
	regular	daily	regular	daily	regular	daily	regular	daily	regular	daily	regular	daily
All	92.4	48.4	40.2	9.0	12.7	2.3	14.7	4.0	7.8	1.1	37.9	6.6
Affluent classes	97.5	75.3	43.3	11.2	60.6	22.1	41.3	15.4	36.8	9.3	60.2	22.3
Executives	91.8	66.9	40.6	7.3	24.6	6.3	28.8	9.1	21.8	6.3	49.3	16.3
With good command of French language	96.9	57.8	52.0	12.9	20.7	5.9	22.3	6.7	17.9	2.4	43.9	11.2
Further education	99.5	67.1	49.5	12.7	50.1	15.4	43.3	14.5	42.9	12.1	62.5	27.7
No education	88.7	41.8	33.5	7.4	7.6	0.3	9.0	2.3	2.2	0.0	33.5	2.5
Housewives	89.5	51.4	38.3	13.7	6.1	0.4	9.7	3.4	3.6	0.0	31.1	2.0
Basic French	90.4	42.2	35.2	6.8	8.4	0.2	10.9	2.6	2.6	0.4	34.3	4.3

Note: 'regular' means at least once a week

It is evident that there are a far greater number of viewers of transnational television than there are owners of the equipment to receive it. This arises from something characteristic of much of sub-Saharan Africa and which assists greatly the spread of TV viewing – the widespread community-based lifestyle and climate that encourages open-air activity. It is easy to watch TV even if you do not have a set. It is also true that direct broadcasting via terrestrial rebroadcasting, which takes place at certain times, will contribute to the high audience levels achieved by some francophone transnational services. In spite of the great differences between social classes and at the very least between the levels of education and knowledge of French, transnational television stations have clearly made inroads even among those with only modest income since 1995.

Six years later, it is the demographic groups that were already the most receptive towards these channels that have improved their access.

TABLE 5.3 Percentage of households with direct access to transnational TV channels and video recorders, Abidjan, June 2001

	Satellite dish	MMDS	Subscribers to Canal Horizons	Video recorders
All	3.5	6.3	7.0	23.9
Affluent classes	41.7	53.8	73.0	89.3
Executives	22.0	25.1	38.3	55.7
With good command of French language	45.4	21.6	25.1	45.4
Higher education	37.2	42.8	64.0	82.6
Uneducated	0.5	1.7	2.1	10.4
Manual workers	0.5	5.6	2.4	18.5
Housewives	0.9	2.2	2.2	13.6
Basic command of French	1.3	2.0	2.7	17.1

As shown by Table 5.4, similar rates of growth are found for the actual audiences reached.

Surveys in Côte d'Ivoire show that audiences for all television are much lower in rural areas. Audiences for transnational television are low outside the major towns. Even in towns outside Abidjan, audiences are smaller and this is linked to much lower levels of access to the necessary household equipment and generally lower levels of subscription to paid-for services. For example, in Bouaké, only 3.3 per cent subscribed to Canal Horizons while the figure in San Pedro was 4.6 per cent. Satellite dish ownership in Bouaké was only 1.9 per cent of households and 3.2 per cent in San Pedro. In Bouaké, only 2.9 per cent of households were connected to MMDS. Access to any transnational TV service was even lower in the other Ivoirian towns surveyed.

International television stations' status as a leading source of news and information endows them with a prominent position. The survey in Abidjan in June 1995 quoted above puts international television stations in sixth place for information on international news, but in second place (after international radio stations) for affluent classes and for those who have higher education, and in third place for executives and employees. International TV reaches second place for information on science and technology and even first place among affluent classes and graduates.

In June 2001 in Abidjan, international television stations ranked in third place as the best source of information about events abroad but in second place (again after international radio stations) for the

TABLE 5.4 Previous day's consumption of television, Abidjan, June 2001 (percentages)

	Any television	Transnational TV	CFI	Canal Horizons	TV5
All	85.8	22.7	3.1	16.5	6.4
Affluent classes	92.3	57.6	5.2	37.7	21.6
Executives	94.5	46.4	4.5	26.6	20.8
Good command of French language	97.2	37.0	5.2	22.0	15.3
Further education	98.1	60.6	9.4	32.8	24.1
Uneducated	78.1	12.6	2.7	10.8	1.7
Workers, craftsmen	81.6	17.1	6.6	10.3	4.9
Housewives	83.3	15.7	0.8	14.9	0.9
Basic command of French	81.8	16.5	3.1	12.8	4.3

well-educated, employees and executives, affluent people and even in second place (as ever after international radio stations) for executives, employees and the well-off, as a leading source of information about an event in Côte d'Ivoire.

International television stations are also received by a significant number of people in Senegal where a local office for Canal Horizons has been set up, and where there also exists a dynamic MMDS network, particularly in Dakar but also in provincial towns. A survey conducted by SOFRES in February 2001 stated that 34.1 per cent of those surveyed subscribed to MMDS, 20.2 per cent to Canal Horizons and that 1.5 per cent had a satellite dish in Dakar-Pikine. The actual number of television viewers, however, is well above that, as Table 5.5 shows.[13]

TABLE 5.5 Previous day's shares of audiences to transnational TV channels, Dakar-Pikine, Senegal, February 2001 (percentages)

	International TV stations	Canal Horizons	CFI	TV5
All	44.2	31.1	15.4	16.0
15–24 years	58.3	43.0	18.9	21.4
Students	69.8	53.6	24.6	25.5
Secondary and higher education	64.4	46.7	24.0	24.9
Employees, executives	63.3	36.2	33.8	27.0
Manual workers	28.7	17.2	9.4	11.5
Affluent classes	73.2	49.8	31.3	32.9
Poorer classes	27.0	21.0	6.8	7.6
Uneducated	23.2	16.6	6.0	5.9

We have retained those categories of people in Table 5.5 who were most likely to watch transnational television stations and those who watched it least. It is interesting to note that even among the latter, ratings are not insignificant. Among other channels in the French digital SAT package, not listed in this table, MCM Africa had a 6 per cent audience on the previous day, while RTL9 had 5 per cent. International television stations ranked in third place in Dakar and Pikine, Senegal, among the leading sources of information about a news event abroad, behind national and international radio stations. For members of the affluent classes, international television came second, just after international radio stations.

In other capital cities in francophone Africa audiences for transnational television can also be high. Figures from Ouagadougou in Burkina Faso show that 16.1 per cent of a representative sample subscribed to MMDS (90.3 per cent of the affluent and 52.4 per cent of the better-educated), 2.9 per cent subscribed to Canal Horizons (39.6 per cent of the better-off). Just 0.9 per cent of the sample owned a satellite dish but 35.6 per cent had watched international television stations over the week preceding the survey and 15.6 per cent the night before. Canal Plus Horizons had been watched by 11.5 per cent during the same week (by 35.3 per cent of executives), TV5 by 29 per cent and CFI by 15 per cent.[14] In Cameroon, foreign television stations benefit from the fact that the national television network CRTV does not fulfil the expectations of its audience. The digital package offered by SAT is watched by 58.5 per cent of the viewers of Yaoundé, at any time. The most popular channels are Euronews (34.7 per cent), RTL9 (31.5 per cent), Canal Plus Horizons (29.7 per cent), followed by CFI and then TV5.[15]

The influence of transnational television stations can be measured according to the greater or lesser number of viewers who watch them and also by the length of time that is spent watching them. These television stations meet a need for information that is not supplied at present by the national public television services, especially in times of crisis. This is particularly noticeable for the better-educated and executives who are also the main listeners to international radio stations.

TABLE 5.6 RTL9's audience in Cameroon, December 2001 (percentages)

	Douala	Yaoundé
All	57.3	56.9
15–24 years	66.9	65.6
Employees, executives	70.9	64.3
Manual workers	57.0	47.0
Pupils, students	69.3	76.5
Housewives	55.9	49.4
Uneducated	41.4	39.9

The influence of transnational television stations in francophone cities is all the greater since national television stations fail to meet the expectations of viewers because of their inadequate local output. This is evident in the two major cities of Cameroon, where television, commonly transmitted either by cable or by MMDS, enables a sizeable audience to access RTL9, whose programme *Ça va se savoir* (*It will be found out*) exposes personal and private disagreements on air. Table 5.6 illustrates RTL9's weekly audience.[16]

Transnational television channels are received less in those countries where television itself is less widespread. The gap widens, however, between the capital and the remainder of the country, between the leading classes and the well-educated and the rest in every country. In 2000 at Niamey in Niger, only 5 per cent of adults were connected either by satellite or by cable, despite the fact that in the course of the week preceding the survey, 17 per cent had watched TV5 and 10 per cent CFI.[17]

As far as Chad is concerned, there is only a survey dating from 1993 by ASA, at which time CFI reached 2.4 per cent of a sample of the population in the capital, N'djamena, TV5, 2.1 per cent and CNN 1 per cent. Yet 59 per cent watched neighbouring Cameroon's television, an interesting example of cross-border television, where a foreign channel attracted more viewers than the national television, which did not even broadcast every day.

Transnational television channels will have an increasingly important role to play in francophone Africa, which has already been greater than elsewhere on the continent. Programmes from foreign broadcasters account for an important part of the schedules of many national public television channels and account for an even greater part of the schedules of the emerging private television stations. They widen the gulf that separates city dwellers from rural inhabitants and the poorest from the wealthiest, all the more according to the level of education and of French language. Transnational television channels, however, whether received by satellite or by the intermediary of an MMDS or cable operator, are on the increase among the public of large francophone cities, especially among the ruling classes and the young. This undoubted influence can be expected to increase in the years ahead, not least because throughout francophone Africa, national broadcasters are hampered by financial problems and government control that limit their creativity.

Lusophone Africa

Portuguese-speaking countries have also developed a network of transnational television stations, a development led to a large extent by channels based in Portugal and Brazil. There is the Portuguese international TV station, RTPI,[18] as well Lusovisao which, in a similar way to TV5, has since July 1999 been distributing the output of Portuguese television stations and that of the five Portuguese-speaking African countries. MGM Latin America provides some of its service from Brazilian sources and the Brazilian giant, TV Globo International, is also available from satellite. There is now also a children's service known as the Panda Channel originally targeted at children between four and fourteen years in Portugal but now on satellite for lusophone Africa.

RTPI is probably the most important of these. It signed agreements in 1994 and 1995 with all five lusophone countries. In January 1998 it launched a special Africa service, RTP Africa, which is available as a free-to-air terrestrial service in Angola. Lusovisao was created on a trial basis, to establish the exchange of programmes between Portugal and the five lusophone countries in Africa. The Portuguese group Visabeira, whose activities – in addition to radio and television – also extend to industry, tourism and property, joined forces with telecommunications providers in Mozambique to introduce TV Cabo in Maputo and later in Beira and in Nampula. TV Cabo broadcasts CNN, Cartoon Network, Sky News, RTPI, RTP Africa and also other channels for sport, cinema and news.

South Africa's MultiChoice, which we describe in some detail in the next section, has also moved into lusophone countries. Multi-Choice Angola was launched in 1998, first being confined to Luanda but now also accessible in Cabinda, Lobito and Namibia. In 2002 it registered 20,000 subscribers, especially those who wished to view TV Globo.

Direct access to satellite services in lusophone Africa might not be widespread but has shown rapid growth in some places. For example, in Mozambique in 1995, only 1 per cent of urban homes in Maputo and 3 per cent in Beira had cable or satellite television. By 2001, 5 per cent of urban homes had access to satellite television, 8 per cent in Maputo, 6 per cent in Chimoio, 3 per cent in Beira and 1 per cent in Nampula.[19] For the most part, direct-to-home satellite services reach only the wealthiest sections of the public in Portuguese-speaking countries. Many more are reached, as in the rest of Africa, through rebroadcasting on terrestrial services.

The development of television has been rapid in the main cities of lusophone countries. For example, in Mozambique, between 1995 and 2001 the number of daily television viewers climbed from 60 to 74 per cent in Maputo and from 46 to 60 per cent in Beira. Over the same period, weekly viewing (otherwise called television's weekly reach) had increased from 74 to 91 per cent in Maputo and from 51 to 75 per cent in Beira.[20]

The cable service TV Cabo reckons that it will be available in 15,000 homes in Maputo in a few years. In Luanda, the capital of Angola, in 1996, 3 per cent of homes had access to satellite television, but RTP Africa was also received via cable. The state TV station, TPA, broadcast a schedule in which 60 per cent was imported programmes, particularly from CNN, CFI and RTPI. In Luanda as a whole, 67 per cent of households received television, and these statistics for access remind us that here, as in many other countries in Africa, most audiences see the content of transnational television through the mainstream terrestrial services, rather than from satellite direct or cable and MMDS.[21]

Anglophone Africa

The two major English-language players in transnational television in anglophone Africa are both South African. They are MultiChoice Africa and TV Africa, while a number of content providers, most of them from outside Africa, utilize these broadcast-publishers to get their services to viewers on the continent. Other satellite services are beginning to emerge.[22]

MultiChoice is the pre-eminent content carrier in anglophone Africa. The parent company, MultiChoice Holdings Investments Limited (MIH), operates subscription services across the whole of Africa, as well as the Middle East, Greece and Thailand. It emerged from MNet, South Africa's first private television channel. Historically, MNet was only a terrestrial channel and was available only in South Africa. It began broadcasting in 1986, breaking several decades of SABC's broadcasting monopoly. Initially it was a joint venture of four newspaper publishers: Nationale Pers (Naspers) owned the greatest share, while Republican Press, Allied Publishing and Times Media Limited held equal shares. In 1998, Naspers acquired control over MIH from the other press groups. Its subsidiaries included MultiChoice (which was simply a distributor platform and subscription management service), MNet, the content provider and scheduler for analogue terrestrial subscription television in South Africa, and M-Web, the Internet portal. The following year MIH Limited celebrated its initial public offering on the Nasdaq and Amsterdam stock exchanges. In 2002 the cycle was completed, with the whole conglomerate of MIH Limited and MIH Holdings becoming wholly owned subsidiaries of Naspers. Naspers restructured itself as a holding company with five subsidiaries: Multi-Choice Investment Holdings (MultiChoice and MNet); M-Web (internet portal); Media24 (print newspaper titles and online news service); Nasboek (book publishing and retailing) and Educor (private colleges and business schools). In this way, the Naspers/MultiChoice stable is an outstanding example of cross-media ownership and control, making full use of the synergies and cost-efficiencies of such an arrangement, while at the same time fully exposed to some of the pitfalls of over-enthusiastic expansion.

An analogue service, distributed via satellite, was launched to more than twenty African countries in 1992. Its subscriber management division became so successful that the company was able to build on it, hiving it off from the rest of the business, and renaming it MultiChoice Limited (MCL) in 1993. Both MCL and MNet traded on the Johannesburg Stock Exchange as linked units until 1995. The first transnational joint venture was entered into with Namibia in 1993. Digital satellite services were offered across Africa in 1995, utilizing the C-band on PAS4 satellite. With the delivery via satellite, the bouquet of channels was enlarged significantly. This was the beginning of DSTV (Direct Satellite Television), a subsidiary of MultiChoice. At this point, MNet and MultiChoice were formally separated, with the latter changing its name to MultiChoice Investment Holdings (MIH). During the next few years, MultiChoice expanded beyond Africa: into Greece in 1995, Thailand two years later and China in 1999. That year, the transmission moved to PAS7 satellite and in 2000 the launch of the Eutelsat W4 satellite opened up the Ku-band services to sub-Saharan African and the Indian Ocean Islands. Asia was the next stepping stone, and 2001 saw the acquisition of 46.5 per cent of QQ (China), a satellite television service on the China mainland. The year also heralded the launch of an Indian and Portuguese bouquet on the DSTV satellite service in southern Africa. Thus within a single decade, MultiChoice expanded horizontally, moving from being a terrestrial pay-television platform in a single country, to a multi-platform provider across the African continent.

At the time of writing, MIH Limited owns operations that span over fifty countries, providing entertainment, interactive and e-commerce services. The group employs over 6,000 collaborators, 690 of whom are based in their Randburg headquarters in South Africa. The group claims over two million paid-up subscribers in Africa, the Mediterranean and Asia, 1.25 million of whom are in Africa. Fifty-seven per cent of African customers subscribe to the digital platform (DSTV): 705,000 households in South Africa and a further 251,518 in the remainder of sub-Saharan Africa. The analogue service accounts for 339,422 households in South Africa and 12,798 in the rest of Africa.[23]

Critics point out that with a monthly subscription of US$60, the reception of these services is limited to foreign nationals and the local elite, and thus they do not contribute to the enrichment of the local states, either culturally or economically. Prices are much higher for this service than for the francophone transnationals outlined earlier, and this has meant that audiences and access to transnational television have so far been much lower.

In a show of optimism that characterized media industries worldwide at the turn of the millennium, MultiChoice diversified further, investing in the interactive television operating system, Open TV, in 1997. This venture proved to be untenable and in 2002, MultiChoice's shares in Open TV were sold to an American company, Liberty Broadband Interactive Television, a subsidiary of Liberty Media, for US$17 million.

The MultiChoice group is able to leverage its business into four areas: content aggregation, subscriber management, platform development and marketing and branding. Within Africa, MultiChoice Africa operates under three different business models, together with a programming and technology support sector. Under the joint venture model, MIH undertakes a partnership with local entrepreneurs or state broadcasters, in which each party has a partial shareholding and a joint management strategy. Joint ventures trade under the name of MultiChoice and the country, e.g. MultiChoice Zambia, and have full access to MultiChoice Africa's nerve centre in Randburg through satellite communication, allowing for technology transfer and fully staffed customer-service support. Franchises carry a MultiChoice identity, while the parent company provides management, infrastructure, training and marketing support. As with joint ventures, they are facilitated through a fully online connection to the central computer system. Independent agents comprise a network of entrepreneurial agents who sign up subscribers and instal DSTV. These companies trade under their own business names, while also promoting the MultiChoice Africa brand. A list of the countries in which MultiChoice Africa operates, arranged by business model, is provided in Table 5.7.

TABLE 5.7 MultiChoice business models by country

Joint ventures	Franchises	Independent agents
Botswana	Angola	Benin
Ghana	Ethiopia	Burundi
Kenya	Malawi	Cameroon
Namibia	Mozambique	Comoros
Nigeria	Swaziland	Congo (Brazzaville)
Tanzania (mainland)	Zimbabwe	Congo (DRC)
Zambia		Côte d'Ivoire
		Equatorial Guinea
		Eritrea
		Gabon
		Gambia
		Madagascar
		Mali
		Mauritius
		Niger
		Rwanda
		São Tomé and Principe
		Senegal
		Sierra Leone
		Tanzania (Zanzibar)
		Togo

MultiChoice Africa is a broadcast-publisher and subscription manager. In its former guise, MCA packages channels, some fully imported from America, Europe or Asia, others compiled from imported programming together with locally commissioned programming through its sister company, MNet, and broadcasts these as channel 'bouquets' to subscribing clients. These clients are served with programme guides, both printed in magazine form as well as electronically available on screen. As a subscription manager, the company administers contracts with, and receives payment from subscribers; operates a call centre for subscriber service; and co-ordinates the supply and servicing of decoders to subscribers.

As a subscription business, all the MultiChoice television programming is encrypted. The system in use is the Iredeto System, for which they have the agency in Africa (and large parts of Mediterranean Europe). Encryption implies the scrambling or encoding of the signal, which is then decoded at the point of delivery through a television-top decoder. Clients not in good financial standing are simply 'cut off' – i.e. the ability to decode the signal is discontinued. MultiChoice operates two distinct systems of distribution – encrypted terrestrial broadcasting and encrypted broadcasting via satellite. The latter is available on both the analogue and digital platforms, although strong moves are being made to 'migrate' all subscribers on to the digital platform.

MultiChoice operates three satellites over Africa: PanAmSat 7 for Ku-band coverage of southern Africa, PanAmSat 10 for C-band coverage of sub-Saharan Africa; and Eutelsat W4 for spot beam coverage of Nigeria and broadband coverage of the rest of Africa. Further capacity of Ku-band services was recently rolled out on the back of the Eutelsat W4 at a cost of US$10 million. The Ku-band operates at a much higher frequency than the older C-band, and has a much smaller footprint with more power. This means that it covers a smaller area across the continent, requiring a greater number of transponders. The advantage of the Ku-band, however, is that it requires far smaller (and less expensive) satellite dishes than other bands, allowing for a greater consumer uptake of satellite technology. The Ku-band also allows for greater reach and penetration of coverage across the continent through the significantly large portion of spectrum allocation devoted to this service. Whereas PanAmSat 10 has allocated the C-band a spectrum width of 5,925–6,425 MHz to the uplink, and 3,700–42,000 to the downlink, the Ku-band on PanAmSat 7 has a double set of spectrum width in each direction: 13,750–14,000 GHz and 14,000–14,250 GHz uplink, and 10,950–11,2000 GHz and 11,450–11,750 GHz downlink. This means there is far greater bandwidth available (i.e. the amount of data a transponder can carry), making possible parallel channels for language dubbing in additional languages.[24]

One of the advantages of digitalization is the opportunity to amortize the content over a number of different content delivery platforms, notably the Internet. As part of the MultiChoice Investment Holdings Ltd Group, the content acquired by MNet and DSTV is used to cross-promote the African M-Web Internet operation. Interactive television is in its infancy, exemplified mainly through the electronic programme guides, but some territories do have access to embryonic services in e-mail, gaming and home shopping, all of which promise to be a major part of future development.

Growth in the satellite television market will be determined most directly by the expansion of a middle-class consumer base able and willing to afford the subscription fees for the service. Beyond this, three other factors will play a role:

- the increase in bandwidth capacity, which will allow the delivery of high-speed, bulk data on a point-to-point basis, while at the same time facilitating a drop in the cost of transmission services;
- the growth of interactive applications, such as e-mail using the television/satellite connection, which will encourage a diversification of the services on offer to consumers, adding value and creating greater demand; and
- the ability to store content on decoders through Home Media Service without the intermediary use of a VCR, thus fundamentally changing the way in which consumers interact with television viewing.

MIH, through the terrestrial broadcaster MNet, has three wholly owned, 'proprietary' brands: K-TV for children's programming, Super Sport for sports coverage and Movie Magic for movies. Each of these channels is made up of both commissioned local programming together with programming produced elsewhere and dubbed or subtitled into the local language. The Movie Magic service acquires exclusive pay-TV rights to premier movies, notably from the Disney, Columbia Tristar/Sony, Warner Brothers, Fox, MCA/Universal, Paramount, MGM and Dreamworks Studios.[25]

All three of these services or brands play out on the terrestrial service available in South Africa, MNet, which is a broad-spectrum

entertainment channel, supplemented by specialist Super Sport channel. Further channels provided by MNet include the partially interactive reality TV show, *Big Brother*, which in 2003 was produced as
Big Brother Africa, with an all-African cast, living together in a game
house until all but one is eliminated.

The analogue and digital services available via satellite are delivered as DSTV, a direct-to-home service, and provide various bouquets
of channels. In addition to those already mentioned, fully imported
channels such as Discovery, National Geographic, Hallmark, BBC
Prime and Cartoon Network are also included. Twenty-four-hour
news channels – BBC World, CNN International, Sky News and
China News – provide a mainstay of programming. Some of the
channels are of international standard, while others are created by
their sellers for specific world regions. BBC Prime, for instance, is
a twenty-four-hour entertainment channel offering a selection of
the best British domestic programming emanating from the BBC.
The line-up of programming is decided by the BBC, and sold as a
package, tailored for different regions of the world, thus obviating
the necessity for the carrying satellite service to apply for individual
programme rights. CNN too has an international edition tailored
for Africa. Foreign-language programming in French (including Canal
Plus and TV5), Italian and German is available as a standard part of
the bouquet, while specialist bouquets, provided for an additional fee,
for Indian, Portuguese and Arabic viewers are also available.

The only available detailed audience data for MultiChoice services
by satellite apply to the South African portion of the viewership. They
confirm that viewers are mostly to be found among the high-income
earners, government officials and expatriates.

Another prominent channel is SABC Africa, the external service of the South African Broadcasting Corporation, South Africa's
state-owned broadcasting body. The channel was created by an
amalgamation of two previously separate channels. Its namesake,
SABC Africa, was a news, current affairs and documentary channel
beamed at the rest of the continent, while Africa-2-Africa, an all-
entertainment channel, was launched in September 2000, in order to
provide a satellite channel broadcasting entertainment made in Africa,
for Africa. On 1 April 2003 a hybrid channel was launched, drawing
programming from both sources. The channel is housed on the DSTV
platform operated by MultiChoice, reaching forty-nine countries. The

channel also serves as an overnight feed on SABC2, one of the three domestic SABC terrestrial channels. In terms of content, the channel has a dual content strategy – to provide news and current affairs, as well as entertainment programming. Most of the weekly programming is based on the news / current affairs format, while weekends are predominantly entertainment. The stated philosophy is to 'celebrate the positive side of Africa and being African'. Some programming, approximately a quarter of the airtime, particularly lifestyle, news and current affairs programmes, are specially commissioned for the channel, while a special effort is made to source African movies. Two African-produced dramas are broadcast every week, representing countries such as Tunisia, Egypt, Burkina Faso, Zimbabwe, Guinea Bissau, Cameroon and Ethiopia. For the most part, however, the programmes are rebroadcasts of material shown on the terrestrial channels in South Africa. The majority of programming is broadcast in English, with considerable subtitling in African languages, French and Portuguese.

Detailed audience data for SABC Africa are available only for South African viewership.[26] The audience profile is predominantly male and predominantly middle-aged. The channel attracts the top two socio-economic groups on the Living Standards Measurement index, i.e. those with over US$2,500 per household per month.

TV Africa started broadcasting from South Africa in July 1998. Founded by Barry Lambert and David Kelly and financed by Zephyr Management, the Africa Investment Fund and the South Africa Enterprise Development Fund, it draws its revenue from advertising rather than subscription. At the time of writing its network provides satellite services to thirty-four African television channels based in twenty-four countries, including Ethiopia, Tanzania, Lesotho, Swaziland, Zambia, Nigeria and the key francophone territories. TV Africa broadcasts between three and eighteen hours of sports and entertainment programmes every day. These are received mostly by commercial television stations. Most of TV Africa's programmes are in English, but it is also providing some French-language content to partners in Benin, Burundi, Gabon, Niger and Togo. Charles Zougoua, TV Africa's director for West Africa, has described the network's mission as being 'to bring Africans sport and entertainment programmes'.[27] TV Africa is able to sell time to advertisers within a programme package delivered via terrestrial stations to audiences in several countries.

This is a formula also being used by another satellite TV service supplier, African Broadcast Network, as we outline later.

Much of the programming of TV Africa is similar to that provided by MultiChoice/DSTV, with the latter having the rights to encrypted broadcasting while TV Africa holds territory rights to the free-to-air transmissions. African-produced programming on TV Africa emanates mostly from Nigeria and Ghana, although these programmes are in short supply. The local affiliates, spread in the twenty-four countries throughout Africa, produce the news programmes where these are available. The estimated reach of TV Africa through its affiliates is 62.1 million.[28]

TV Africa seeks to make use of existing terrestrial broadcasters to reach audiences and to sell access to those audiences to media buyers – advertisers of consumer goods and services targeting African consumers. TV takes a relatively low share (about 20 per cent) of sub-Saharan Africa's advertising expenditure. This will grow, but the total cake is not large and television's share is not likely to reach the levels found elsewhere of 40 per cent and more. TV Africa's growth is likely to be slow. Audiences to terrestrial stations are also of less interest to some of the higher-spending advertisers, who are more interested in the wealthier audiences reached by satellite and cable services.

A third African satellite television service has recognized this problem and is seeking other ways of obtaining funding. The African Broadcast Network's aim is to reach mass audiences through partnerships and deals with Africa's mostly state-owned TV stations. It began broadcasting in January 2001, and is a UK-registered company, whose satellite service is based in Johannesburg. As with TV Africa, the idea is to provide a continent-wide programme stream to terrestrial TV stations. While most of TV Africa's affiliates are private stations, ABN seeks to serve the larger state-owned stations, which also reach the largest audiences at present and remain the dominant force in most markets. Like TV Africa, ABN offers access to TV audiences in several countries as a media package to advertisers. ABN does its sales through a large and influential British media sales company.

ABN's programme offer began with a chiefly US mix of popular drama series, soaps, comedy and sport. It plans to introduce more African programming as the system succeeds and grows. It has also been able to offer the Africa Cup of Nations football. The company owns the African Barter Company, whose ability to create deals involving exchanges rather than the use of scarce hard cash has made the proposition more viable.

The ability to offer audiences in several African countries to advertisers in single deals is a major strength of both TV Africa and ABN. But ABN believes that the future of the venture depends on other forms of funding. Its chief executive, George Twumasi, recognizes that many members of African TV stations' audiences, being financially weak, are of little or no interest to commercial advertisers. But, he points out, they are of great interest to those organizations committed to improving Africa's health, education, systems of government and general development. ABN has therefore created a not-for-profit sister organization, the African Public Broadcasting Foundation. This will have two objectives. The first is to 'kick start the production of a greatly increased volume of indigenous programmes in entertainment, education and information'.[29] This leads to the next objective, although it would be better described as a means to the end of the first objective. This is to seek aid from development agencies, both government and non-government organizations, who see the benefit for the African poor in developing better television services. Twumasi believes that without this kind of non-commercial assistance it is unlikely that there will ever be enough cash resources to bring African television 'to the level where it can match services elsewhere in the world'.[30] There are already many expressions of interest and support, especially to provide television services through satellite delivery that have a purpose beyond entertainment and which will serve Africa's urgent need for poverty alleviation and development. ABN has made an impressive start. It provides a daily satellite service of between one and two hours at prime time, and services are carried in the daily schedules of terrestrial stations in ten countries.

Conclusion

Sub-Saharan Africa's TV market is financially the weakest in the world. It is also, thus far, weak in terms of indigenous content. This situation is unlikely to change with any speed. What will change in the field of transnational television services by satellite will be the successes and failures of the different approaches we have outlined. We have seen the dominance of European and South African initiatives in which the rest of Africa south of the Sahara has played relatively little part, at least so far as production is concerned. There is huge potential for the future, but television is an expensive medium and the risks of failure high. A major problem in writing this chapter lies in making any predictions for what might succeed.

Transnational television stations play a role in sub-Saharan Africa that varies greatly from one country to another. There has been more activity in francophone countries than elsewhere, although this imbalance now seems to be changing. In many countries it already forms a major part of the television landscape and especially in the television consumption habits of the upper classes and of young urban people. Transnational television activity throughout the continent can be expected to continue to grow while the public service broadcasters continue to be weakened by a lack of adequate resources to meet audience needs and demands. ABN, TV Africa and some of the francophone and lusophone enterprises may be able to break through this by bringing a greater pan-African element and especially in ABN's case, if it is successful, by the pooling of resources for more and better indigenous production.

There are two potential developments. The first is linked to the possible development of a pan-African satellite channel. At this stage only the television industry in South Africa is of sufficient size to provide the momentum to make this happen, although the ABN might also be able to raise sufficient interest and involvement through creating and developing the required partnerships. The second relates to the development of new partnerships between African and Western television stations, which would allow the former to express themselves while using the logistics and technical know-how of the latter. Nevertheless the freedom of expression of African television stations is hindered by the conservative attitudes of African governments, which continue to control most television production and transmission on the continent

Notes

1. Accurate and reliable statistics for Africa are hard to find. The BBC's international research department estimated in 1999 that there were 29 million TV sets in sub-Saharan Africa, about one for every twenty people. This compares with Asia and North Africa, where there is one set for every six people. See Graham Mytton, 'From Saucepan to Dish', in Richard Fardon

and Graham Furniss (eds), *African Broadcast Cultures* (Oxford: James Currey, 2000), pp. 21–41. As far as TV transmitting facilities are concerned, there are several African countries with only one terrestrial domestic broadcaster. In many countries, satisfactory reception can be obtained only in and around the major urban areas. See *World Radio TV Handbook* (Oxford: WRTH Publications, 2003).

2. Of the forty-eight countries south of the Sahara, nineteen can be classified as francophone, and seventeen as anglophone. Additionally three countries can be classified in both camps. Five lusophone countries, one Spanish-speaking and three that do not fall into any of these categories, make up the remainder.

3. Personal correspondence, Lynn Mansfield, SABC GM Strategic Planning, Radio, 16 May 2003.

4. André-Jean Tudesq, *L'Afrique noire et ses télévisions* (Paris: Anthropos-Ina, 1992), and André-Jean Tudesq and George Wedell, *Television and Democracy in Africa*, Report for the EEC (DG8), September 1996.

5. MMDS is sometimes described as a cable service without cables. It uses a high-frequency transmission system to carry several TV services in a package similar to what one might have from a cable service that can be received in any household subscribing to the service and with the specialized receiving equipment necessary.

6. Perhaps the best-known outcome of this co-operation is TV5, referred to later, a global TV service that seeks to reflect the cultural product of this grouping of francophone countries.

7. Hervé Bourges, a friend of socialist President Mitterrand, was initially appointed to head the French state's international radio service, Radio France International. He later moved on to other government-appointed posts in the media before going to SOFIRAD.

8. The francophone Canadian province.

9. This and other pieces of information about the situation in Côte d'Ivoire refer to the situation before the outbreak of fighting between government and rebel forces in late 2002. Many aspects of the television landscape were changed by this conflict and the long-term situation remains unclear.

10. See previous note.

11. For access to much contemporary audience data we are grateful to Jean-Marc Belchi, head of the research department at CFI, to Daniel Nobi, director of the research department at RFI, both in Paris, and Marie Dziedzic at the research archive of the BBC World Service in London.

12. The various tables for Côte d'Ivoire have been provided by Etudes Médias of HPCI, Hilmar Peter Consultants International.

13. Sofrès, *Etude sur les moyens d'information du Sénégal* (Paris, February 2001).

14. HPCI Média, *Etudes médias: Ouagadougou* (Burkina Faso) (Paris, March 2000).

15. HPCI Média, *Etudes médias: Douala, Youndé* (Cameroon) (Paris, December 2001).

16. Ibid.

17. Immar, *Etude des moyens d'information: Niamey* (Niger) (Paris, April 2000). Other surveys found similar low levels of household access to satellite TV. There were only 0.5 per cent of the sample possessing a satellite dish in a survey completed in February 2000 in the three principal towns of Madagascar. In a survey in Cotonou, Benin, only 1.5 per cent had a satellite dish although 12.3 per cent had access to MMDS.

18. RadioTelevisão Portuguesa Internacional the Portuguese equivalent of CFI. It carries some commercial advertising but it is a state enterprise.

19. BBC World Service, *Media Survey: Mozambique* (London: BBC, 2001).

20. Ibid.

21. BBC World Service, *Media Survey: Angola* (London: BBC, 1996).

22. As this book was going to press, TV Africa went into liquidation. Its services to Nigeria and Ghana have been taken over by a new company: Proudly Africa. Its other services have ceased. It is a reminder that commercial international TV in Africa is a precarious undertaking given the relative poverty of the continent, the underdevelopment of its television services and the low level of revenue from advertising. Further references in this chapter to TV Africa refer to the situation in mid-2003 before the collapse. At the time of going to press, only its activities in Nigeria and Ghana survive, under the Proudly Africa name.

23. <http://www.multichoice.co.za/ourbusiness>. Consulted June 2003.

24. <http://www.panamsat.com/global_network>. Consulted June 2003.

25. Some of these films and programmes are available on terrestrial channels in the various territories.

26. SAARF TV audience data 2003.

27. Quoted in the Ivorian daily newspaper *Le Patriote*, 8 June 2000.

28. Estimate provided by the broadcaster.

29. George Twumasi, 'Television: Africa's Future Media Opportunity', *The Channel*, January–March 2003, p. 20.

30. Ibid.

CHAPTER 6

· ·

The Transnational and the National: Changing Patterns of Cultural Influence in the South Asian TV Market

David Page and William Crawley

§ THE past fifteen years have transformed the media scene across South Asia.[1] At the beginning of the 1990s state broadcasters had a practical monopoly of television audiences in their own national territories – apart from some transnational viewing off air in border areas. The video industry that emerged in the 1970s also allowed largely pirated films and copies of television programmes to be distributed outside their primary market. But this did not substantially affect the sense of impregnability of the national broadcasting networks and the regulatory systems that controlled them. Debate about broadcasting regimes focused largely on state control of the system. Attempts to modify that system – principally in India – concentrated not on diluting the monopoly but on introducing an element of autonomy and diversity in the running of state broadcasters and the editorial policies they followed.

By the new century the television universe incorporated competition between the terrestrial systems and the new cable and satellite channels, which were rapidly catching up, and in some places overtaking, the terrestrial broadcasters. The terrestrial sector was still dominated by the state broadcasters, with Sri Lanka the only significant exception. The satellite sector was overwhelmingly developed by the private sector and the most successful satellite networks were transnational in their ownership and operation, though increasingly country- and language-specific in their target audiences.

In response to these developments, state broadcasters in India and Pakistan extended the range of their own services, starting satellite channels catering to regional and niche audiences, sometimes with notable success. But it was the private satellite sector that was instrumental in changing the cultural and programme priorities of television, first of all in entertainment and later increasingly in information and news as well.

Between the extra-territorial satellite system and the state broadcasting networks a new industry grew up, which was effectively the gatekeeper for the satellite channels and to a growing extent for the terrestrial broadcaster as well. Wholly indigenous, the cable industry developed by providing an affordable distribution channel to transnational and global broadcasters. These networks initially remained largely outside state or national control. But the indigenous character of the cable industry made it an early candidate for state regulation.

The process by which the content providers battled with the distributors for a greater share of the revenue generated by satellite broadcasting was more complex. It was affected more by the opportunities and imperatives of the market and of new technologies than by government action or regulation. In general, the higher the stakes for investment the greater the investor's need for a regulated system to protect his investment. The role of the state, so recently challenged and undermined, had to be reinvented.

But despite the state's gradual recognition that it has to play a more active role as a regulator, the new television scene in South Asia is still characterized more by the number of channels than by the diversity of their content. The pursuit of similar commercial formats across both state and private channels has reduced the scope for programming serving a public purpose, and to some extent real choice for the viewer. At the same time, the opening of new channels in regional languages has provided a genuinely new and welcome element of choice, catering for substantial audiences that were barely noticed before. The process has also made accessible additional services in languages spoken or understood across South Asian national boundaries. This has increased the potential for regional transnational broadcasting to become a vehicle of cultural influence, information and news, though there are also some significant contrary trends.

In the first phase of the satellite revolution, the dominance of Hindi programming in the northern subcontinent raised fears for other cultures in neighbouring countries and within India itself. These were particularly acute in Pakistan, where the state broadcasting system had been used to develop a distinctive national culture, but they were also felt in Bangladesh and Nepal and in regions of India like Bengal and Maharashtra.[2] But by the late 1990s, two developments were helping counter this trend. One was the advent of cheaper satellite technology, which made the launching of services for smaller cultural markets more financially viable, and the second was a move by the popular Hindi-language channels towards subscription financing. As far as cross-border influences in India and Pakistan are concerned, this second trend was reinforced after 2001 by a deterioration in relations between the two countries and a clamp-down on cable operators relaying programmes from across the border. By 2003, therefore, a different pattern of cultural influence was emerging.

This article examines these trends and investigates the reasons for them. It aims to explore changes in the Indian and other South Asian television markets both at a national and a transnational level. It looks first at the working of the Indian satellite TV market, the validity of theories that only those with deep pockets would be able to survive, and the growth of regional media and news channels within the country. It then assesses the recent diversification of TV markets in Pakistan, Bangladesh and Nepal and changing patterns of media influences in the northern subcontinent. After an examination of new government approaches to media regulation, the chapter finishes with a look at civil society responses to these prevalent trends.

The 'Deep-pockets' Theory: India's Experience Revisited

At the turn of the century, marketing insiders in India had predicted the collapse of many or most of the weaker channels, which were only reaching a small share of the country's cable and satellite audience. The burgeoning growth of new channels would be trimmed, they argued, as they foundered on the rock of financial reality. Only those with the deepest pockets would survive and they would eliminate or swallow up the smaller channels. The giants included Star TV, backed by Murdoch's global News Corporation, Sony Entertainment Television, a branch of the Japanese multinational media hardware and software giant, and Zee TV, owned by the expatriate Indian businessman, Subhash Chandra. At that stage, Zee was in a share-owning alliance with Murdoch's News Corp, both collaborating and competing successfully with the multinationals, and it was on its way to becoming a global presence. This was not just through its success in building audiences for satellite television in India, but through its dominance of the worldwide television market for communities of Indian origin, and the appeal of popular Indian cultural programmes in Asia, Africa, the Middle East and increasingly in Europe and America.

By 2003, the Star network had acquired a dominant position in the battle for Indian and to some extent for wider South Asian regional audiences. Sony was well established as a major competitor in the entertainment field and looking to break new ground with its distribution alliance with NDTV. MTV India was holding its own well as a locally focused music channel and offshoot of the global youth music network. Zee, at one time the market leader, was attempting to regain its pre-eminence after a period of lacklustre programming and poor financial results. But this battle between the giants continues to be a competition in which innovation in programming, even single new programmes, has been able to alter the balance significantly. Star was able to consolidate its lead after 2000 on the basis of one highly successful programme – *Kaun Banega Crorepati*, the Hindi-language version of the global quiz game *Who Wants to be a Millionaire?* With Star's initiative, Zee lost ground and for two years or more had difficulty making up the leeway. But its management could argue with some justification that the number one position can be won as well as lost.

In the battle between the channels to prove the superiority of their programming, the TAM ratings are the leading evidence. After a programme revamp in December 2002, Zee Cinema claimed to have re-established its lead over rival channels Max, Star Gold and B4U Movies as the leading Hindi movie channel. It attributed this to better packaging, shorter breaks, innovative programmes, marketing-driven scheduling of films and better quality of film prints. Star Gold countered with its own claim to be in the lead both at weekday prime time and at weekends. Star Gold has launched initiatives like dubbed versions of Hollywood blockbusters in a move to challenge Zee Cinema's larger library of Hindi films.[3]

The validity of the deep-pockets theory as the key to survival in the Indian market at one level is incontestable. In the once highly diversified cable business, the smaller operators have given way to larger companies, which can afford to invest in more sophisticated technology. From the 1995 Indian Cable Regulation Act to the 2002 Conditional Access Bill, Indian government regulation has focused on the distribution system rather than the content provider. Tens of thousands of small-scale neighbourhood cable operators achieved a notable success in establishing cable connections to more than 40 million homes. But in moving the advantage away from the small cable operators towards the bigger franchised Multi Systems Operators, regulatory measures have been working in favour of the more sophisticated technologies and the companies that have the technical resources and financial muscle to provide them.

The companies that have taken advantage of their technical superiority include Zee's own cable arm, Siti Cable, the Hinduja-owned communications group IndusInd Media and the Raheja-owned Hathway Cable company. But if these big companies have enjoyed an advantage in relation to small cable operators, they face stiff competition from each other. When Murdoch sold his US$300 million share in Zee in September 1999, there followed a complex battle over access to distribution systems owned by the Zee subsidiary Siti Cable. At the time, Zee claimed access to 4.8 million homes through its cable subsidiary. But following the split with Zee, Star was able to negotiate directly with these cable operators to carry its programmes and avoid the disadvantages it was thought the divorce from Zee would bring. Whereas the Hinduja-owned company retained direct control over the deals negotiated by all its cable subsidiaries, and even appointed the managers of the Multi Systems Operators it used, Siti operated a system of indirect franchises with the cable operators, which allowed them the freedom to negotiate with other broadcasters, even bypassing its main franchising partner. In an industry where control of the signal is all-important, these differences revealed weaknesses in Zee TV's ability to control the distribution of its own programmes.

The link and then split between Murdoch's News Corp and Zee TV revealed some contradictory pressures in the adaptation of global satellite TV to the Indian market. The original link had shown a mutual advantage to both sides: for Zee TV in forging a link with a global media company, for Star in affording access to the Indian-language market that provided the real mass audience. At the time, neither Star nor Zee appear to have foreseen that Star would move so strongly into the Indian-language market itself, creating a conflict of interest with its Indian partner. The strategic alliance between them was undermined when the strategy on one side changed. But the global/local antithesis was clearly demonstrated.

The Hinduja-owned IndusInd Media and Communications in turn provides an example of a local television distribution system being drawn into technical reliance on a global network. With an estimated value of US$500 million, IndusInd Media is India's largest Multi Systems Operator. It has been playing a central role in the takeover of smaller cable operators and the corporatization of the cable TV industry. In April 2003, it announced a deal with a Swiss company, Kudelski, by which a wholly owned subsidiary of Kudelski (Nagravision SA) would provide the Indian company with the means of encrypting and deploying IndusInd's pay-TV services.[4]

The development of the cable market in South India provides another instance of corporate consolidation of this gateway media industry. The cable TV business in Chennai started in the early 1990s as in other parts of India with many small operators. The first corporate player to enter the Chennai market was the Raheja-owned Hathway Cable. The consolidation of smaller players was accompanied by allegations and denials of strong-arm tactics and sabotage, still a potent element in the competition between local cable operators in cities throughout India.[5] The Hathway Cable group started to buy out operators and in those areas where it was not able to do so, the company promoted competition actively. Small players responded by forming consortia to challenge the increasing presence of Hathway and began offering more community-based services.[6] With the growth of expensive fibre-optic technologies, however, it was impossible for these consortia to survive for long, unless their losses were financed by more profitable partners or subsidiaries. In the absence of any legal protection for the community-based consortia, regulatory moves were opening new opportunities for the bigger players. Eventually, the Chennai cable market came to be dominated by two players: Hathway itself, which remained strong in the south of the city, and Sumangali Cable Vision, an offshoot of the Sun TV group, which became the main player elsewhere.

The commercial strategy of the broadcasters in extending subscription TV services, and the willingness of the Indian viewing public to take them up in large numbers, has also increased the pressure on the smaller cable operators. It is they who have to bear the financial costs of investment in the hardware needed to promote this change and the enhancement of choice for the Indian domestic viewer. As more and more satellite channels have moved to subscription, costs have risen for the smaller operators, with the possibility of serious losses if a major channel such as Star were to revert to free-to-air. In early 2003, Star would not rule out such a reversion if the move to subscription were to lead to a big loss of viewers. Instead, Star's chief operating officer turned the criticism back on the cable operators, arguing that their lack of transparency in reporting had prevented the co-operation between cable operators and broadcasters which would have made conditional access unnecessary.[7] The introduction of conditional access systems in India's leading metropolitan cities in September 2003 seemed certain to reinforce the dominance of the large players.

Multiplier Effect of Cheaper Satellite Technology

But in other ways the Indian market was changing during the late 1990s in favour of the smaller media entrepreneur. One reason was the greater number of available satellites and the falling costs of access to satellite transponders, which brought down the previously huge costs of investing in television satellite broadcasting. This resulted in the opening of many new regional language channels, principally by already established companies: Zee, Tara (with some nominal investment from Star) and the Andhra-based Eenadu group. Zee and Tara opened channels in Bengali, Marathi, Gujarati and Punjabi, though Tara could not sustain all these outlets. Eenadu moved into many different language markets and by 2003 had the largest bouquet of regional channels after Doordarshan. The Bangladesh and Pakistan markets also saw the growth of nationally focused satellite channels, offering competition to state broadcasters.

In India, a second trigger was the volatility of the market itself and the opportunities it offered to those with winning programme ideas and innovative strategies. As Zee TV and Sony found to their cost when faced with Star TV's *Kaun Banega Crorepati*, the basis of competitiveness could be altered within the space of a few months by a successful new programme and a schedule that attracted and retained audiences. Consistently successful producers and production companies such as Ekta Kapoor's Balaji Telefilms (which is listed on the stock market) have been able to flourish across different channels

– including Sony, Sahara and Star – with *Kyunki Saas Bhi Kabhi Bahu Thi* and other serials. A third factor has been the attraction of entrepreneurs towards the new medium for reasons of prestige and influence rather than its likely profitability.

In the late 1990s, the failure of Business India TV was seen as an object lesson to others. The Business India group, publishers of the highly profitable journal of the same name, invested and lost heavily in this channel, later known as TV-I. The experiment was beset with problems from the start. It was beamed from a Russian satellite that was not easily accessible. It was unable to secure a place on the prime cable band at a time when a majority of TV sets had access to at most a dozen channels. It was unable to put on air the bouquet of channels regarded as essential for a serious broadcaster. Its programming – a mixture of Hindi and English news, current affairs and general entertainment – depended on building an audience preference for its targeted brand of quality information and public service broadcasting. But as channels multiplied providing twenty-four-hour news or sport, nature and wildlife, travel, entertainment or films, the audience moved between them with greater rapidity and less regard for channel loyalty. The channel closed in 1998. Its failure had seemed to clinch the argument that news channels were inherently unprofitable, unless backed by a profitable bouquet of entertainment and sports channels.

But in more recent years others who were not considered in the 'deep-pockets' league have survived. Sri Adhikari Brothers, though relatively late-comers in the television entertainment scene, were by 2003 posting healthy profits with SAB TV, a general entertainment channel started in 2000, with a late-night current affairs or discussion element. They had been successful since 1985 as software suppliers to Doordarshan and other channels, and retained copyright in many of these programmes, giving them a good base from which to start as an independent broadcaster. The B4U ('Bollywood for You') company runs a pay film channel and a free-to-air music channel of its own as well as supplying other channels. In international markets, B4U Movies contributes almost 85 per cent of the company's revenues. In India, however, the music channel contributes an almost equal share.[8]

News channels, some of them stand-alone, have also shown healthy profits. The Living Media group, publishers of the fortnightly news magazine *India Today*, established a successful twenty-four-hour news channel, Aaj Tak, originated and broadcast in Hindi, and followed this up with the launch of a second news channel in English called Headlines Today. Aaj Tak found a ready market because of its use of colloquial Hindi, its professional news operation and its extensive network of reporters across the north of the country.

Prannoy Roy's New Delhi Television (NDTV) has been an extraordinary success story in terms of influence, but its recent history also illustrates the commercial fragility of a channel that appeals primarily to an elite English-speaking audience. NDTV, a news production company that had previously worked with CNN and Doordarshan, signed an agreement to supply the news content to the Star News channel after Rupert Murdoch cut his links with the BBC World TV channel in 1996. It made a big impact on behalf of the global Murdoch network, winning larger audiences in India than longer-established foreign news broadcasters such as CNN and the BBC. But as part of the Star bouquet of channels, it remained dependent on its relationship with Murdoch and vulnerable to changes in Star's strategy. As the end of its contract with Star approached, NDTV considered a number of possibilities to broaden its appeal and its revenues. Ultimately, the end of the contract in April 2003 became the cue for NDTV's launch as a broadcaster in its own right, both in English and Hindi. Star had already been downplaying NDTV's profile. Its contract with NDTV did not give Star editorial control, and Star's management were uneasy when the central government criticized NDTV for its reporting of the Gujarat riots in March 2002. Star TV's CEO went so far as to say in interviews in July 2003 that NDTV's news had been biased,[9] a sign perhaps of a willingness on the part of Star to take a soft line with the establishment where the reporting of its news channel is concerned.

Media observers expected that NDTV would have a struggle to survive on its own.[10] But after much speculation about its future, it announced a distribution partnership with Sony Entertainment Television's One World Alliance. This alliance with Sony gives the company a strong base from which to establish a new profile. This was the first step that the conservative Japanese company had taken into what used to be considered the sensitive market of news broadcasting. It is an important sign of the way in which – both commercially and politically – attitudes to news broadcasting in South Asia have changed.

NDTV's move mirrors the thinking other broadcasters and production companies have been pursuing in setting up strategic alliances. For example, Raghav Behl's TV 18 has developed its earlier co-operation with the Singapore-based Asian Business News, later taken over by CNBC. Though TV 18 had to be radically cut back with the advertising recession in the late 1990s, its association with CNBC was consolidated as a partnership in 2002 and by early 2003 was proving profitable.

In 2003, Sahara TV, which was launched in 2000, extended its media interests with a plan to open up to thirty new city-based Hindi TV news channels. The main national news channel, Sahara Samay Rashtriya, made a favourable impact when it went on air in the middle of the year and regional bulletins derived from the national channel followed. The Sahara TV venture, which complements similar initiatives in the print media in the state of Uttar Pradesh and in Delhi, may have been motivated as much by the potential for political influence in the Hindi belt as by the return on revenue, but Sahara is consciously making its news balanced. Overt political links have proved the downfall of channels which depended on them entirely when their patrons' political fortunes have been reversed. The Tamil channel, JJTV, owned and controlled by the AIDMK leader, Jayalalitha, closed after she and her party lost political control of the state of Tamil Nadu in 1996.[11] But politically affiliated channels that show more even-handedness in political reporting have found a more permanent niche. The successful Sun TV group retains close political links with Tamil Nadu's former ruling party, the DMK. But Sun TV, with separate English and Tamil news channels, has retained a mass following because of its more sophisticated news policy.

A strong local and regional specialism – both in terms of language and programmes – has been shown convincingly to be a major element in the success of news channels. These are also the elements subject to the greatest official and local sensitivity. Global approaches that do not take this into account are unlikely to succeed in attracting mass audiences, though they may retain respect as niche players. Channels like BBC World and CNN retain significant niche audiences for international news, but being broadcast exclusively in English does limit their mass appeal.[12] Their second limitation is the relative lack of Indian content both in news and general programming, compared to the strong coverage of Indian news provided by Star, Zee and Aaj Tak. Star's decision – after it ended its contract with NDTV – to concentrate on Hindi news bulletins and to drop its English-language service is also a significant indicator of the balance between profitability and influence in the now much more crowded Indian television news market.

Changing Patterns of Cultural Influence

Despite the strengthening presence of international satellite broadcasters on the South Asian media scene, it seems that the initial lively concerns about Western cultural influences have all but evaporated. By the mid-1990s, the adoption of global technology and the adaptation of global formats to Indian culture and conditions had fully localized Indian satellite TV and for the rest of the decade channels like Zee, Star and Sony became the dominant players in the northern subcontinent. For India's neighbours, however, the dominance of these 'Indian' satellite channels provoked concern both about Indian news bias and about what they saw as an invasion of specifically Indian cultural values and perspectives in the field of entertainment. News bias was perceived particularly in the reporting of the Kargil conflict and in coverage of the sharp decline in relations between India and Pakistan, which put South Asia at the centre of global fears of a possible nuclear conflict after 1998. This remains a central and unresolved issue of transnational broadcasting in South Asia. But in other respects the balance of cultural influence has changed significantly in recent years. India's pre-eminence as South Asia's media superpower, once largely uncontested, is now more muted. Both within India itself and in neighbouring countries, new satellite services aimed at Pakistani, Bangladeshi and Indian regional audiences have proved they can make ends meet and there is a greater degree of media pluralism. If the 1990s witnessed a massive growth in cross-border audiences for Indian programmes, ten years later the emphasis is far more on the diversification of national media markets. This greater media pluralism, however, has come about almost entirely through the growth of the satellite sector and is mainly confined to entertainment and news programmes. Except in Sri Lanka and Nepal, governments have been slow to license terrestrial competition for state broadcasters.

Satellite Responses to the Growth of Hindi Dominance

The early salience of Hindi entertainment and sports channels in the Bengali-language marketplace, whether in West Bengal or Bangladesh, gave way in the late 1990s to a flowering of Bengali-language satellite channels which began to counterbalance the earlier trend. In Bangladesh, Channel I and ATN Bangla, both founded in 1998, attracted sizeable audiences in the urban areas, while in West Bengal three new satellite channels were launched in 2000 vying with Doordarshan for the Indian Bengali audience. However, none of these channels developed a significant audience across the border. Of the three channels targeting the West Bengal market, Tara Bangla, an independent off-shoot of Star TV, attempted to serve both Bengals and for a period had a news correspondent in Dhaka, but its quest for credibility in Bangladesh remained elusive. The other two – Alpha Bengali, a Zee TV subsidiary, and ETV Bangla, part of the Hyderabad-based media empire of Ramoji Rao – made less effort and were less successful. Despite the potential advantages of scale to be derived from addressing the entire Bengali-language universe, only DD7, Doordarshan's Bengali satellite channel, with its diet of old black-and-white Bengali movies, had any sizeable impact on the other side of the border. Indian interest in Bangladeshi channels was, if anything, more limited.

In Pakistan, the state initially responded to the satellite onslaught from across the border by consolidating all terrestrial television broadcasting under its own control. In 2000, it terminated Pakistan TV's contract with Shalimar Television Network, which had commissioned and broadcast entertainment programmes from the independent sector, and devoted the same resources to a PTV news and sports channel.[13] By 2001, however, despite earlier concerns that the market would not support them, rival satellite channels in Urdu began to emerge, and two years later there was also a Sindhi channel, uplinked from Dubai and broadcasting four hours each day. The first to appear was IndusVision, an entertainment channel with a diet of drama and film-based programmes, supplemented later by separate music and news channels. Run by Ghazanfar Ali, a former film producer, Indus made a significant impact with its music channel, particularly after the government ban on Indian music channels, but it never really capitalized on its early advantage and was soon outrun in the race for advertising by ARY, a competitor with more financial resources and more varied programming. ARY was the first channel to make a serious dent in the government's news and current affairs monopoly, broadcasting hard-hitting interviews and current affairs discussions on Pakistani subjects.[14] Both these channels were permitted to uplink from Pakistan, though this privilege was not extended to GEO, the satellite channel of the Jang group, launched in August 2002 after a long and politically troubled gestation period. The launch of GEO by the country's leading Urdu newspaper group had been held up in the late 1990s because of differences with the Nawaz Sharif government over political reporting. But part of the reason it was discouraged, undoubtedly, was that it offered the prospect of strong competition for state-controlled Pakistan TV. Since its launch, GEO's considerable news resources have enabled it to offer detailed coverage of political events across the country and it made a real mark during the general elections of October 2002. In a short time, therefore, the growth of the satellite sector in Pakistan has resulted in a similar transformation of political reporting to that achieved in India in the mid-1990s. As one commentator put it: 'Pakistanis have been desperate for TV news and are enjoying watching politicians squirm on live TV. Years of exposing wrongdoings in print seem inconsequential when pitted against half an hour of grilling on TV.'[15]

If Bangladesh and Pakistan saw the growth of independent satellite channels serving national audiences, in Nepal, by contrast, international influences increased. With their ready understanding of Hindi, Nepali audiences continued to watch a range of channels aimed at the Indian market either directly or through the country's burgeoning cable systems. By 2002, the Kathmandu-based SpaceTime Network had consolidated its control of the cable market, not just in Kathmandu but in smaller towns elsewhere. At that stage, it was reported to have a subscriber base of about 200,000 and to offer forty-seven channels compared with twenty-two in 1998.[16] In July 2001, SpaceTime also responded to demands for Nepali programming by launching Channel Nepal, a satellite channel offering a diet of soap operas, music and quiz programmes broadcast for five hours per day. But the channel did not win a reputation for quality. It developed sizeable audiences for its Nepali entertainment programmes but its news resources were limited and its bulletins sometimes looked dated because of the delays involved in uplinking from Singapore. From September 2003, the channel was able to uplink directly from Kathmandu.[17]

Nepal TV, the state-controlled channel, also launched a satellite service in July 2001, responding both to domestic compulsions and to the demands of the Nepali-speaking diaspora in India and elsewhere. Satellite distribution improved the efficiency of feeds to local trans-mitters and made broadcasts more accessible to those with dishes in remoter parts of the country. It also put state-controlled television in a better position to serve Nepalis throughout the South and West Asian regions. But the competitive balance with external satellite channels in Nepal is changing only slowly.

Reinforcing the Local: The Role of Terrestrial Competition

In 2002, the government of Nepal took a significant step towards media diversification when it licensed the Kantipur group (which already runs a successful newspaper and one of the country's most popular radio stations) to set up a national terrestrial television station. It also gave permission to Image Channel, which runs an FM radio station in the Kathmandu valley, to start a terrestrial metro channel. Both channels started broadcasting in July 2003, though they were not rebroadcast on SpaceTime network. Given the track record of the Kantipur group in particular and the limited size of the market, this development seemed likely to put state-run Nepal TV under serious financial pressure. It also raised obvious questions about cross-media ownership and the transparency of licensing procedures. A government-appointed committee did recommend limiting owner-ship to two media but the new government that came to power in June 2003 more or less ignored its recommendations.

If the market supports both channels, it will certainly increase media pluralism in Nepal, even if it results in some narrowing of the programme range. But the Nepali television market will never be able to support the same degree of diversification as the larger Pakistani and Bangladeshi markets and counterbalancing India's cultural influence in Nepal remains a much more challenging proposition. Until recently, Nepal had concentrated on diversifying its radio market, licensing a range of different independent stations, some strictly commercial and some more community-oriented. Its new television initiatives are more straightforwardly commercial, but they also reflect a widely held per-ception in Nepal that the most effective way of countering new cultural influences is to strengthen the Nepali media themselves.

Sri Lanka embarked on this same trajectory in the mid-1990s with the licensing of active competition in its own terrestrial sector. By 2000, the state-run television station, Rupavahini, faced competition from three other terrestrial channels in Sinhala and two in Tamil. Many of these channels relayed programmes which originated on satellite channels. Dubbed Hindi soap operas are popular with Sinhala audiences and programmes from South Indian TV stations like Sun TV and Raj TV are relayed by local broadcasters to Sri Lanka's Tamil population. But Sri Lankan audiences for direct satellite programming remain very small.

We have argued elsewhere that Sri Lanka's experience demonstrates that the introduction of terrestrial competition offers a way of strengthening the local at the expense of the global, or at least of managing the global on more local terms.[18] The Sri Lankan model is not without its shortcomings. Licensing policy is less than transparent. Competition in the TV market is so intense that there is little scope for diverse programming. Outside the news and current affairs field, which has attracted serious advertising, the emphasis is almost entirely on mass entertainment. As a result, the state sector in particular has come under intense pressure and has had to cut staff and commercialize its programmes. Nevertheless, Sri Lankans act as gatekeepers, outside influences are mediated by local editors, and the appeal of the channels is not restricted to urban viewers. These are important cultural and social advantages in a globalizing world.

What has seemed a viable policy in the smaller countries of the region has not yet taken root elsewhere. In Bangladesh, the establishment of Ekushey TV in 2000 looked like the beginning of a similar trend. But despite its considerable popularity, the station was closed down in 2002 after a change of government and a series of court cases. Ekushey TV shared Bangladesh TV's transmission facilities and had the same extensive reach in both urban and rural areas. Its news and current affairs programmes proved more credible than those of the state channel and it both provided entertainment and adopted a public service broadcasting agenda, giving space to socially relevant programming which the satellite-only channels almost completely ignored. Some of its participatory programmes for young people were particularly admired. But it ultimately fell foul of the bipolarity of Bangladesh politics and the failure of the two main parties to develop a consensus on media policies. The owner of the channel, A. S. Mahmud, was a businessman with close links to the then prime minister, Sheikh Hasina Wajid, but once the Awami League was voted out of office and the legality of the station was questioned the licensing procedure did not stand the test of legal scrutiny. There was widespread agreement that the channel had contributed significantly to media diversity in the country, but the option of maintaining it with modification was not pursued. The court made no recommendations on this issue and the new BNP government of Begum Khaleda Zia chose to close it down.[19] Whatever its origins, Ekushey TV proved an uncomfortable experience for the politicians, not least because it reached the country's politically important rural audiences. Satellite TV, with its largely urban following, is seen as much less of a threat to the status quo because it plays largely to urban audiences who already enjoy a vibrant print medium.

Regulatory Developments in South Africa

As far as government perceptions are concerned, the most striking change over a ten-year period is that a multi-channel television environment is now seen not so much as an invasive threat to be repulsed or contained as a technology to be managed and exploited for its revenue potential. Subsumed within the highly profitable new communications market, broadcasting is no longer seen primarily as a cultural tool and vehicle for information and nation building. The state monopoly of television broadcasting has ended. The competitive and commercial pressures on state broadcasting have been acknowledged. The guidelines and goalposts of the state broadcasters have been irrevocably shifted. Values of public service broadcasting have changed even if they have not been disavowed. Viewers are no longer dependent on the state broadcasters; many have abandoned them altogether.

In these circumstances, the pressure to rescue state broadcasters from being vehicles for government propaganda has eased. The once powerful arguments for autonomy for the state broadcaster have been weakened. In a competitive market the state has become the underdog. Moreover, because privatized channels have for the most part failed to adopt a public service agenda, protagonists of the state now argue that the national broadcaster has a right and an obligation to make the government's voice heard.

In the case of India the loss of monopoly has been softened by the fact that the major international and domestic satellite broadcasters are geared predominantly to the Indian market and Indian sensitivities. Star News and Zee News, for all their pretensions to be global, have in practice echoed and reinforced Indian government attitudes, and their management consciously accepts that they are under an obligation to do so. When the new in-house Star News went on air at the beginning of April 2003, the network created a holding company, ostensibly with a majority Indian shareholding, to comply with a ceiling of 26 per cent on the foreign ownership of channels that had the right to uplink from India. The move was vigorously criticized by Star's commercial rivals.[20] The Indian government allowed Star extra time to comply with the regulations, but at the end of July the outcome was still subject to judicial proceedings.[21]

While maintaining government control of the state broadcasters, national governments have been drawn into legislating on the nongovernment sector because of the rapid development and growing convergence of media and communication technologies. Regulation as a means of maintaining a state broadcasting monopoly is no longer viable. But the need for regulation to facilitate the introduction of new technologies and to provide a framework of competition is something that India and Pakistan have broadly recognized and are seeking to implement. It is forecast that in the next ten years there will be 100 million TV homes in India alone (70 million currently), and 15–20 million homes with computers (currently 3–4 million). The dynamics of both telecommunications and broadcasting and the digital technologies that are becoming standard for both of them are pointing in the same direction: towards a common system of regulation.

Nepal was the first country in South Asia to bring information, broadcasting and telecommunications under one ministerial roof. Over the past three years, India has been moving slowly in the same direction and similar pressures exist in other countries. The Indian government published a draft Communication Convergence Bill in 2000, setting out a framework of regulation that would incorporate existing telecommunications and broadcasting and consolidate the ministries of information, technology, communications and information and broadcasting. It proposed the establishment of a new Communications Commission of India, which would become the single regulatory authority for IT, communications and broadcasting.

The bill was introduced into parliament – the Lok Sabha – in August 2001. Two years on, sections of it were still strongly contested and by the end of July 2003 it had attracted no fewer than seventy-seven amendments, without having been put to a deciding vote. But the principle it incorporates, of allowing broadcasting competition under licence, though not clearly defined, holds the promise of being a major liberalizing measure. Ten years ago, the idea that there would no longer be a separate ministry of information was regarded as a fantasy, if only because of the strong vested interests of the bureaucracy and the perceived need for direct control by government agencies of key instruments of information. Today that prospect is enshrined in the proposed legislation.

Business people in the communications industry have welcomed the bill as promoting a competitive regulatory environment, allowing a level playing field to an unlimited number of entrants to the market. Its critics do not dispute the need for some form of licence or registration for cable networks, uplinking stations and radio and TV transmission facilities, all of which use the radio frequency spectrum. But they are suspicious both of mandatory obligations placed on service providers and discretionary powers retained by the proposed regulatory authority. They would prefer to let the market determine the number of licences granted, rather than see the commission impose restrictions to prevent one or more service providers from becoming dominant at the expense of others. Some influential voices in the industry argue against provisions of the bill that will require content providers to be licensed at all, citing the freedom of the print media and publishing as the proper benchmark of comparison. They are wary of intervention by the commission in setting tariffs for the provision of services. They oppose a provision that would oblige foreign satellite broadcasters to be free-to-air. They argue that the industry itself should be self-regulating, setting the technical standards and programme and advertising codes, and that the commission should intervene only when self-regulation is seen to be ineffective or inadequate.[22]

Efforts to secure agreement on the new bill have taken place, however, against a background of continuing government resistance to media diversification and decentralization. Despite the growing de facto devolution of power to the states, the government in New Delhi retains tight control of media policy throughout the country. The Supreme Court ruling in 1995 that the airwaves are public property had still not been given legislative effect eight years later. The BJP, the dominant force in national government since 1997, has retained full control of Doordarshan and All India Radio and has not allowed Prasar Bharati, which was set up as an autonomous corporation to run the two services in 1997, to operate with any degree of independence. It has, however, given uplinking rights to satellite channels in majority Indian ownership, like Sun TV, Eenadu, NDTV and Aaj Tak, while denying them to internationally owned corporations like Star and Sony. It is in effect treating these satellite channels as if they were part of an Indian terrestrial sector, though it has not yet attempted to set standards for them or to discuss programme issues with them. The fact that India, the largest and most culturally complex of all South Asian countries, has resisted the licensing of any independent local or community radio stations (so far it has licensed community radio only on a restricted basis for educational purposes) is further evidence of the resilience of the centralizing mindset that characterizes its bureaucratic elite. The fact that satellite television has now been operating for nearly ten years, attracting large audiences in different regional languages without precipitating the separatist tendencies such bureaucrats fear, has apparently had little effect on government thinking in this matter.

Pakistan has witnessed a number of false dawns in electronic media liberalization but there have been some promising developments recently, despite the country's political difficulties. The country's military ruler, General Pervez Musharraf, held out the prospect of a more diverse media environment in his first broadcast to the nation in October 1999. But progress in honouring this pledge was much slower than anticipated. The departure within eighteen months of his adviser on media matters, Javed Jabbar, who was the chief architect of the proposed reforms, marked a setback. But with the establishment in March 2002 of a new electronic media regulatory authority, PEMRA, the way was cleared for the licensing of private television and radio stations. By May 2003, PEMRA had issued over twenty-five licences for the establishment of private and commercial FM radio stations in Pakistan's leading cities, with permission for local news and current affairs programmes, and with the first stations on air later the same year, Pakistan's radio market was soon substantially transformed. PEMRA had also issued five licences for satellite TV stations, including permission to uplink from Pakistan.

It had licensed over 950 cable operators and was in the process of setting lower fees for operators serving populations of fewer than 50,000, a measure of the spread of cable to the smaller conurbations. It was still studying the feasibility of issuing licences for terrestrial television and for the non-commercial use of electronic media by public interest organizations.[23]

PEMRA is the first regulatory broadcasting authority to be set up in South Asia, and although it owes its origins to an ordinance passed under a military government it is in the process of radically altering the media landscape in Pakistan. It is not as independent of government as it might wish to be, but its board reflects a wide range of expertise, both government and non-government, and its provincial complaints commissions are entirely drawn from civil society. The national broadcasters, PTV and the Pakistan Broadcasting Corporation, which remain under direct government control, are excluded from its remit, but its decisions on private sector media development are likely to shape the future of those organizations as well. It remains revenue-driven in its licensing policies and has missed a chance to create a more diverse FM radio environment – as has been the case in India – but unlike in India it has not put restrictions on news broadcasting, which should enable these stations to play a wider role. One critical area for the future concerns cross-media ownership. The PEMRA rules initially prohibited the award of licences to entrepreneurs from existing media, despite the fact that cross-media ownership was not entirely ruled out in the original proposals.[24] This prohibition was challenged by the Jang group and in July 2003 the cabinet amended the ordinance to remove the restriction.[25] With Jang's GEO channel, uplinked from Dubai, fast emerging as the dominant satellite TV player, the group is becoming the market leader in both the print media and satellite TV. A licence for GEO to uplink from Pakistan was requested as a recognition of existing realities, but there is also a danger that it could open the way to further consolidation of the media sector and the creation of over-powerful interests.

Civil Society Responses

The South Asian media market is now largely dominated by the ethos of satellite TV, with its uncomplicated pursuit of the bottom line and its reliance on a mixture of soap operas, game shows and news. This new thrust to broadcasting has been reinforced by the impact of economic liberalization on the state-controlled media: there is an increasing expectation that they will fund themselves. As a result, the state sector in most countries is now as dependent on advertising as its commercial rivals, with obvious implications for target audiences and programme diversity. TV as a whole, including state TV, increasingly focuses on the urban middle class, which has the spending power, and ignores, or pays less attention to, audiences in the rural areas.

The new dominance of the market has given rise to a fear voiced by Hameed Haroon, the CEO of Pakistan's Dawn newspaper group, at a conference in Delhi in 2000 that 'size has become the sole consideration for the survival of a culture'.[26] Indian journalist M. J. Akbar acknowledged the same problem when he commented that 'India is likely to become a media, entertainment and information superpower in the region and this will have both a political impact and social consequences'.[27] These fears have been allayed to some extent by the growth of national and regional satellite TV, although the new channels have tended to follow existing entertainment formats and have not offered the kind of alternative programming many viewers would like to see. There is, in fact, a perception in many parts of South Asia that where there was previously one juggernaut (the state), there are now two (the state and the market), but that the voice of civil society is still not being heard. As a Pakistani documentary maker put it: 'We have the bureaucracy and we have the market but we do not have the community. We have the consumer but we do not have the citizen.'[28]

Hopes that the state might be able to rectify these imbalances by creating a broadcasting industry that better represents the diversity of South Asian societies and is more accountable to their various publics have so far been unfulfilled, though this is less true in the smaller countries than elsewhere. In India, Pakistan and Bangladesh, political and security concerns have limited the impact of media reform, although Pakistan now seems to have broken out of this mould. There is still a great deal to play for in the development of national policy in this area. But it seems clear that the inclinations of governments and bureaucracies are instinctively against diversification and devolution, and that it will come about only if there is sufficient pressure from civil society.

One way that pressure is exerted on governments is through newspapers, although they have tended to be much better at defending their own territory than acting as champions of the electronic media. They are also, in many cases, subject to the same commercializing trends as the TV channels. The Bollywood stars and the TV game shows provide copy for the gossip columns and a steady stream of advertising revenue for papers like the *Times of India*. The two media feed off each other and the voice of the media critic is only dimly heard. There are some outstanding media critics – but they are relatively rare in India and much less evident in neighbouring countries.

There are a number of active pressure groups – of which women's groups are the most successful – which lobby the industry and the regulators. Women's groups have found much to object to in the great expansion of satellite television, whether in soap operas or in adverts. There is much stereotyping of women's traditional roles as well as a general demonizing of the working woman. Women's groups, whether in India or in other countries, have been trying to make their voices heard on such matters, though in many cases without much success.

One of the most effective pressure groups in this field is the Centre for Advocacy and Research, a Delhi-based organization which began as an advocacy group concentrating on women's issues but has since broadened its remit to include the disabled and other marginalized groups. It owes much of its success to its thorough research and to its development of viewers' forums in different parts of India. Consequently, when it engages with commercial TV channels, it does so on the basis of chapter and verse and the views of established monitoring groups on particular programmes. It has had some success in persuading channels to change the way that disability is portrayed and its experience suggests that they find it difficult not to address civil society concerns when put forward in this systematic way.

Another major area of concern is the lack of media coverage of issues relating to development – which affect some 40 per cent of the population of South Asian countries, particularly in the agricultural sector. This is a field in which the state sector's traditional responsibility, particularly on TV, is being watered down under growing commercial pressures and where the new satellite media are doing virtually nothing. Radio is the obvious choice for work in this field, but in India, Pakistan and Bangladesh radio stations serving the rural areas remain a government monopoly and are more attuned to serving central authority than their particular localities.

One positive general development is the increasing recognition among donors of the role that the media can play in winning local support for initiatives such as the national Poverty Reduction Strategies backed by the IMF and World Bank. Well-made radio and TV programmes can spread effective messages about AIDS or leprosy or the education of girls. But it is important that these strategies are not deployed from the top down only. A vibrant civil society is one which has the capacity to reflect on its own dilemmas, not just to hear other people's solutions to them. Developing the resources of civil society to fight for its own media is a longer-term investment but one that will ultimately pay a higher return in terms of the democratization of society and the safeguarding of local cultures.

Cross-border Hostilities and the Prospects for 'South Asian' Media

Although the growth of satellite television has provided cross-border audiences with new insights into life among their neighbours, at times of tension and hostility it has demonstrably exacerbated tensions. Pakistanis watching Indian television during the Kargil confrontation of 1999 found that private channels like Zee and Star were 'more holy than the Pope'.[29] There was little to choose between Doordarshan and its commercial rivals. Patriotic feeling and government control of access to information contributed towards a similarity of perspective among Indian channels and provided a powerful argument among Pakistanis for more diversification of their own media. Zee TV's proprietor, Subhash Chandra, admitted that Pakistanis had cause for complaint, but he put the lack of balance down to the fact that Pakistan had not permitted Zee TV to set up a bureau in Islamabad.[30] Pakistani officials accused Zee more generally of squeezing out the Pakistani point of view. Other critics of Zee's performance contrasted its South Asian broadcasts during the dispute with the more news-neutral service it developed for its audiences in Europe, among which people of Pakistani origin formed a significant proportion. Patriotism and economics were evidently more at odds in Europe than they were in the subcontinent.

Zee TV came under fire again in Nepal in 2000 at the time of the hijack of the Indian airlines jet to Kandahar. At that time, its allegations that Nepal had provided a base for Pakistani military intelligence to orchestrate the hijack plunged relations between the two countries to a new low.[31] The channel was also strongly criticized in Bangladesh in 2002 for its reporting of a border incident in which a number of Indian soldiers were killed in crossfire. Here too the station was accused of taking a strongly nationalistic line and contributing to a marked deterioration of relations.[32]

These various incidents have prompted some introspection about the role of the media – whether print or electronic – in perpetuating negative stereotypes and demonizing the 'other'. An India–Pakistan media retreat organized by *Himal*, the South Asian news magazine, and Panos South Asia, in May 2002 produced a thoughtful exchange of views among practitioners.[33] Indian journalists were critical of a lack of professionalism on their own side in covering aspects of the Kargil confrontation. Barkha Dutt of Star TV, who had made her name for her reporting of the conflict, talked of the pressure of events and of 'subliminal nationalism that creeps in'. In her view, 'one of the reasons why television failed in Kargil is that TV is still a very young medium in India and does not really have very senior reporters'.[34] Mushahid Hussain, who had been Pakistan's information minister at the time, said that 'nation, mindset and market come together in a particularly potent form on such occasions'. He drew a distinction, however, between the attitude of Zee and Star TV: 'I requested Zee and Star to air our perspective. Star agreed. Zee refused.'[35]

The meeting highlighted restrictions on access for journalists as a major impediment to building understanding, although there was also a feeling that increased interaction at workshops and conferences between Indian and Pakistani journalists was slowly making a difference to the level of reporting. Such a generalization did not apply, however, to the Urdu-, Hindi- and other-language newspapers on which most Indians and Pakistanis rely. Interaction between journalists from these papers was much more limited and their coverage of the other country tended to be restricted to stories that showed it in a bad light.

Although efforts to strengthen Indo-Pakistan relations by improving people-to-people contact have a long if tortuous history, the need to build media bridges between the two countries is receiving serious attention only now. A major study of the South Asian media funded by the United Nations Development Programme was published in 2002 and is to be followed by a number of initiatives to build greater understanding across the Indo-Pakistan divide.[36] These are not restricted to television, but they include the commissioning of television programmes on subjects of mutual interest, capacity building for television journalists, monitoring of television programmes and increased networking among TV journalists. The aim is to raise funding for these initiatives from donors and from media organizations in the two countries, although raising this counterpart funding is likely to prove challenging.

With satellite technology becoming more affordable, the setting up of genuinely South Asian channels, providing news on the region as a whole and not just on individual countries, should become a more distinct possibility. Language differences across South Asian borders are less of a barrier than they are within India itself, where they are providing opportunities for diversity in broadcasting on a unprecedented scale. It is the nature of the new television technology that it can cater for such diversity. The question is whether the market in all its forms – no longer necessarily a mass market but smaller niche markets – can in practice deliver the variety and diversity that the technology makes possible. And if the market cannot deliver, are there other ways in which the potential can be realized?

The creation of more 'South Asian' media has been held back among other things by hostility between India and its neighbours and lack of progress in improving trade relations. So long as advertisers see no practical value in appealing to audiences beyond national markets, channels aimed at the great Indian middle class or at Pakistani or Bangladeshi audiences have little incentive to appeal to viewers beyond national borders. To this extent, national governments still call the shots in the much more complex media world that has emerged over the last decade. The growth of satellite news services has provided for greater reflection of opposition views and helped create a new platform for political debate. This has had its greatest impact, however, within national political space. There is much cross-border viewing but much less representation of cross-border views. Transnational broadcasters may operate partly outside national systems of regulation, but they need to be on good terms with governments in their key markets. When political tensions rise,

India bans the relaying of PTV on Indian cable systems and Pakistan bans the relaying of Indian satellite channels. The growth of Pakistani and Bangladeshi satellite channels has helped to counter the dominance of Indian satellite channels in these national markets. But it has not contributed much so far to the creation of a broader South Asian civil society, which the satellite revolution has the potential – and indeed in negative as well as positive ways has already done quite a lot – to foster.

Notes

1. This chapter draws on workshops and discussions set up by the Media South Asia Project under the auspices of the Institute of Development Studies at the University of Sussex, supported by the Ford Foundation, and held in Delhi, Mumbai, Chennai, Kolkata, Colombo, Dhaka, Kathmandu and Karachi over the period 2000–02. The authors are grateful for the contribution of the participants in those meetings, fuller accounts of which are available on <http://www.thehoot.org/mediasouthasia>. They are especially indebted to advice and assistance given by Sevanti Ninan, Bhuvan Lall, Rama Bijapurkar, Deepa Bhatia, Deepak Thapa, Beena Sarwar, Agha Nasir, Nalaka Gunawardene, Rajendra Sharma and Afsan Chowdhury. They are grateful to Vanita Kohli for permitting access to information from her book *The Indian Media Business* (New Delhi: Sage, 2003).

2. These 'shared perceptions of marginalisation' are documented in detail in David Page and William Crawley, *Satellites over South Asia: Broadcasting, Culture and the Public Interest* (New Delhi: Sage, 2001). See, in particular, pp. 184–202 and 223–47.

3. A. C. Nielsen Television Audience Measurement, *Cable and Satellite*, 'Hindi Speaking Markets', 2–8 February 2003, <http://www.indiantelevision.com>. Consulted June 2003.

4. *Business Standard*, Mumbai, 17 April 2003.

5. See Sevanti Ninan, 'Will the Cable be Cut?', *The Hindu*, 25 May 2003.

6. For an account of cable operations in South Chennai, see Page and Crawley, *Satellites*, pp. 311–13. See also *Venkatachari Jagannathan*, 1 November 2002 and 24 December 2002 <http://www.domain-b.com>. Consulted March 2004.

7. Interview, Sameer Nair, CEO Star TV, New Delhi, January 2003.

8. For Sri Adhikari Brothers, see <http://www.indiainfoline.com/comp/srad/0507a.html>. Consulted March 2004; for B4U, see <http://www.screenindia.com/fullstory.php?content_id=3047>. Consulted July 2003.

9. See Surajeet das Gupta's interview with Star TV CEO, Peter Mukerjea, *Business Standard*, 24 July 2003.

10. Interview, Rama Bijapurkar, Mumbai, January 2003.

11. See Page and Crawley, *Satellites*, pp. 205–6.

12. BBC World Service radio programmes in Hindi and other Indian languages have also seen a sharp downturn in audiences as local satellite television extends to a mass audience. See http://www.bbc.co.uk/pressoffice/pressreleases/stories/2002/04_april/16/worldservice_audiences.shtm>. Consulted June 2003.

13. See Page and Crawley, *Satellites*, pp. 280–1.

14. ARY capitalized on the news interest created by 9/11 and broke new ground with its daily current affairs shows and phone-ins to political leaders. See, for example, Omar R. Quraishi's report on ARY's interview and phone-in with MQM leader, Altaf Husain, *Dawn* (Karachi, 18 May 2002), also available on <http://www.dawn.com/2002/05/18/fea.htm>.

15. Muna Khan, *Dawn* (Karachi, 27 December 2002), <http://www.dawn.com/events/lifestyle2002/Is17.htm>. Consulted June 2003.

16. See Deepak Thapa, 'Media Profile of Nepal', pp. 7–8 (February 2003), <http://www.crossboundarymedia.net.shtm>. Consulted March 2003.

17. Ibid., pp. 12–13. Communication from Rajendra Sharma, Radio Nepal, Kathmandu, 28 March 2004.

18. See Page and Crawley, *Satellites*, pp. 257–60.

19. For an account of the rise and fall of Ekushey TV and its significance in the context of Bangladesh politics, see 'Bangladesh Media in Times of Transition', a paper presented to a seminar organized by Mass Line Media in 2002, published in Afsan Chowdhury, *Media in Times of Crisis* (Dhaka: Shraban Prokashoni, 2003), pp. 125–31.

20. See Sevanti Ninan, 'Star under Attack', *The Hindu*, 20 July 2003.

21. See Business Standard Corporate Bureau, 16 and 23 July 2003, <http://www.rediff.com>. Consulted July 2003.

22. See US India Business Council comments on Draft Communications Convergence Bill, <http://www.tiaonline.org/policy/submissions/USIBC ConvergenceSubmissions.pdf>, consulted July 2003; Kiran Karnik, 'Karnik on Convergence', 9 January 2002, <http://www.thehoot.org/story.asp?sectio n=&storyid=webhoothootL1K0910226&pn=1>, consulted July 2003; Bhuvan Lall, Executive Director, Indian Broadcasting Foundation, interview, January 2003.

23. Saleem Gul Shaikh, Chief Executive of PEMRA, interview, Islamabad, May 2003.

24. Javed Jabbar, former federal minister for information and broadcasting, electronic media freedom, '14 Issues', *Dawn*, 7 February 2003.

25. See *Dawn*, 22 and 24 July 2003.

26. Hameed Haroon, 'The View from beyond India's Borders', paper presented to the conference on 'South Asian Broadcasting in the Satellite Age' (New Delhi, 8–9 December 2000).

27. M. J. Akbar, remarks made at the same conference (New Delhi, 8 December 2000).

28. Shireen Pasha, speaking at a workshop on 'Culture and Communication in the Satellite Age' (Karachi, 18 April 2001).

29. Imran Aslam, former editor of the *News*, interviewed for the documentary 'Michael Jackson Comes to Manikganj' by director Nupur Basu (2000). See also Indian Institute of Mass Communications, 'The Media and Kargil' (1999). 'Information War Media: A Victim or a Tool', <http://www.thehoot.org> 9 August 2002. Consulted July 2003.

30. Subhash Chandra, interviewed for the documentary 'Michael Jackson Comes to Manikganj' by Director Nupur Basu (2000).

31. See Page and Crawley, *Satellites*, p. 246.

32. See 'Conflict Reporting: Contrast and Commonalities', a report prepared for the South Asian Forum on Human Rights, quoted in Afsan Chowdhury, Bangladesh Media Profile, pp. 3–4 (February 2003), <http://www.crossboundarymedia.net>. Consulted March 2003. An updated version of this profile is also published in Afsan Chowdhury, *Media in Times of Crisis*, pp. 79–114.

33. See *Himal*, June 2002, 15(6), pp. 10–27.

34. Ibid.

35. Ibid.

36. The Cross Boundary Media Project has set up a website at <http://www.crossboundarymedia.net>, where its research profiles of different South Asian countries and its plans for the future are available.

CHAPTER 7

The Transnationalization of Television: The Indian Experience

Daya Kishan Thussu

§ THE international television scene has profoundly changed in the past decade or so with the proliferation of satellite and cable television channels as a result of digitalization and the availability of privatized communication satellites. The resulting growth of multi-channel networks has made the global televisual landscape much more complex. Gone are the days when national broadcasters addressed a common public space, which in most countries had been a characteristic of television since its invention. Before media globalization, with the possible exception of broadcasters from major powers such as the United States, television networks traditionally saw themselves as operating within and for the nation state, making programmes for citizens rather than consumers. With the globalization of the US model of commercial television, national broadcasters, though still receiving the highest audience share, no longer have a monopoly on the airwaves. The availability of myriad channels has given viewers in many countries an ability to access simultaneously a vast array of local, national, regional and international networks. The viewer as consumer is the premise for a media system driven by advertising.

This chapter aims to explore, through the example of Indian television, the complexities involved in the transnationalization of television. Televisual images from India are now increasingly becoming part of a global cultural experience – whether of fashion, film, popular music or television. Such developments raise fundamental questions about transnational media flows and the need to rethink the question of media and cultural imperialism. The market-driven broadcasting environment has enabled Indian and foreign (mainly but not exclusively Western) television companies to create a transnational

Indian television audience, drawing primarily on the huge Indian diaspora but also catering to the larger conglomerations of South Asian populations scattered across the globe.

Globalization and Television Traffic

The deregulation and liberalization of the broadcasting and tele-communications sector and its rapid privatization in the 1990s, partly as a result of free-market trade regimes set up under the auspices of the World Trade Organization, has contributed to the creation of a global marketplace for media products. Although the General Agreement on Trade in Services (GATS) has exempted the broadcasting, film and cable industries, convergence in the industry, with multimedia conglomerates offering video programming, computing and telecom networks over the same technological infrastructure, has blurred the distinction between broadcasting and telecommunications. The current round of world trade negotiations is likely to liberalize further the trade in global television products, since Article XIX of the GATS contains a built-in agenda for rapid liberalization in audio-visual services, thus strengthening the position of the champions of free trade in the audiovisual sector and creating a global agora which offers many challenges as well as enormous opportunities.

There is little doubt that the main beneficiaries of such liberalized trading regimes have been the mainly US-based global media conglomerates – Disney, Time Warner, News Corporation – given that they own multiple broadcast and cable networks and production facilities and dominate television content and delivery mechanisms. Deregulation and privatization of broadcasting across the globe and the relaxation of cross-media ownership restrictions, coupled with mergers and acquisitions, have ensured that the media companies have broadened and deepened their existing interests, aided by new methods of delivering content, namely digital satellite, cable and the Internet. The convergence of media and technologies, and the process of vertical integration in the media industries, have led to the concentration of media power in a few large corporations, which have used an array of strategies, including the regionalization and localization of managerial staff and programme content, to acquire new and retain traditional audiences in a heterogeneous global market.[1]

One result of these changes is the US domination of the global television export market: in 1999 the USA accounted for 85 per cent of light entertainment exports; 81 per cent of television movies; 72 per cent of drama; 63 per cent of feature films; 60 per cent of children's programmes and 37 per cent of factual television programming.[2] The grossly unequal trade in television and film products from the media-rich North, and within it the Anglo-American core, to the media-poor South was at the heart of the debates on the so-called 'Dallasization' of global culture, which provided much of the material for the media and cultural imperialism theses.[3]

Arguably this traffic has become more pronounced in the era of multi-channel television. The largely Western-owned audiovisual industry is one of the fastest-growing global industries, as digital technologies have facilitated both the development and delivery of a whole new range of products and services (pay-per-view, interactive TV, video-on-demand, web TV). This has given new relevance to the media and cultural imperialism arguments: the growing flow of consumerist messages through Western-owned or -inspired television has been seen by some as evidence of a new form of cultural imperialism, especially in the global South.[4] Some have argued that the extensive reach of US-based media, advertising and telecommunications networks have helped the USA to use its 'soft power', to promote its national interests.[5]

Creation of a Transnational Television Audience

While there is no doubt that the increasing traffic in televisual programming and the resultant globalization of as powerful a medium as television has tended to increase Western (more specifically, US) cultural influence in the world, the global flow of cultural products is not as straightforward as the exponents of the media/cultural imperialism theses often claim. Some 'peripheral' countries have emerged as exporters of audiovisual products to an increasingly complex global television market,[6] while Western-based media conglomerates have also had to adapt to local market demands. In the burgeoning literature on media globalization, much less attention has been given to how 'other' broadcasters have astutely made use of the possibilities offered by new technologies and a market-driven broadcasting environment.[7]

A market-driven mediascape has made it possible to beam a range of specialized channels across the world, some in local or national languages, giving wider choice to consumers and opening up their window on the world. In addition, they have also contributed to freeing up airwaves from state control, virtually the norm among many countries in the global South, where state-controlled broadcasting had been little more than a mouthpiece for ruling parties or governments.

One largely under-researched aspect of the deregulation of broadcasting has been how it has acted as a catalyst for the extension of private television networks from countries like India to the lucrative Western markets, aiming primarily at diasporic audiences. Looking beyond the traditional view of Western domination of international television exports, it is discernible that the traffic of televisual products is not just one way – from the West (and within it, the Anglo-American axis) to 'the rest', even though it is overly weighted in favour of the former. Evidence shows that new transnational television networks are presenting images from the South across the globe, feeding into and developing emergent 'diasporic public spheres'.[8]

Satellite television has opened up possibilities for transnational broadcasters to cater to specific geocultural markets based on linguistic affinities, thus contributing to the creation of supranational public spaces.[9] An increasingly interconnected and globalized economy has facilitated the movement of people – what Appadurai has called 'ethnoscape' – from one geographical location to another, in search of new or better jobs. The internationalization of a professional workforce employed by transnational corporations, international non-governmental organizations and multilateral bureaucracies as well as of services such as higher education has also boosted demand for transnational television. The issue of identity is central to members of such diasporic groups, often living 'between cultures'.[10]

India and the Transnational Television Bazaar

Television in India has undergone a process of rapid expansion and globalization as a result of market liberalization, evident in the availability and growth of Indian television channels not only within India but also catering to a large South Asian diaspora outside its borders. Indian television is now available in five continents. In Britain, for example, Indian channels – Zee, Sony, Star Plus, B4U (Bollywood for

You) – available on Sky's digital network, have dedicated viewerships. Indian television companies are increasingly trying to get into the lucrative US market, where the Indian diaspora comprises one of the richest strata of society: of the nearly two million people of Indian origin living in the USA, the investment firm Merrill Lynch estimates, there are 200,000 millionaires among them. They have an average income of over US$60,000, compared to the national average of about US$39,000, making them America's wealthiest immigrants.[11] In the United Arab Emirates, a vast majority of the population consists of foreign workers from the Indian subcontinent, making the oil-rich Gulf region a key target for television networks based in India.

To make sense of the transnationalization of Indian television, it is important to understand the national context of television, which in India experienced profound changes since the early 1990s, accelerated by the combined impact of new communication technologies and the opening up of global markets. At the beginning of the 1990s there was no television industry worth the name in India, which until 1991 had just one state-controlled channel, Doordarshan, little more than a mouthpiece of the government of the day and notoriously monotonous. By 2003, more than 100 channels – some joint ventures with international broadcasters – were operating in India. This expansion demanded new programme content – from news to game-and-chat shows, from soap operas to 'reality TV' – which have been provided by a burgeoning television industry that is increasingly going global.

The liberalization of the Indian television industry revolutionized broadcasting in what used to be one of the world's most protected media markets.[12] Gradual deregulation and privatization of television transformed the media landscape in the country – evident in the exponential growth in the number of television channels and the resultant expansion of mainly Western transnational media players into India, one of the world's biggest television markets.[13]

India's rapidly expanding economy and a pro-market government, coupled with an established satellite network, made the Indian market an extremely attractive proposition for transnational broadcasters. Combined with this was the huge number of potential consumers – a large, growing and increasingly Westernized middle class, estimated to be 200 million, providing global media corporations with unrivalled opportunities for running a wide array of satellite channels.

Cable and satellite television have increased substantially since 1992, when only 1.2 million Indian homes had cable and satellite television. According to the 2002 National Readership Survey, there were nearly 384 million television viewers in India, with cable and satellite penetration growing to 40 million homes.[14]

While they started out with mainly Western programmes, however, the global players such as News Corporation have been forced first to Indianize, then regionalize and finally localize, their programming to suit the range and variety of cultural and linguistic tastes encompassing the Indian market.[15] As Table 7.1 shows, entertainment-led channels dominate the cable and satellite market, with the top three – SET MAX (part of Sony Corporation), Star Plus (constituent of Rupert Murdoch's News Corporation) and Sony TV (owned by Sony Corporation) – belonging to major global players.

TABLE 7.1 Market reach of cable and satellite TV – the top ten channels

Channel name	Type	Market reach (million of homes)	Market share (%)
SET MAX	Entertainment/ sport	8.3	12.2
Star Plus	General	7.2	10.5
Sony TV	General	7.1	10.4
Zee TV	General	6.3	9.2
Ten Sports	Sports	5.9	8.6
Zee Cinema	Indian films	5.7	8.3
Star Sports	Sports	5.6	8.2
DD2	General	5.4	7.9
Aaj Tak	News and current affairs	5.1	7.5
Star Gold	Hindi movies	4.8	7.0

Source: Data from TAM Media Research, *Cable and Satellite TV Magazine*, May 2003.

The Triumvirate Take Over

Despite the proliferation of cable and satellite channels in India, the market is shared between three major players: Star, Sony and Zee. Like media conglomerates elsewhere, they have taken over smaller competitors to present a mixed bouquet of programme offerings to reach the national as well the diasporic audience. These three have also been crucial in the expansion of Indian television networks outside India. Zee network, India's first private Hindi-language and most successful satellite channel and the first to think in terms of global markets, was launched in 1992 by the Essel Group of Indian entrepreneur Subhash Chandra, only a year after Western television networks started beaming to India. Unlike Western broadcasters, whose largely US-made programmes were watched by the English-fluent urban middle classes with aspirations to a Western way of life, Zee began by offering Hindi-language programmes, targeting the mass market and also the diasporic one, skilfully developing indigenous programming and adapting Hindi derivatives of Western formats, such as game-and-chat shows, leisure programming and quiz contests.[16]

Zee also contributed to the evolution of a hybrid media language – Hinglish (a mixture of Hindi, India's main language, and English, the language of international media). The use of Hinglish has been an important factor in the expansion of Indian television outside the borders of the country. The deployment of such a hybrid language on its all-music channel Music Asia (now renamed Zee Music) contributed to the popularization of Hinglish, particularly among the youth – a trend that in subsequent years seems to have influenced much of Indian television. The idea behind using a mixture of Hindi and English was to expand the channel's reach beyond the Hindi-speaking regions of India and, crucially, to cater to the South Asian diaspora – part of an ethnically, linguistically and religiously diverse group – which would be more amenable to a hybrid variety of television and demonstrate greater empathy with hybridized languages.

Members of the South Asian diasporic communities, especially second and third generations, who have grown up within other cultures, may speak a myriad of languages, but most of them at least understand some Hindi, due largely to the popularity of Hindi films. Catering to the taste of a younger generation, growing up on the diet of MTV and its local clones, Zee was following a trend that began in the Hindi movie industry, which increasingly uses Hinglish words and phrases in film dialogue and in songs. Advertising companies too have cashed in on this trend with Pepsi's call for '*Yehi hai* [only this is] the right choice, baby', breaking new ground in postmodern advertising.

Other indications of the transnationalization of the Zee network is the increasing use of English subtitles in its programmes, to meet the demands of the new subscribers. Within the diasporic groups itself, Zee is increasingly aiming to reach language-based niche audiences. In Britain, it already runs Zee Alpha Punjabi channel and has recently acquired a majority stake in ETC Networks (prominent in music and Punjabi television) and in Padmalaya (catering to the South Indian market and the Tamil diaspora). The diasporic market, especially in Europe and North America, is crucial for the transnationalization of Zee – during 2002, more than 16 per cent of its revenue came from outside Asia.

By 2002, Zee was broadcasting in more than eighty countries and claiming to have access to 225 million viewers globally. Apart from Asia and the Middle East, where its target market is of 50 million households, it had 172,000 subscribers in North America, 135,000 in Britain, 73,500 in the Caribbean and 37,500 in Africa. In 2002, Zee entered a joint venture with AOL Time Warner, making it 'the largest pay offering network' in India, reaching over 35 million television households.[17]

As its annual report for 2001–02 states, Zee is 'India's largest and only fully integrated media and entertainment company', which enjoys what it calls a 'strong presence across most of the entertainment

TABLE 7.2 Indian television's triumvirate

Star bouquet	Sony / Discovery	Zee-Turner bouquet
Star Plus	SET MAX	Zee TV
Star News	Discovery	Zee Cinema
Star Movies	Animal Planet	Zee News
Star World	CNBC	Cartoon Network
Star Gold	AXN	CNN
Star Sport	NDTV	HBO
Vijay		
Channel [V] India		
National Geographic		
Adventure One		
ESPN		

Sources: Company websites, trade press.

value chain'. The first link in this chain is content production: it is the largest producer of Hindi-language television programming and has recently started to produce feature films. The 2002 film *Gadar – Ek Prem Katha*, was the biggest blockbuster in Indian cinema. The second is 'content aggregation', demonstrated in its presence across the different programming genres – entertainment, news, cinema and music in Hindi and English, six regional language channels and zeenext.com. Services provide the third link of the chain. These include broadcasting live events and educational services which reach more than 225 million viewers globally. Finally, distribution – cable and direct to operator – completes the chain. Zee owns Siti Cable, India's largest cable network, an 8,000-kilometre network of two-way cable, reaching 6.5 million households in forty-three cities.

The second major player in the Indian market is Star (Satellite Television Asian Region), part of Rupert Murdoch's News Corporation, which proudly claims to be 'setting the pace of media in Asia', broadcasting forty services in eight languages and reaching more than 300 million viewers in fifty-three countries. Over 120 million people watch Star every week.

Star TV was the first major global player to recognize the demand for Western, mainly American, programming for an Indian audience growing up on the dull and drab Doordarshan, when, in 1991, it started beaming a five-channel satellite service in English (Plus, Prime Sports, Channel V, the BBC World and Movie), which became an instant hit with the English-fluent urban elite. It realized, however, that if it had to make a profit the channel would have to make programmes in a language that a majority of Indians understood and on themes with which the masses would be able to identify.

Having been in the Indian market for over ten years, Star's fortunes in India changed dramatically after its flagship channel Star Plus launched *Kaun Banega Crorepati*, an Indian version of the successful British game show *Who Wants to be a Millionaire?*, hosted by India's best-known film star Amitabh Bachchan.[18] In 2003, it had become the most popular private channel in the country – with an average of forty out of the top fifty shows every week. In 2003, Star claimed to be reaching more than 31 million homes in India. Given the international nature of Star TV, however, these programmes were reaching a large trans-Indian and even a trans-Asian audience. In 2003, the Star bouquet included:

- Star Plus (entertainment channel, available in Europe on the Sky digital platform and on the digital cable TV platforms, NTL Home and Telewest also available in Middle East and the Philippines);
- Star News (twenty-four-hour news in Hindi also available in Europe, Middle East, the Philippines and Thailand);
- Star Movies (Hollywood blockbusters);
- Star World (available across Asia and featuring US programmes such as *The Simpsons*, *Ally McBeal*, *Friends*, *NYPD Blue* and *Dharma and Greg*);
- Star Gold (Hindi films, and available in Middle East and in Thailand);
- Star Sport (live sporting events, also available in East and Southeast Asia);
- Vijay (catering to the Tamil market in Southern India);
- Channel [V] India (all-music channel, also available in Middle East, East and Southeast Asia);
- National Geographic (documentary channel also available in East and Southeast Asia and in Middle East);
- Adventure One ('adrenaline-pumping action from around the world' also available in Australia, Europe, Middle East, East and Southeast Asia);
- ESPN (all-sport channel, available in East and Southeast Asia).

In March 2003, Star revamped the content of Star News, moving from news in English produced by NDTV[19] to twenty-four-hour news in Hindi produced in-house. It is flashier, tends towards infotainment and emphasizes metropolitan news. For example, its daily *City 60* programme focuses exclusively on news events in India's major cities. The channel has a new team of anchors and reporters and twenty-one bureaux across the country. The move to Hindi may have been engineered by market logic, as shown by the fact that within one week of this switch Star News ratings almost doubled.

The third main player of the Indian television industry is Sony, part of the Sony conglomerate. Entertainment has been at the heart of Sony's agenda in India. Since its launch in 1995, Sony Entertainment Television has aimed to provide family entertainment. Three years later, AXN (animation, action and adventure channel) was added to the Sony platform and, in 1999, SET MAX (sports network) was included. It can draw on the resources of Columbia TriStar

International Television, a Sony Pictures Entertainment company, which calls itself 'the biggest entertainment powerhouse of America'. Apart from India, SET is also available in the USA, Europe, Australia, Middle East and Africa.

That entertainment may not be enough to sustain such a hetero-geneous audience has forced Sony to enter into a partnership with Discovery Channel (operational in India since 1995). By 2003, Sony was claiming to reach 29 million homes while Discovery had sub-scribers in 21 million households. The motto of this so-called One Alliance – a joint venture between Sony and Discovery – is 'eight different channels – one aim – total entertainment'. Sony is seen in over 28 million households in South Asia and in the Middle East.[20]

Like Zee and Star, Sony too is aiming to reach a transnational Indian audience. SET Asia became the first South Asian entertain-ment channel to launch on the UK digital satellite platform in 1999. By 2003, it was available on Sky digital, cable NTL and Telewest broadband. It has sponsored community events for the Asian diaspora in Britain, prominent among them being the 'Sports Personality of the Year Awards', 'Britain's Richest Asians' and the Bradford Mela, one of Britain's biggest annual Asian fairs. Having established itself in the UK market, Sony has expanded into other international mar-kets: in Denmark via Tele Danmark; in Norway and the Netherlands via UPC and in Portugal via Cabovisão. In Canada it is on ATN (Asian Television Network); in the USA on Dish Network; in Russia on Kosmos TV and in South Africa on DSTV. Since February 2003, SET Asia is also available on Arab Digital Distribution platform in the Middle East – as part of ADD's dedicated Asian entertainment channel bouquet, Pehla.

Apart from these three big players, regional television networks have ambitions to be transnational in their operations. Prominent among them is the Tamil-language Sun TV, started in 1993 as India's first regional private channel. Within a decade, it had acquired an audience of 40 million around the world. Since 2002, Sun TV has been available on Dish Network in the USA, which also distributes five Hindi channels and one Urdu channel besides channels in fourteen other languages. Apart from India and the USA, the programmes of Sun TV are accessible in Sri Lanka, Malaysia, Singapore, Europe and Australia.

While the cable and satellite market has been shared by the three major networks, the state broadcaster Doordarshan, traditionally drab but now market-driven and competitive, continues to provide both entertainment and education to the vast majority of India's population, for whom it remains their window to the world.[21] Despite fierce competition from foreign-owned and -operated television networks, Doordarshan boasts the biggest audience share in India. It is the largest terrestrial network in the world – in 1980 the national network covered only 25 per cent of India's population and only 14 per cent of the area of the country; by 2002, it could reach nearly 90 per cent of the population and nearly 78 per cent of India's landmass.

In parallel with entertainment-led private networks, Doordarshan too is dependent on advertising revenue, yet it continues to uphold its public service role, as evidenced by its claim, on its website, that 'it strives to carry messages in its programmes on means of population control and family welfare, agricultural information and knowledge, preservation of environment and ecological balance, highlighting the need for social welfare measures for women, children and the less privileged'. The programme content of its flagship channel, DD1, is broadly divided into 47 per cent entertainment, 38 per cent information (including sport) and 15 per cent education. One indication of its public service ethos is the launch in 2000 of Gyandarshan, a dedicated twenty-four-hour educational channel now accessible to an estimated 20 million viewers in cable homes. Apart from more than twenty regional channels, Doordarshan also operates DD Metro (for major cities), DD Sports (launched in 1999, the first dedicated sports channel in India, which is now an encrypted channel, given the potential for sports earning) and DD Bharati (for arts and culture).

A competitive broadcasting environment has forced Doordarshan to look for subscribers outside India. Since 1995 Doordarshan has run an international channel, DD India, with its mission 'to build bridges of communication with Indians living abroad and to showcase the real India; its culture, its values, its tradition, its modernity, its diversity, its unity, its agony and its ecstasy ... '.[22] To generate extra revenues, Doordarshan has also repositioned its sports channel as 'Live Indian Sports Channel', with rights to telecast sporting events, most notably cricket, which has a dedicated trans-Indian audience. Available on PAS-10 satellite, it can be accessed in thirty-four countries, including in the Middle East, parts of the former Soviet Union, South Asia, Europe and Africa.

Localization of the Global or the Globalization of the Local?

The above survey of the television scene in India and its increasing transnational character demonstrates that in the cable and satellite market it is the three major global players who dominate the sector. The triumvirate of Indian television – Star, Zee and Sony – have been instrumental in localizing the global and globalizing the local. They have recognized and then cultivated a transnational Indian audience for their programming.

Zee's was a pioneering effort in this regard. It teamed up with Rupert Murdoch's Star TV – from 1993 to 1999 – to raise its international profile, most significantly to get on the BSkyB network in the UK. Such alliances also opened up possibilities of developing programmes with other broadcasters in South Asia – the drama serial *Tanha* (*Lonely*), telecast on Star Plus, was a result of creative co-operation between television artists from India and Pakistan, the two major rivals in South Asia. The series was written by a Pakistani author, but produced and directed by an Indian with cast from both countries. Zee tried to produce and distribute its programmes on its own when it bought back its share from Star in September 1999 (perceiving it as a rival), but realized that the pressures of a competitive and crowded marketplace necessitated alliance with a global giant. It now has a joint venture with Time Warner to remain competitive. Both Sony and Star are already part of major transnational operators.

The transnationalization of Indian television has been a boost for the movie industry, as many dedicated film-based pay channels have emerged during the late 1990s. At the heart of the Indian entertainment industry are the country's huge film factories, which have an annual turnover of almost 20 billion rupees (approximately US$425 million) – slated to hit Rs60 billion (approximately US$1.25 billion) in the next five years. By the end of 2003, Indian movie exports are expected to be in the region of Rs70 billion (approximately US$1.5 billion), targeting a South Asian diaspora of more than 30 million people. It is the world's second biggest film industry, with 800 million tickets sold annually. Although still very small in comparison with export earnings of Hollywood, this represents an interesting development, given the overwhelming dominance of the US film industry in global film production and distribution.[23] The Indian entertainment industry is expected to treble in size – from Rs154 billion (approximately US$3.3 billion) in 2000 to nearly Rs600 billion (approximately US$12.5 billion) by 2005, according to a report entitled *The Indian Entertainment Industry: Envisioning Tomorrow*, prepared for the Federation of Indian Chambers of Commerce and Industry by Arthur Andersen.[24]

The globalization of the Indian film and television industry has been accompanied by a growth in Indian television programming elsewhere.[25] It is significant to note that B4U, Britain's round-the-clock digital television channel for Hindi movies, was launched in London in 1999 and only subsequently became available to subscribers in India. This global dimension is to be seen in the marketing strategies of Indian television and film companies. In 2000, for example, the first international Indian film awards, billed as the 'Bollywood Oscars', was broadcast from London's Millennium Dome to more than 122 countries, reaching 600 million viewers. The ceremony, promoted by Wizcraft International Entertainment, brought together Indian film and music stars with US Oscar winner Angelina Jolie, Chinese star Jackie Chan and Australian pop singer Kylie Minogue.

In the twenty-first century, while the West continues to set the international cultural agenda, non-Western cultures are more visible than ever before. The popular Indian music director Allah Rakha Rahman's collaboration with British composer Andrew Lloyd Webber on a successful musical, *Bombay Dreams*, was seen as an example of this trend towards cultural globalization. In 2001, the New York-based Indian director Mira Nair's *Monsoon Wedding*, a light-hearted account of a wedding in a wealthy family in India, was awarded the Golden Lion for best picture at the Venice Film Festival. The British Asian director, Asif Kapadia's *The Warrior* won the London Film Festival's prestigious Sutherland Trophy. A cover story in the magazine *Newsweek*, 'Bollywood Goes Global', intoned: 'The West may have the biggest stalls in the world's media bazaar, but it is not the only player. Globalization isn't merely another word for Americanization – and the recent expansion of the Indian entertainment industry proves it.'[26]

One of the fastest-growing sectors of the Indian economy, the entertainment industry has rivalled the Indian information technology sector as one of the most successful export earners. In 2002 alone, according to consulting firm KPMG, the entertainment industry grew by more than 6 per cent to a size of Rs166 billion (approximately US$3.5 billion) with television contributing the maximum to growth. KPMG has projected a 20 per cent annual growth rate for the entertainment industry until 2007, which would take its revenues to Rs419 billion (approximately US$9 billion).[27]

As Indian and Indian-oriented television businesses begin to integrate fully with the US-dominated global economy, it is likely that Indian television will become more visible in the international broadcasting arena. However, what kind of television will it be? If the diasporic audience becomes the focus of attention for programme makers is it possible that they might privilege themes and programmes, in Hinglish, for the NRI (the famed non-resident Indian)? Already, there is a clear bias in favour of programming for urban middle-class Indians on private television networks: according to a recent study conducted by the New Delhi-based Centre for Advocacy and Research, nearly 60 per cent of the serials on Zee, Sony and Star Plus were set in upper-class homes; while middle-class families figured in 14 per cent of the serials, the lower classes did not feature at all.[28]

As in many other countries, globalization in relation to India has profoundly influenced its media cultures, forcing it to redefine its place in the world. This influence, however, has been a two-way process. There has been a lot from India – popular music, film, fashion, literature, computer software – which has been globalized in the 1990s as a result of marketization. In the twenty-first century, television from India is likely to become part of transnational television culture – after all, every sixth person in the world is of Indian origin.

While the transnationalization of Indian television demonstrates a growing reverse traffic in television flow, it is questionable whether there is a corresponding decline in Western media influence internationally. It is unlikely that Indian television is being watched by a non-Asian audience in the West, apart from occasional forays into the 'exoticism' of Bollywood. There is a temptation to see such developments as having a potential to evolve into counter-hegemonic channels at a global level to check US domination of the airwaves. The globalization of Indian networks, however, has occurred only after making alliances with transnational media conglomerates. How much of this is Indian television and to what degree is it about hybridization and appropriation of global genres of television? Networks such as Zee are arguably merely clones of the US model of market-led television, susceptible to the same kind of commercial pressures.

Finally, the output of such networks remains relatively small and their global impact is restricted largely to the diasporic communities, their primary target market. Therefore it is unlikely to have a significant impact on US hegemony of global television cultures. Nevertheless, it can safely be said that transnationalization of television has ensured a blurring of cultural boundaries, a mixing of genres and languages and a contraflow in traffic, a process still in its infancy and one that merits close monitoring.

Notes

1. Robert McChesney, *Rich Media, Poor Democracy: Communication Politics in Dubious Times* (Champaign: University of Illinois Press, 1999); Daya Thussu, *International Communication: Continuity and Change* (London: Arnold, and New York: Oxford University Press, 2000); Jean Chalaby, 'Transnational Television in Europe: The Role of Pan-European Channels', *European Journal of Communication*, 17(2) (2002), pp. 183–203.

2. Mark Balnaves, James Donald and Stephanie Hemelryk Donald, *The Global Media Atlas* (London: British Film Institute, 2001), p. 55.

3. Herbert Schiller, *Communication and Cultural Domination* (New York: International Arts and Sciences Press, 1976); Oliver Boyd-Barrett, 'Media Imperialism Reformulated', in Daya Thussu (ed.), *Electronic Empires: Global Media and Local Resistance* (London: Arnold, 1998), pp. 157–76.

4. Herbert Schiller, *Information Inequality: The Deepening Social Crisis in America* (New York: Routledge, 1996); Thussu, *International Communication*.

5. Joseph Nye, 'Soft Power', *Foreign Policy*, 80 (1990), pp. 153–71.

6. John Sinclair, Elizabeth Jacka and Stuart Cunningham, *New Patterns in Global Television: Peripheral Vision* (Oxford: Oxford University Press, 1996).

7. Thussu, *International Communication*.

8. Arjun Appadurai, *Modernity at Large: Cultural Dimensions of Globalisation* (Minneapolis: University of Minnesota Press, 1996).

9. UNESCO, *World Culture Report: Culture, Creativity and Markets* (Paris: United Nations Educational, Scientific and Cultural Organization, 1998).

10. Homi Bhabba, *Location of Culture* (London: Routledge, 1994).

11. Chidanand Rajghatta, 'Merrill Estimates 200,000 NRI Millionaires in US', *Times of India*, 14 May 2003.

12. Monroe Price and Stefaan Verhulst (eds), *Broadcasting Reform in India: A Case Study in the Uses of Comparative Media Law* (New Delhi: Oxford University Press, 1998).

13. Manas Ray and Elizabeth Jacka, 'Indian Television: An Emerging Regional Force', in John Sinclair et al. (eds), *New Patterns in Global Vision*, pp. 83–100; Srinivas Melkote, Peter Shields and Binod Agrawal (eds), *International Satellite Broadcasting in South Asia: Political, Economic and Cultural Implications* (Lanham, MD: University Press of America, 1998); Daya Thussu, 'Localizing the Global: Zee TV in India', in Daya Thussu (ed.), *Electronic Empires*, pp. 273–94; David Page and William Crawley, *Satellites Over South Asia: Broadcasting, Culture and the Public Interest* (New Delhi: Sage, 2001).

14. Dionne Bunsha, 'The Rise of Print', *Frontline*, 19(14), 6–19 July 2002.

15. Manjunath Pendakur and Jyotsna Kapur, 'Think Globally, Program Locally: Privatization of Indian National Television', in Mashoed Bailie and Dwayne Winseck (eds), *Democratizing Communication? Comparative Perspectives on Information and Power* (Cresskill, NJ: Hampton Press, 1997), pp. 195–217.

16. Daya Thussu, 'Localizing the Global: Zee TV in India', in Daya Thussu (ed.), *Electronic Empires*, pp. 273–94.

17. Zee TV website: <http://www.zeetelevision.com>. Consulted June 2003.

18. Sevanti Ninan, 'Wake up Zee', *The Hindu*, 20 October 2002.

19. New Delhi Television – India's most professional news network, producing news and current affairs programmes in both Hindi and English. Since April 2003, it has operated as a separate channel available on Sony's bouquet. See Table 7.2.

20. Sony Entertainment Television website: <http://www.setindia.com>. Consulted June 2003.

21. Doordarshan Audience Research Unit, *Doordarshan 2001* (New Delhi: Doordarshan Directorate General, 2002).

22. Doordarshan website: <http://www.ddindia.com>. Consulted June 2003.

23. Toby Miller, Nitin Govil, John McMurrie and Richard Maxwell, *Global Hollywood* (London: British Film Insitute, 2001).

24. 'Entertainment Sector Projections', *Cable and Satellite TV*, Mumbai, July 2001.

25. Carla Power and Sudip Mazumdar, 'Bollywood Goes Global', *Newsweek*, February 2000, pp. 88–94.

26. Ibid., p. 88.

27. 'Bollywood Flicks Dazzle Overseas Markets', *Times of India*, 28 May 2003.

28. Roli Srivastava, 'Indian Soaps Wash Hands of Middle Class', *Times of India*, 20 September 2002.

CHAPTER 8

Trans-border Broadcasters and TV Regionalization in Greater China: Processes and Strategies

Joseph Man Chan

§ THE patterns to which television products are internationalized have drawn unfailing interest from scholars, researchers and policy-makers over the last few decades. This has to do with the important ideological influence that is assumed of television in identity politics. One major approach to trans-border television is derived from the theory of media imperialism that stresses the asymmetrical relationship between the Western centres and the peripheries of the East and the homogenization of culture.[1] Underlying this critical stance is the perception that cultural sovereignty and cultural diversity are at risk. Since the 1980s, studies emerged to call for a reconsideration of media imperialism because of the rediscovery of the nation state,[2] the audience's active reception of televisual texts, and the elaboration of more sophisticated patterns of television interactions across borders.

Although globalization is an elusive concept,[3] it is central to contemporary discourse on world media and culture.[4] The surge in such discourse has given renewed interest to the role of the nation state and the issue of cultural homogenization in this age of globalized communication. To both critical or globalization theorists, the nation state is susceptible to the influence of transnational agencies and is rapidly losing its relevance as communication technologies evade national boundaries and overcome distance.[5] At the same time, the proliferation of Hollywood products in the cultural market has led some researchers to lament the standardization of culture, resulting in what is characterized as 'the unification of the world under the signs of Mickey Mouse and Bruce Willis'.[6]

Is there a role for the nation state as television becomes more globalized? Will this globalization result in the homogenization of television culture? Informed by these two general questions, this study attempts to illustrate, through the formation of the Greater China television market, how the nation state is all but dead and how regionalization should be brought in to make up for the deficiency of the globalization perspective in accounting for the patterns of trans-border television. Another simple purpose of this chapter is to provide an account of how the Greater China television market is being formed by focusing on how television at different levels interacts in shaping television in this region. I will examine the strategies and processes the major players adopt in exploiting this regional market. The implications of the resulting patterns for our understanding of television regionalization and globalization will also be discussed.

The Centrality of the China Market

The term Greater China may be interpreted in several ways, ranging from the political or economic integration of Taiwan, Hong Kong and mainland China to cultural exchanges among people of Chinese descent around the world.[7] This article regards Greater China as 'the economic, political and cultural space defined by the interactions among its three primary constituent parts – Hong Kong, Taiwan and mainland China'.[8] Although Hong Kong became reunified in 1997 with China, which also claims Taiwan as an integral part, the three regions represent different political, economic and cultural systems. I will therefore treat their television configurations in a separate manner. Television that spans the regional boundaries can be considered as trans-border or transnational, depending on the ownership and the national-geographical origin of a television player.

Among the three constituents of Greater China, Hong Kong and Taiwan are by themselves marginal markets to transnational television corporations because of their small sizes. Hong Kong is a city with 7 million people, whereas Taiwan is a region populated by about 24 million, about half of whom live in urban areas. These two places, however, do not all escape the eyes of transnational players because of their general affluence. To the transnational players, any extended market beyond their homeland will only add to their revenue by recycling what they have already produced. But mainland China is the market they covet. Indeed, the China market is also what the broadcasters of Hong Kong and Taiwan crave for.

The China market owes its appeal to its large population size, being four times that of the American people and constituting one-fifth of humanity. The populations of many of its provinces match, if not surpass, those of the large countries in Western Europe. Given that China is still a developing country with the majority of the population living in rural areas, the economic value of the China TV market should not be equated to the population size. What is of value to the transnational and cross-border advertisers is primarily the urban population. The TV market potential of China is uneven, with the greatest potential residing in the big cities along the coastal region.

The value of the China TV market is supported by the high rate at which its economy has been growing since the early 1990s. At the initial stage of Chinese development, transnational advertising was effective only in making the product brands known to the public who, however, did not have any real purchasing power. Mass consumption set in as a major urban lifestyle in the metropolitan areas in China in the early 2000s. While the per capita income in these areas is meagre by Western standards, it indicates that some Chinese can now move their eyes from consumer items such as television sets and washing machines to cellular phones, automobiles and even private apartments. The urban affluent do not just dress to keep warm but to demonstrate their status and identity. Travelling in and outside the country has become a favourite pastime for many people during weekends and vacations. All this consumption has rendered television advertising a formidable business, which has been growing in double digits in the last decade.[9] What attracts the transnational television players is not necessarily the current value of the China market but its potential. It is therefore strategic for transnational players to secure their position in China, even before it fully opens up. One will miss the whole point in any discussion on Greater China television if mainland China is not given a central place in one's analysis.

Television Systems in Greater China

The television systems of the three constituent parts of Greater China are as different as their political configuration. Hong Kong was a British colony that was transformed into a Special Administrative

Region of China that retains autonomy under the scheme of 'one country, two systems'. Taiwan, a political rival of the Chinese Communist Party for over half a century, is a new democracy ruled by the Democratic Progressive Party after ousting the Kuomingtang Party in 2000. Mainland China is a socialist nation trying to modernize itself by economic reforms and an open-door policy.

Table 8.1 highlights the differences among the television systems in terms of ownership, policy towards trans-border television, audience characteristics and exports. Television in Hong Kong operates primarily within a market structure the parameters of which are set by the government regulators.[10] Unlike regulatory regimes in many other parts of the world, the licensing conditions under which broadcast television was introduced to Hong Kong did not impose minimum requirements for the inclusion of local content. While the government has set some limits on the publication of pornographic and politically sensitive materials, the government's interference in mediated content is minimal in practice. Without an explicit and elaborate cultural policy, Hong Kong is virtually a free port in information, as there is no strict control over the flow of media in and out of Hong Kong. Consequently, Hong Kong television has to face competition from the world.

Hong Kong has one of the world's largest Chinese television programme libraries and is an important regional exporter of audio-visual products.[11] Hong Kong television productions have proved to be very popular in overseas Chinese markets too. The means of distribution include videos, cable and satellite television, piracy and spillover (in Guangdong area). The major markets include Taiwan, China, Southeast Asian countries and Chinese overseas communities in North America and Europe. Hong Kong television first made its name in Taiwan and later in China in the 1980s. Hong Kong television programmes owe their competitive edge in China and Taiwan to higher production quality, quick tempo, the availability of well-known stars and the touch of modern living. With the novelty effect of Hong Kong television waning and the rising competition of domestic products, only selected television programmes from Hong Kong can draw the crowds they once did.

Taiwan has a long history of authoritarian rule, which ended as the Kuomintang (KMT), the former ruling party, embarked on a liberalization and democratization programme in 1987.[12] However, television

TABLE 8.1 TV systems in Greater China[13]

	Mainland China	Taiwan	Hong Kong
TV ownership and control	State monopoly, all party-controlled; being commercialized	Major stakes of terrestrial TV owned by KMT, the military, or government; run as commercial enterprises with ideological constraints; by law, all political interests must withdraw shares before 2006	All are privately owned with the exception of a quasi-public broadcaster; minimal regulation
Policy towards trans-border TV	Moving from cultural anti-foreignism to a less severe form of cultural protectionism; censorship and quota control; granting limited landing rights to selected trans-border TV broadcasters	Restricting imports to different fixed ratios in terrestrial TV and cable networks; open to HK-run and foreign TV channels in cable TV, showing at least 20 per cent local programmes	Foreign ownership of terrestrial TV allowed up to a total of no more than 49 per cent; free flow of programmes; foreign channels carried in cable networks
Audience characteristics	Pop. approx. 1.3 billion, approx. 40 per cent urban, very diverse	Pop. approx. 24 million, approx. 75 per cent urban, relatively homogeneous	Pop. approx. 7 million, approx. 95 per cent urban, homogeneous
Programme exports in Greater China	Limited; selected programmes are popular in Hong Kong and Taiwan; exports via satellite TV, videos and programme sales	Selected programmes are popular in China and Hong Kong; exports via satellite TV, videos, programme sales, barter trade and piracy	Programmes are in general popular in China and Taiwan; exports via satellite TV, videos, programme sales, piracy and spillover

in Taiwan is strongly susceptible to the influence of KMT, the military, the government and the Democratic Progressive Party – the ruling party. Control goes with ownership: the board directors and managers of each station have been appointed by people closely affiliated with the interested parties. Although these free-to-air broadcasters are controlled one way or the other by political interests, they are run as profitable enterprises, resulting in a commercial model that has grown out of the government–business alliance and oligopolistic competition.[14] Of equal importance to the terrestrial broadcasters in Taiwan are its cable networks, which enjoy a penetration of over 76 per cent and offer more than ninety channels.[15]

With the gradual opening of the China market and the penetration of satellite television from Hong Kong, Taiwanese broadcasters are developing a more acute sense of international marketing.[16] Taiwanese television dramas, including martial arts stories, period, romance and contemporary serials are very popular in China. Taiwanese dramas are characterized by their emphasis on traditional values and virtues such as fidelity, loyalty, thrift and the like. Such treatment of traditional values appears to have aroused a strong resonance with the Chinese audience. Taiwan started its first television exports to Hong Kong in 1971. In more recent years, mainland China has become a more important market for Taiwan, and since the early 1990s, Taiwanese programmes have begun to enjoy some revived interest in Hong Kong.

State-owned and party-controlled, television in China has been undergoing important changes, such as the relaxation of ideological control and regulation control during the reforms in the last two decades.[17] Cultural anti-foreignism, which prevailed during the radical years, has subsided, making way for the inflow of Western or capitalist lifestyles. Before the reforms, the only foreign programmes that were broadcast were imported from other socialist nations.[18] Today, stations are allowed to broadcast programmes originating from Hong Kong, Taiwan, the United States and other parts of the world, provided that they get political clearance from government and do not exceed the given quota.[19] This applies to both broadcast and cable television, especially during prime time.

In general, only selected television programmes from China are popular in Hong Kong and Taiwan. Hong Kong audiences find the Chinese programmes dull, and their ideological tone overbearing.

Not until the late 1990s did Taiwan allow its television stations to broadcast TV programmes from mainland China. Some of the period television drama serials proved rather popular among Taiwanese audiences. China has become more aware of the importance of exporting its programmes in the 1990s. CCTV, the state broadcaster, established Channel 4 to broadcast programmes over satellite for audiences in Taiwan and Hong Kong. The audience, however, is insignificant.

Major Players

Television players in Greater China are of three types: 1) global players such as News Corporation and Time Warner, which have significant television operations in many parts of the world; 2) regional players such as Phoenix TV, which focuses primary on regional broadcasting; and 3) national players such as China's CCTV and HK-TVB, which treat regional broadcasting as an extension of their domestic operation. The global players may simply make their home programmes available to Asia in general and Greater China in particular. CNN, BBC, HBO, ESPN, MTV and Discovery Channel are the notable examples. The global players may also set up specific channels to target the whole of Greater China or its constituent parts. The Chinese Channel of News Corp's Star TV and Time Warner's Chinese Entertainment TV are good illustrations. The national players form the basic fabric of regional broadcasting as they take part in programme trades, joint productions and local distribution. For the more powerful players such as CCTV and HK-TVB, they can set up custom-built channels for the purpose of regional broadcasting. Channel 4 of the former and the TVB8 of the latter are examples of this kind.

Table 8.2 captures some of the more important television players in Greater China. Although Hong Kong pales in its market size, it stands out as the centre of broadcasting in the region because of its geopolitical position, advanced communication infrastructure and rule of law. Subsequently, it has become the headquarters for quite a few trans-border television operations.

Before I proceed to generalize the strategies and processes of trans-border television in Greater China, I deem it necessary to illustrate each type of broadcaster (global, regional and national) with one example.

TABLE 8.2 Trans-border TV players in Greater China (in alphabetical order)

TV Players and content	Headquarters	Primary target audience
Asia Plus (entertainment)	Taiwan	Greater China
BBC World* (news)	UK	Greater China
Bloomberg TV Asian Channel* (financial news)	USA	China
CCTV		
• Channel 4 (general, in Mandarin)	China	Greater China
• Channel 9 (general, in English)	China	Greater China and world
CNBC Asia Pacific* (financial news)	Singapore	Asian region
Discovery Channel* (information)	USA	Greater China
• Animal Planet (information)		Greater China
Hallmark	USA	
• Asia Channel* (movies)		China
• Taiwan Channel (movies)		Taiwan
• Kermit Channel (education)		Taiwan/China
Japan Entertainment TV* (JETV) (entertainment)	Japan	China/Taiwan
Macau Five Star TV* (youth pro- grammes, news and entertainment)	Macau	China
MTV Mandarin*# (music)	USA	HK/China/ Taiwan
NHK World Premium* (general)	Japan	China
Phoenix TV	Hong Kong	
• Phoenix Chinese*# (general & entertainment)		HK/China
• Phoenix Movie*# (movies)		HK/China
• Phoenix InfoNews* (news)		Greater China
Star TV	Hong Kong	
• Star Movie* (movies)		Greater China
• Star World (entertainment)		HK/Taiwan
• Star Sports* (sports)		Greater China
• Channel V* (music)		Greater China
• ESPN* (sports)		Greater China
• National Geographic* (science & geography)		Greater China
• Adventure One (adventuring)		HK
• Fox News* (news)		HK/China

TABLE 8.2 Continued

TV Players and content	Headquarters	Primary target audience
• Xing Kong Wei Shi*# (entertainment, in Mandarin)		China
• Star Mandarin Movies (movies, in Mandarin)		Taiwan
• Star Chinese Channel (general, in Mandarin)		Taiwan
Taipei International Satellite TV	Taipei	Eastern parts of China and North America
• CTV, TTV, CTS (general)		
• News and Info Channel (news)		
• Movies Channel (movies)		
• Family Channel (education)		
• CSTV (general)		
• MSTV (propaganda)		
Time Warner		
• CETV*# (entertainment)	Hong Kong	China
• CNN* (news)	USA	Greater China
• HBO* (movies)	USA	Greater China
• Cinemax Asia* (Movies)	USA	Greater China
• Cartoon Network (Cartoons)	USA	Greater China
TVBI	Hong Kong	
• TVB8* (entertainment)		China
• Galaxy* (drama)		China
• TVBS (general)		Taiwan
• TVBS Newsnet (news)		Taiwan
• TVBS Golden (entertainment & music)		Taiwan

Notes: * with landing right in three-star or better hotels and selected entities in China   # with landing right in the Guangdong province

News Corp's Star TV: A global player Star TV, a subsidiary of News Corporation, is the largest satellite broadcaster in Asia, broadcasting forty services in eight languages to more than 300 million viewers in fifty-three countries from its Hong Kong base since 1991. Besides India, China is Star's major target market. The News Corp of Rupert Murdoch made an en-route into China in 1996 through investing in

Phoenix TV, Star TV's joint venture with Li Changle, a mainland Chinese with a military background. In late 2001, Star TV's venture into China came to another breakthrough when landing rights were granted to its new entertainment channel in Guangdong province.[20] The twenty-four-hour Mandarin channel, Xing Kong Wei Shi, was subsequently launched in early 2002 via cable TV operators to one million Guangdong households. In return, News Corp's Fox Cable Networks will carry China Central Television's (CCTV) English-language channel CCTV 9 in the USA.

It did not take long for Star TV to realize that its original idea of pan-Asian broadcasting was not feasible. In 1994 it divided the services into the northern and the southern arenas, with China as the main target in the former and India as the main target in the latter. The immediate success of Zee TV, Star TV's joint venture in India, which was broadcast in Hindu, further confirmed the need for Star TV to go local. As a result, Star TV continuously sought joint venture opportunities in the region. Reinforcing this pattern is the success of Phoenix TV in China. After struggling for more than a decade, Star TV is less a regional broadcaster and more a conglomeration of half a dozen local broadcasters slugging it out market by market.[21]

Phoenix Satellite TV: A regional player Phoenix Satellite TV was a joint venture between Star TV and two corporations with a strong China background. Phoenix was listed on Hong Kong's second board Growth Enterprise Market (GEM) in October 2000. The Phoenix channels are targeted to all Chinese viewers in the region. With China as its target market, it took Phoenix TV four years to be receivable in about 42 million mainland householders or 13 per cent of households with TV sets, either through cable TV or direct satellites.[22] One reason for Phoenix's popularity is that it provides a programming mix that the state broadcaster, CCTV, fails to provide. Its strength lies in the lively soap operas, sports and variety shows. Phoenix TV's edge over CCTV is also based on its relatively liberal treatment of news, which attracts educated Chinese viewers.

Legally, Phoenix TV is allowed to broadcast only to certain restricted areas, but in reality many cable operators carry its channels on an illegal basis. Phoenix allows the latter to download its programmes free of charge. The turning point for Phoenix's venture into the China market came in early September 2001, when two Phoenix channels were given approval to broadcast in Guangdong through its cable television network.[23] In the few years since its inception, Phoenix has grown into a three-channel station, offering general programmes, movies and news respectively. While it has yet to secure landing rights in Taiwan, it received limited landing rights in the whole of China at the end of 2002.[24]

HK-TVB: A 'national'-turned-regional player The Hong Kong-based HK-TVB plays a significant role in the development of trans-border TV in Greater China. It owes its influence to its active international marketing efforts and the popularity of its programmes. Like that of its local competitor, Asia TV in Hong Kong, TVB's broadcast signals spill over into Guangdong, outperforming the domestic broadcasters.[25] Such penetration was done without open permission from the central authority. It was not until 2003 that the Chinese government formally gave TVB and ATV landing rights in Guangdong. It remains to be seen, however, if arrangement will be made for Hong Kong channels to translate their popularity in Guangdong into advertising dollars.

TVB's launching of Galaxy in 1998, which included two twenty-four-hour Mandarin-language satellite channels, namely, the TVB8 and TVB Xing He Channel, marked its ambition in regional broadcasting. The footprint of these satellite channels covers China, Southeast Asia, Australia, Europe and North America.[26] TVB8 features a combination of entertainment, infotainment and musical programmes that are found to be popular in most Chinese communities. These satellite channels were first encrypted for restricted viewers in the mainland. The resultant limited reach, however, led TVB to revamp TVB8 and make it a free-to-air channel in 2001.[27]

An economically more profitable satellite television venture is TVB's launching of TVB Super Channel for the extensive cable networks in Taiwan in 1993.[28] Adopting the strategy of tailoring its programmes to the Taiwan market, TVBS quickly emerged as a formidable television player in Taiwan, whose performance is known to have an important impact on the partisan terrestrial broadcasters.

Formation of Regional TV

In Western Europe, trans-border TV is generally received through cable networks or direct-to-home satellite broadcasting. These forms of transmission prevail because European regulators do not forbid broadcasting from outside. As mainland China is rather restrictive in its approach to foreign media, DTH is used only by individuals willing to defy the formal rules on satellite signal reception. In the 1990s, foreign broadcasters were formally allowed, at best, to have their programmes carried in cable networks at three-star hotels or above and units pertaining to foreign exchanges. Star TV and Phoenix TV belong to this group. But such accessibility is rather limited. They achieve greater penetration when some community and city cable networks take the risk and carry the satellite signals on their own. Penetration as such varies over time, as the regulators fluctuate in legal enforcement. There is strong incentive for some networks to take the risk because they are badly in need of programmes to fill up all the airtime and to attract subscribers with more appealing programming.

It is wrong to assume that China is totally successful in fending off trans-border television. What resulted occasionally was a form of 'suppressive openness',[29] meaning that some audiences in the country were provided with access to foreign broadcasters despite restrictive regulation. The restrictive policy was not enforced because the nation state had lost its political will to enforce it to the letter and the network operators had become too delinquent. When legal defiance is common, 'suppressive openness' may be legalized and changed into 'regulated openness'. This observation applied to China when it formally allowed some foreign broadcasters, including Phoenix TV, Time Warner's Entertainment Television (CETV), the Hong Kong-based Asia TV (ATV) and Television Broadcasts (TVB) and others to have their signals downlinked to Guangdong cable networks.

This marks an important change in China's policy towards foreign broadcasting. Penetration is allowed on a massive scale as far as reception is confined to a pre-defined area, Guangdong in this case. It can be argued that this is merely a formalization of Hong Kong television's spillover: many people in the Pearl River Delta were allowed, by default, to receive Hong Kong television signals.[30] Indeed, the signals were carried by the cable networks in Guangzhou and elsewhere, only with the Hong Kong advertising replaced by local ads.

Regulated trade is a long-established form of trans-border television in Greater China. Hong Kong was the first to export its programmes to both mainland China and Taiwan. Although they were highly popular, cultural protectionism on both sides of the Taiwan Strait has led to restrictions on the proportion of imported programmes, especially during prime time. Programme trade is therefore only partially subject to the dictates of the market and never took off as a significant source of revenue for television stations in all three regions. However, trade remains a formal channel for the three regions to share programming. The success of some programmes such as the martial arts television series from Hong Kong, the Judge Bao series from Taiwan and the *Three Kingdoms* and other costume drama from mainland China have demonstrated that Greater China has the real potential to be a unified television market.

The quota limitation in China has led television players in Hong Kong, Taiwan and elsewhere to form joint production units with Chinese television stations or production houses to produce programmes for consumption in all three regions. Forming joint ventures not only helps them evade the restrictions on programme importation, but also to take advantage of the comparative advantages of each place. For instance, the costume drama *Princess Huanzhugege* is a joint production made with capital from Taiwan, scenes from China, and acting and production personnel from all three places. A great success, the series has inspired many to follow suit. As China wants to separate television delivery from production, it has encouraged the growth of private or semi-private production houses. The control over the ownership of a production house is not as tight as it is with television ownership, thereby opening up ways for international corporate players to get involved in television production and financing in China. But the right to broadcast programmes remains in the hands of the television station and the party.

The penetration of television in Greater China can take other more subtle forms, such as piracy and format imitation. In their attempt to attract subscribers, the cable networks in some towns in mainland China go so far as to broadcast pirated Hong Kong and Taiwanese television programmes. They obtain these programmes by recording off the air in the Pearl River Delta and Fujian Province. These programmes are than duplicated as videos and broadcast without official permission in cable networks in the more remote areas. Some of the more popular television series are pirated and sold as videos. People keep their own libraries and circulate these videos among friends. With the introduction of broadband, some television programmes are also put on the Internet for people to download. This happens most often among university students, who have ready access to the Internet.

In Hong Kong and Taiwan, television formats, such as that of the British programme *Who Wants to be a Millionaire?*, are sometimes officially imported and paid for. But most of the time, television from the West and Japan is an important source of inspiration for television in Greater China. The transfer of television format and even content can thus take place via diffusion, resulting in the convergence of television forms. Programmes from around the world are readily available to television producers and managers, who treat them as models. This explains why some Chinese are surprised to find that the 'innovative formats' found at home are regular features in Western television when they have a chance to travel overseas.

Trans-border TV Strategies

As mentioned earlier, cracking the China market is the most important goal for trans-border television players from outside China. Several strategies are emerging. As illustrated by Star TV, self-censorship is essential in order to avoid antagonizing the Chinese government. Rupert Murdoch's decision to take BBC off the China bouquet has been widely interpreted as an attempt to appease the Chinese government in order to get permission to get into the mainland. Persistent efforts finally paid off when China gave Star TV limited landing rights and did not object to its forming a joint venture, Phoenix TV, with two China-linked corporations. The desire to keep away from ideology results in depoliticization. This also applies to other players such as CETV and Phoenix TV. The former boasts that it offers entertainment only, shying away from sex and news. Phoenix TV carries news, but it also takes care not to step too far beyond the Chinese Communist Party's ideological boundaries. It openly admits that it has a team in Shenzhen, the neighbouring city of Hong Kong, to review programmes to ensure that they abide by China's general censorship standards.

Another common strategy of trans-border television is to head-quarter in Hong Kong. There is a historical reason that led to the emergence of Hong Kong as the broadcasting hub of the region:

it is the place where regional satellite television pioneer Star TV started, and it has always been open to foreign ownership and imported programmes. Centrally located in Asia, it has a state-of-the-art communications infrastructure. In addition, it has a vibrant domestic television industry teeming with personnel knowledgeable about television in Greater China and the West. The rule of law also guarantees that trans-border television is largely a level playing field for all players. Although Taiwan aspires to be the broadcasting hub in the Asia-Pacific region, its project is endangered by the island's relatively weak legal tradition and shaky political environment. The political advantage of headquartering in Hong Kong is that it is designated as a Special Administrative Region of China which has autonomy in running its internal affairs. This enables Phoenix TV, among others, to exploit such freedom and broadcast news and information that would be forbidden were it located in China, thus giving it a competitive edge over CCTV.

Localization is an important lesson to be learned in satellite broadcasting. Star TV initially dreamed of becoming a pan-Asian broadcaster, with one set of programmes for the whole of the Asia-Pacific region. It quickly learned that this does not work, as Asian culture and regulatory standards are so diversified that country-specific programming is warranted.[31] The success of Zee TV in India, and the later success of Phoenix TV in mainland China lend strong support to the need for localization. Localized programming can take place at various levels, including the use of language, repackaging, programme mix, marketing strategies and the like. CETV intends to employ production houses in mainland China to provide programmes. TVB of Hong Kong repackages and dubs some of its Cantonese programmes for Galaxy. Without some form of localization, it is virtually impossible for a trans-border television broadcaster to appeal to the audience in a given market on a large scale.

Trans-border broadcasters cannot just wait for formal approval to enter China's television market. While they may keep on prodding the Beijing authorities for permission, they often resort to the strategy of networking to surmount the difficulty. The lure of profit has motivated a constant search for innovations on all parties to exploit the leeway allowed within the Chinese system. Very often networking (or *guanxi*) is mobilized as a way to evade formal restrictions, resulting in the downlink of foreign satellite television signals, the exchange for advertising time, and the formation of joint ventures in production or other forms of television operation. All these arrangements would not have been possible without understanding from both sides and the intricate connections that the Chinese partner has with the television regulators and personnel in China. By the creative use of such intricate webs of social connections, China is opening itself up to Hong Kong and Taiwanese television in an evolutionary manner, attesting to the subversive forces of networking and profiteering.

Theoretical Implications and Concluding Remarks

In a nutshell, the patterns of trans-border broadcasting in Greater China are very much a reflection of the evolution of changes in the regulatory regimes in its constituent parts. Programme trade is the most enduring channel of television exchange because it came into place in the 1980s. When foreign television was banned in China, spillover was an important mode of diffusion, especially in the Pearl River Delta. It was the contest of will between audience and censors that determined the rates of penetration. Piracy also plays an important role in bringing in trans-border television. This is true especially for restricted but popular programmes. The granting of landing rights in Guangdong and limited landing rights elsewhere marks an important stage in which China formally allows the entry of trans-border television on a relatively large scale.

The occasional success of selected television programmes in the whole of Greater China demonstrates that trans-border television has a strong potential. Trans-border television has reached an evolutionary stage at which interactions among players from the constituent parts are increasing, resulting in programme trades, joint ventures and other kinds of exchange. It is premature to expect Chinese television to open to the world completely. The success of selected trans-border programmes in the region, however, testifies to the existence of common cultural tastes in Greater China. The popular culture of Taiwan and Hong Kong, including television programmes, pop songs and movies, is very influential in China. The sharing of a common popular culture constitutes and is constituted by regional television. The interactions of television cultures represent what Jonathan Friedman refers to as the consumption of palatable cultural difference.[32] On the one hand, the audience is socialized to the familiar and yet different imported programmes. At the same time, viewers are entertained by products that try to integrate elements from all three places, including the combination of artistes, producers, formats and stories.

At this juncture, I would like to return to the questions raised at the beginning of the chapter in regard to the role of the nation state and the prospect of cultural homogenization. First of all, the state is facing challenging conditions such as the expansion of transnational media corporations, increasing liberalization and privatization of media systems worldwide and the development of cable and satellite technologies.[33] These challenges have indeed weakened the capability of nation states to exercise power and maintain information sovereignty. As the case of Greater China attests, however, it is really too early to declare the irrelevancy of the state. In spite of the advent of communication technologies such as satellite and cable, ideological and regulatory differences still constitute the limiting factor in the formation of the Greater China television market. The political and ideological boundaries continue to prevent the free flow of capital, personnel and programmes between China and the other two Chinese societies. Like other countries that practise media protectionism, China is afraid of external ideological influence that may threaten the status quo, corrupt the public mind and cause social instability.[34] China is still wary of alien forces coming from Hong Kong, Taiwan and the West that may undermine the socialist system. Such ideological concerns result in the prohibition of foreign satellite television reception, censorship and quota controls. All these restrictions have prevented trans-border broadcasters of Hong Kong and Taiwan from taking full advantage of the promise of the China market. As in other countries, formal regulation still rests in the hands of the national political and commercial elite.[35] The nation state continues to play a critical role in regulating communication across national boundaries and the development of a national cultural industry. Indeed, the nation state, as in China, even plays a key role in managing the globalization process itself.[36]

Political considerations in Taiwan also hinder the formation of regional television in Greater China. Inherited from an authoritarian rule that guaranteed oligopoly and profit, Taiwan's television system remains susceptible to heavy influence from the major political parties and government. Political suspicion between Taiwan and China has led to restrictions on programme imports from the mainland. Taiwan and China are at a stalemate, trying to outsmart one another in negotiations. The principle of reciprocity has become a tool by which Taiwan tries to prevent Chinese television from penetrating its home market. Up to the present, Taiwan bans CCTV Channel 4 from its territory, stating that landing rights will be given only under the condition of reciprocity. All these political and ideological barriers across the Taiwan Strait demonstrate the key roles that nation states may play in the future development of the Greater China television market.

The second theoretical concern is whether globalization will result in cultural homogenization. My account of the formation of trans-border television in Greater China can provide only a partial response to this question, as it is confined to the analysis of the industrial and institutional levels. It shows that the globalization of television is an extraordinarily complex phenomenon that necessitates examination at the local, regional, national and global levels. Of particular importance in the case of Greater China are the national and regional levels, echoing the call for attention to regional television by Joseph Straubhaar and John Sinclair and colleagues.[37] The multi-level perspective is different from the uni-directional flow of the past, with the USA as a dominating centre conceived in the theory of media imperialism.[38] It represents increasing flows of capital, programmes and cultures in regions defined by geographical locations and cultural proximity.[39]

The case of Greater China shows that the influence of regional broadcasters is more prominent than that of global players, particularly when they make no attempt to offer tailor-made programmes. Programmes co-produced by regional players are in general more popular than their Western counterparts. The dissemination of television around the world is an uneven process, with the American domination stronger in certain parts of the world. In Greater China, American TV does not form the largest segment of screen time, nor does it produce the most-watched programmes.

The Greater China trans-border television market does not stop at geographical boundaries. There are growing signs that it extends to include productions from its neighbours – Korea and Japan – whose programmes, through videos and television, have gained large followings first in Taiwan, then in Hong Kong and finally in China. While these television programmes may not be the most popular, they prove to be attractive to the middle classes and the younger generation. Inspired by these productions, the Taiwanese and Hong Kong producers imitate their formats. Given the strong need for cheap programmes to fill up the unlimited airtime, mainland China has been importing more and more programmes from Japan and Korea. The growing popularity of programmes from these neighbouring countries reinforces the previous emphasis on regionalization rather than globalization in the discourse on international television.

Television culture, however, is not spreading by simple imitation. As of now, the television industries in Greater China are developing differently. In China, television is an integral part of the propaganda machine; in Hong Kong, it is a cultural industry; in Taiwan, it is transforming itself from a cultural arm of the ruling political party into a more autonomous cultural industry. In the process of reconfiguration of television in China, it is beyond doubt that models from the West and Hong Kong are often a source of inspiration. When the country borrows from outside, it has the tendency to appropriate what is best for its interest, thereby creating a hybrid culture. Pure imitation is rare, television culture being Westernized, regionalized and reinvented at the same time. Parallel to this is the need for localization on the part of trans-border broadcasters. Star TV, for instance, has to offer tailor-made content and repackage its programmes for a given market in China and elsewhere. As far as hybridization and localization form parts of the equation of trans-border broadcasting, there is no reason to be pessimistic about the homogenization of television culture.

This said, we should not ignore the ways by which television cultures are converging. The penetration of trans-border television places competitive pressure on terrestrial and domestic broadcasters by offering alternative programming and more balanced news reporting. For instance, the popularization of TVBS in Taiwan, a satellite television service initiated by HK-TVB, exerts strong pressure on Taiwanese terrestrial broadcasters to expand their ideological boundaries by allowing news and commentaries more critical of the ruling party and to enlarge the quotas on Chinese and Hong Kong programming. Similar pressure exists in China. As trans-border television gains a foothold in China, terrestrial television has to come up with competitive strategies. The most logical way is to give its television operations the same degree of autonomy in heading off the competition. This partly explains why CCTV was allowed to broadcast the Second Gulf War live and to give it twenty-four-hour attention. Without a freer hand, it is going to suffer greater audience loss to Phoenix TV, which took the war as another opportunity for rapid growth. The market success of CCTV will in turn spark off imitations on the part of other Chinese broadcasters. That explains how television innovations from within and without are diffused in China. This chain reaction inevitably leads to some degree of cultural convergence.

Notes

1. Herbert Schiller, *Mass Communication and the American Empire* (Boston, MA: Beacon Press, 1969); Oliver Boyd-Barrett, 'Media Imperialism: Towards an International Framework for the Analysis of Media Systems', in James Curran, Michael Gurevitch and Janet Woolacott (eds), *Mass Communication and Society* (London: Edward Arnold, 1977), pp. 116–35; Oliver Boyd-Barrett, 'Media Imperialism Reformulated', in Daya Kishan Thussu (ed.), *Electronic Empires: Global Media and Local Resistance* (London: Arnold Press, 1998), pp. 157–76.

2. E.g. Chin-Chuan Lee, *Media Imperialism Reconsidered* (Beverly Hills, CA: Sage, 1980); Joseph Straubhaar, 'Beyond Media Imperialism: Assymmetrical Interdependence and Cultural Proximity', *Critical Studies in Mass Communication*, 8(1) (1991), pp. 39–59; John Sinclair, Elizabeth Jacka and Stuart Cunningham, 'Peripheral Vision', in John Sinclair, Elizabeth Jacka and Stuart Cunningham (eds), *New Patterns in Global Television: Peripheral Vision* (Oxford: Oxford University Press, 1996), pp. 1–32; Chris Barker, *Global Television: An Introduction* (Oxford: Blackwell Press, 1997).

3. Cees Hamelink, 'The Elusive Concept of Globalization', *Global Dialogue*, 1(1) (1999), pp. 1–9; Havid Held and Anthony McGrew, *Globalization/Anti-globalization* (Oxford: Polity Press, 2002).

4. E.g. Michael Richards and David French (2000), 'Globalization, Television and Asia', in David French and Michael Richards (eds), *Television in Contemporary Asia* (New Delhi: Sage, 2000), pp. 13–28; Barker, *Global Television*; John Tomlinson, *Globalization and Culture* (Chicago, IL: University of Chicago Press, 1999).

5. Peter Golding, 'The Communication Paradox: Inequality at the National and International Levels', *Media Development*, 3 (1994), pp. 7–9; Malcom Waters, *Globalization* (London: Routledge, 1995); Walter Wriston, *The Twilight of Sovereignty* (New York: Macmillan, 1992); Held and McGrew, *Globalization/Anti-globalization*.

6. Todd Gitlin, 'The Unification of the World under the Signs of Mickey Mouse and Bruce Willis: The Supply and Demand Sides of American Popular Culture', in Joseph Chan and Bryce McIntyre (eds), *In Search of Boundaries: Communication, Nation-States and Cultural Identities* (Westport, CT: Ablex Press, 2002), p. 21.

7. Harry Harding, 'The Concept of Greater China: Themes, Variations and Reservations', *China Quarterly*, 136 (1993), pp. 660–86.

8. Joseph Chan, 'Television in Greater China: Structure, Exports, and Market Formation', in Sinclair, Jacka and Cunningham (eds), *New Patterns in Global Television*, pp. 126–60.

9. Yu Huang and Andrew Green, 'From Mao to the Millennium: 40 Years of Television in China', in French and Richards (eds), *Television in Contemporary Asia*, pp. 267–92.

10. Joseph Chan, Eric Ma and Clement So, 'Back to the Future: A Retrospect and Prospects for the Hong Kong Mass Media', in Joseph Cheng (ed.), *The Other Hong Kong Report 1997* (Hong Kong: Chinese University Press, 1997), pp. 455–82; Clement So, Joseph Chan and Chin-Chuan Lee, '[Mass Media of] Hong Kong SAR (China)', in Shelton Gunaratne (ed.), *Handbook of the Media in Asia* (New Delhi: Sage, 2000), pp. 527–51.

11. Yiu-ming To and Tuen-yu Lau, 'Global Export of Hong Kong Television: Television Broadcasts Limited', *Asian Journal of Communication*, 5(2) (1995), pp. 108–21.

12. Binghong Chen, 'Changes in the Configuration and Operation of the Television Industry in Taiwan', paper presented to the Conference on 'The Prospect and Retrospect of Taiwanese Television' (National Chengchi University, Taiwan, 31 October–1 November 2002) (in Chinese).

13. Adapted from Chan, 'Television in Greater China', pp. 126–60.

14. Lee, *Media Imperialism Reconsidered*.

15. Chen, 'Changes in the Configuration and Operation of the Television Industry in Taiwan'.

16. Chan, 'Television in Greater China'.

17. Zhongdang Pan and Joseph Chan, 'Building a Market-based Party Organ: Television and National Integration in China', in French and Richards (eds), *Television in Contemporary Asia*, pp. 232–63; Huang and Green, 'From Mao to the Millennium'; Ran Wei, 'China's Television in the Era of Marketization', in French and Richards (eds), *Television in Contemporary Asia*, pp. 325–46; Tsan-Kuo Chang, *China's Window on the World: TV News, Social Knowledge and International Spectacles* (Cresskill, NJ: Hampton Press, 2002).

18. Junhao Hong, *The Internationalization of Television in China: The Evolution of Ideology, Society, and Media Since the Reform* (Westport, CT: Praeger, 1998).

19. Yu-li Liu, 'Comparing Cable Television Laws and Regulations in China

and Taiwan', *Mass Communication Research*, 53 (1993), pp. 209–30 (in Chinese); Joseph Chan, 'Media Internationalisation in China: Processes and Tensions', *Journal of Communication*, 44(3) (1994), pp. 70–88.

20. 'News Corp's Star TV Gains Landing Rights in South China', *Dow Jones International News*, 19 December 2001.

21. Owen Hughes, 'Davey Says Plan for Development of Pan-Asian TV Network Unchanged. Star Affirms Localization Strategy,' *South China Morning Post*, 8 April 1998, p. 6.

22. Michael Dwyer, 'TV the Key to Chinese Puzzle', *Australian Financial Review*, 24 October 2000, p. 49.

23. 'Phoenix One Wing Short', *South China Morning Post*, 31 October 2001, p. 1.

24. K. S. Chan, 'HK Phoenix Satellite Gets China Landing Rights', *Dow Jones International News*, 6 January 2003.

25. Joseph Chan, 'When Socialist and Capitalist Television Clash: The Impact of Hong Kong Television On Guangzhou Residents', in Chin-Chuan Lee (ed.), *Money, Power, and Media: Communication Patterns and Bureaucratic Control in Cultural China* (Chicago, IL: Northwestern University Press, 2000), pp. 245–70.

26. Rose Tang, 'TVB Eyes Fresh Revenue Sources as Adverts Fall', *South China Morning Post*, 28 May 1998, p. 3.

27. 'Foreign TV Not So Remote. Guangdong in Line for Foreign TV Broadcasting Breakthrough', *South China Morning Post*, 6 September 2001, p. 1.

28. John Frank-Keyes, 'TVB "Super Channel" Hits Taiwan', *South China Morning Post*, 27 October 1993.

29. Chan, 'Television in Greater China'.

30. Chan, 'When Socialist and Capitalist Television Clash'.

31. Joseph Chan, 'National Responses and Accessibility to Star TV in Asia', *Journal of Communication*, 44(3) (1994), pp. 112–33.

32. Jonathan Friedman, 'Globalization and the Making of a Global Imaginary', in Gitte Stald and Thomas Tufte (eds), *Global Encounters: Media and Cultural Transformation* (Luton: University of Luton Press, 2002), pp. 13–32.

33. Silvio Waisbord and Nancy Morris, 'Introduction: Rethinking Media Globalization and State Power', in Silvio Waisbord and Nancy Morris (eds), *Media and Globalization: Why the State Matters* (Lanham, MD: Rowman and Littlefield, 2001), pp. vii–xvi.

34. Joseph Chan, 'No Culture is an Island: An Analysis of Media Protectionism and Media Openness', in Geogette Wang, Jan Servaes and Anura Goonasekera (eds), *National and Local Cultural Products in the Age of Global Communication* (London: Routledge, 2000), pp. 251–64.

35. Annabelle Sreberny-Mohammadi, Dwayne Winseck, Jim McKenna and Oliver Boyd-Barrett, 'Editor's Introduction: Media in Global Context', in Annabelle Sreberny-Mohammadi, Dwayen Winseck, Jim McKenna and Oliver Boyd-Barrett (eds), *Media in Global Context: A Reader* (London: Arnold, 1997), pp. iv–xxviii.

36. Yunxiang Yan, 'Managed Globalization', in Peter Berger and Samuel Huntington (eds), *Many Globalizations: Culture Diversity in the Contemporary World* (Oxford: Oxford University Press, 2002), pp. 19–47.

37. Sinclair, Jacka and Cunningham, *New Patterns in Global Television*; Joseph Straubhaar, '(Re)asserting National Television and National Identity against the Global, Regional and Local Levels of World Television', in Chan and McIntyre (eds), *In Search of Boundaries: Communication*, pp. 181–206.

38. Schiller, *Mass Communication and the American Empire*; Boyd-Barrett, 'Media Imperialism: Towards an International Framework for the Analysis of Media Systems'; Boyd-Barrett, 'Media Imperialism Reformulated'.

39. Sinclair, Jacka and Cunningham, *New Patterns in Global Television*.

CHAPTER 9

International Television Channels in the Latin American Audiovisual Space

John Sinclair

§ IN order to understand how the globalization of television production and distribution has developed and assumed the ever more intensive and complex forms it has today, language and culture have to be taken into account as primary 'market forces' which can help or hinder the major producers and distributors of television programmes and services in gaining access to markets outside their nations of origin. In this context, it becomes helpful to discard the usual metaphors, such as the 'worlds' which share a common language, in favour of the concept of 'geolinguistic region'.

Latin America within its Geolinguistic Region

Talk of 'globalization' very often turns out really to mean 'regionalization', and regions can be cultural as well as geographical. Thus, a geolinguistic region is defined not just by its geographical contours, but also in a virtual sense, by commonalities of language and culture. Most characteristically, these have been established by historical relationships of colonization, as is the case with English, Spanish and Portuguese. In the age of international satellites, however, not only do former colonies counter-invade their erstwhile masters with television entertainment, but geolinguistic regions also come to include perhaps quite small, remote and dispersed pockets of users of particular languages, most often where there have been great diasporic population flows out of their original countries. This would include the unique case of the Spanish-speaking minorities of diverse Latin American origin who have settled right across the USA.

English may be the world's biggest geolinguistic region, dominated by the USA, but Spanish provides an illuminating case. No other language is spoken in as many countries as the national native language, as distinct from an official one, nor with the same degree of world-regional consolidation. Spanish is outstripping English in its number and distribution of native speakers.[1] It is the 'mother tongue' of some twenty countries in Latin America, and just as the USA contains more than four times as many native speakers of English as does the home of English, the UK, Mexico's population of 103 million is more than two and a half times that of Spain, with its 40 million.[2] That is, Mexico is to the Spanish-speaking world what the USA is to the world's English-speaking community, so far as audio-visual markets are concerned.

Thus, in Spanish-speaking Latin America audiences in a whole host of nations can be addressed by virtue of their more or less common linguistic and cultural heritage as a kind of 'imagined community' on a world-regional scale, a feature of the region that the larger television corporations have been well placed to exploit. Note that the USA also has to be included as part of this region, since, with its over 35 million 'Hispanics' or 'Latinos', it is actually the fifth-largest, and the wealthiest, domestic television market in the Spanish-speaking world.[3]

Furthermore, we are talking here not just of the contiguous geographic region of North, Central and South America, and the Spanish-speaking Caribbean, but the whole geolinguistic entities created by Iberian colonization: that is, the nations of Spain and Portugal themselves have to be included as part of the region in which their respective languages are spoken. The largest Latin American nation, Brazil, does not speak Spanish, but has a comparable history to its Spanish-speaking neighbours. It is the only Portuguese-speaking national market in the continent, and by far the biggest within the whole geolinguistic region of Portuguese. In this respect, Brazil bears a similar relationship to Portugal as Mexico does to Spain.

Thus, the 'Latin American audiovisual space' needs to be seen in the context of a wider 'Latin', or at least Iberoamerican space, which has emerged in the process of new distribution technologies, strategic investments and productive capacities being utilized by those in a position to exploit cultural and linguistic similarities on a global basis.

Televisa-ion and Globo-ization

Now that many countries have had over fifty years of television, it appears that passage through an initial stage of dependence to a maturity of the national market is, if not universal, then certainly a common pattern, of which the Latin American experience is paradigmatic. Crucial in the transition is the growth not just of the audience size, but of domestic programme production, the emergent consensus among observers being that audiences come to prefer television programming from their own country, and in their own vernacular, or if that is not available, from other countries culturally and linguistically similar. Joseph Straubhaar calls this 'cultural proximity': 'audiences will tend to prefer that programming which is closest or most proximate to their own culture: national programming if it can be supported by the local economy, regional programming in genres that small countries cannot afford'.[4]

The development of Latin American national markets for television programming bears out this hypothesis, including the pre-eminence of Mexico and Brazil as 'net exporters' within the region, to follow Rafael Roncagliolo's classification. Venezuela and Argentina are 'new exporters', with Colombia, Chile, and Peru seeking to join them, but coming from far behind, while the rest of the nations in the region, most of which are the smaller nations of Central America and the Caribbean, are 'net importers'.[5]

Concerns in the 1970s about 'picture-tube imperialism' notwithstanding,[6] Latin America has developed its own television programming production and distribution structures, and genres that are popular at local, national and regional levels. A small number of companies, however, have been able to seize a strategic advantage out of emphasizing similarity at the expense of difference, and so build themselves hegemonic positions over the commercialization of linguistic and cultural commonalities within their respective geolinguistic regions.

In particular, two major media conglomerates have arisen in the Latin American audiovisual space: Televisa, based in Mexico, the largest and most influential media corporation among all those countries that speak Spanish; and Globo, rooted in Brazil, the predominant network among all the Portuguese-speaking nations. No single network has ever dominated the USA, the world's largest English-speaking domestic market, to the degree that Televisa and Globo have each secured hegemony over their respective national markets. That is not to say that their home market size is necessarily a competitive advantage just in itself, nor to ignore the actual competition they have to deal with in their home markets, but to see how their domestic market dominance has been the basis upon which they both have been able to make consequential efforts over time to internationalize themselves, such that they have become by far the major players in their respective geolinguistic regions.

Challenges of the Post-broadcast Era

As well as the traditional programme exports upon which Globo's and Televisa's prominence has been built, the geolinguistic space of their domain is now constituted by direct satellite transmission services, and also via investment in foreign broadcasters. Televisa has always been astute in capitalizing upon the advantages of satellite technology, such as in the 1980s when it created a national network of Spanish-language stations in the USA, linked via satellite and fed with programming beamed up from Televisa's most popular channel in Mexico. Televisa also played a major part in initiating PanAmSat, the world's first private international satellite network. Around this time too, it established ECO (Empresa de la Comunicación Orbital) a news and information service drawing on foreign correspondents, rather like an early Spanish-language CNN. This was combined with entertainment programming into a satellite service for international transmission, Galavisión.[7]

In the 1990s, however, satellite and other technologies of the digital, 'post-broadcast' age opened up the Latin audiovisual space to competition from other corporations based outside of the natural language monopolies which Televisa and Globo for so long enjoyed. For one thing, the technical properties of digital compression not only allowed the satellites to transmit many more channels than ever before, whether from the USA, Europe or elsewhere, but also facilitated the provision of multiple audio tracks. This provided the various US-based global corporations with an interest in Latin America with the technical means to cross the language barriers that formerly sheltered the Latin American majors. For example, one image stream, say a Hollywood film on Time Warner's Latin American cable channel

HBO Ole, could be made available dubbed into Spanish or Portuguese, as well as in the English version.

Clearly for the Latin American market, the provision of multiple audio tracks is elemental, but much more culturally sensitive bases for differentiation have now been developed, such as musical taste cultures. Viacom's MTV not only has a separate service for Latin America, and within that, one for Brazil, but has created special programming feeds for Mexico at one end of the Spanish-speaking zone, and Argentina at the other. As well as increasing its total subscribers in the region, this strategy has also attracted local advertisers, in addition to the global ones that one expects to find everywhere on MTV.[8] MTV Latin America represents the kind of challenge that Televisa and Globo now face on their home ground in the era of convergence. Other global channels with special services for Latin America are CNN and the other Turner channels, Fox Latin America, Discovery Channel and the sports channel ESPN. Even by 1996, 90 per cent of television services (that is, satellite and cable signals rather than packaged programmes) imported into the Iberoamerican region were found to be from the USA.[9]

The challenges of convergence are not only at the level of content, but also of carriage, that is, distribution systems. A new era has been initiated by the advent of digital direct-to-home (DTH) satellite delivery, a post-broadcast technology which has encouraged the major Latin American producers and distributors to enter strategic alliances with US satellite and cable services. Such alliances, with their plans extending to Europe as well as Latin America, mark the beginning of a phase that brings Latin American television into the mainstream of globalization.

At the end of 1995, Rupert Murdoch's News Corporation announced that it would lead SkyTV, a pan-regional DTH satellite subscription service consortium, which included both Televisa and Globo, as well as a major US cable corporation, TCI (Tele-Communications Inc). This had been a response to the advent of Galaxy, an initiative announced earlier that year by Hughes Electronics Corporation, the US-based satellite division of General Motors, then owner of the DTH enterprise DirecTV in the USA. This consortium, later to be known as DirecTV Latin America, incorporated Televisa's cable competitor in Mexico, Multivisión, along with TV Abril (Globo's main cable competitor in Brazil), and Grupo Cisneros, owners of

Venevisión, a major television producer and distributor based in Venezuela.

Although smaller in its scale of operations than Televisa and Globo, the Cisneros Group is also a significant regional player, and has taken a very active role in extending the DirecTV service from one country to the next in Latin America. In addition, it is AOL's partner in the Internet service provision (ISP) business, competing with Spain's Telefónica, the market leader. It is also a stakeholder with Televisa in the leading US Spanish-language network, Univisión, and has extensive production and distribution activities in Miami.[10]

Both SkyTV and Galaxy/DirecTV had begun transmission by the end of 1996. Social inequalities in Latin America, however, are such that the potential pool of DTH subscribers is relatively small, and competition has been tough. Eventually Multivisión and TV Abril left the Galaxy consortium, to be replaced by Grupo Clarín of Argentina, another major regional player, one with a base in a country where subscription television has always been strong. Nevertheless, by early 2003, DirectTV Latin America was bankrupt. It was claiming 1.6 million subscribers in twenty-eight countries.[11] This would be somewhat less than half of the total number of DTH subscribers in the region. In any event, the subsequent takeover of DirecTV by News Corporation in the USA, which occurred around the same time, means that News Corp is free to merge SkyTV and DirecTV Latin America into the one service.

In terms of globalization processes, such a strategic alliance of large US-based corporations with the key regional companies is instructive. They represent a kind of global corporate venture: that is, the interpenetration of capital from what used to be called the 'transnational corporation' with 'national' capital from selected major companies of the target region. This is the kind of corporation that is globalizing not only the programme trade but also the trade in television services made possible by convergent technologies. The new kind of alliance has been formed in recognition of the strength which the Latin American companies have, not just in their national, nor even in their world-regional markets, but also the whole geolinguistic regions they have created.

Nevertheless, such alliances raise the question of how robust and resistant might the Latin American geolinguistic markets prove to be in the longer term. What happens when US producers begin to make a large output of material tailored specifically for such major geolinguistic markets other than English? That is, will the Latin American corporations that have built themselves up through exploiting their geolinguistic positions be able to sustain themselves against competition on their home turf from global services in Spanish and Portuguese? We can return to such questions later.

'Cultural Imperialism in Reverse'

As it has been defined in this chapter, and as the regional strategic alliances make clear, there is a Latin audiovisual space that is not just Latin American, but hemispheric, in that it includes North America. Furthermore, it is also transatlantic, in that it extends to Iberian Europe. That is not to say that the international ambitions of the Latin American corporations have proved easy to fulfil. Of particular interest in that regard has been the contrast between Televisa's attempts to gain some influence in Spain, and Globo's corresponding efforts in Portugal.

In 1988, as soon as international satellite reception became legal in Spain, Televisa announced 'the conquest of Spanish-speaking space in Europe', and began transmitting its Galavisión service (incorporating ECO) from Mexico, first on Eutelsat and later PanAmSat. It set up a company to sell advertising, Iberovisa, and installed thousands of free dishes to build an audience. By 1992, however, when satellite dish owners already had about twenty channels to choose from, including European and US-based services, Televisa could not conceal the abject failure of the venture. Furthermore, over the same period, Televisa failed in its bids to secure a share in the private terrestrial licences being granted by the socialist government at that time.[12]

With the advent of digital television and the transition from socialist to conservative government in Spain in 1996, however, Televisa has found its niche, having aligned itself with Telefónica, the dominant private telecommunications company, and later with DirecTV, in the DTH platform, Vía Digital. With this, Televisa has secured an outlet for its programming in Spain, including the Galavisión service. Still, in spite of an apparent fad in the early 1990s, there is evidence that audiences in Spain are less enamoured than those in Latin America with Televisa's major export genre, the *telenovela*.[13]

By contrast, Globo's experience in Portugal has been that it has encountered relatively little political opposition, and not only has it found a ready market for its *telenovelas*, but it has been able to institutionalize its whole style of doing business. This is just as well for Globo. Given that the company faces a language barrier in the Latin American market, the Portuguese connection has been much more significant in Globo's internationalization than Spain has been in Televisa's.

Before the advent of the privatization of television in Portugal in 1990, Globo had links with RTP (Rádiotelevisão Portuguesa), to which it had been selling *telenovelas* since 1977. Although Portuguese companies produced some of their own *telenovelas*, and there were also some imported from the other Brazilian networks, Globo *telenovelas* always were the most popular, so RTP felt it had a trump card in the programming battle that was to come with the privatized era. However, Globo became a shareholder in one of the new channels, SIC (Sociedade Independente de Comunicação). Right from the beginning, Globo took up the maximum allowable to a foreign owner of 15 per cent.

Given that commercial television was a new phenomenon in Portugal, the Portuguese partner was eager to have access not just to Globo programming, but their entire repertoire of commercial and technical expertise. For both parties, this was an ideal strategic investment, putting Globo in a perfect position to take on the tutelage of its Lusitanian protégé. With this backing, SIC soon overtook RTP's market leadership, with audiences embracing Globo's *telenovelas* so much so that Portuguese elites began to worry about 'cultural imperialism in reverse'. Note also that Globo is reaching popular audiences via broadcast television, whereas Televisa reaches the more restricted DTH audience in Spain. Globo and SIC participate in Portuguese DTH as well, as programme suppliers.[14]

What of Iberian commercial ambitions in Latin America? The most significant service is that of Antena 3 TV, Spain's leading terrestrial broadcast network and DTH participant, which began Antena 3 Internacional in 1996. This is a satellite channel of Antena 3 TV's own programming, transmitted throughout Latin America, and also available in the USA, making Antena 3 Internacional as extensive in its global reach to the Spanish-speaking world – Spain, the USA and Latin America – as only Televisa has been in the past, but coming from the opposite direction.

Since 1997, the Spanish telecommunications giant Telefónica has become the major owner of Antena 3, both directly and indirectly. Telefónica itself has a strong international orientation, particularly evident from its acquisition of Endemol Entertainment, and its activities in Argentina, that most 'European' of Latin American nations. Furthermore, Telefónica is a key owner of Hispasat, the Spanish domestic satellite first launched in 1992, which not only serves to carry the Vía Digital signal to its subscribers in Spain, but serves both sides of the Atlantic, including the carriage of Antena 3 Internacional. Hispasat, incidentally, also carries the international service of the national broadcaster RTVE to the Americas, which is perhaps the most serious effort by any national government in the Latin world to provide a service for its geolinguistic region as a matter of policy.[15]

Co-operation Towards a 'Latin Audiovisual Space'

While it would come as no surprise that the national broadcasters of Spain and Portugal are supported by their governments in providing satellite television services to their respective post-colonial worlds, perhaps more striking are various intergovernmental initiatives, mostly aimed at consolidating the Spanish and Portuguese languages and cultures on an international basis, even including one committed to creating a 'Latin audiovisual space' as such. These efforts have been augmented by the activities of international broadcasters' associations and professional bodies. It should be understood, however, that the international orientation of both Spain and Portugal is as modern nations of a united Europe, not one-time imperial centres brooding on their glorious pasts.

As early as the 1960s, Spain was seeking to establish international links between RTVE and Latin American television programme producers, in which a major concern was its interest in the maintenance of the Spanish language under its hegemony, as well as the fostering of news and cultural programming exchanges. The advent of satellite television has given a new kind of vision to these efforts, or to quote the responsible executive of Hispasat:

> Satellites have become a key element for the diffusion of a full range of television channels in markets which are homogeneous for linguistic, cultural or economic reasons. In this way, satellites today are the most appropriate telecommunications infrastructure for the

development of digital television platforms directed to specific linguistic markets, leaping national barriers to form homogeneous markets composed of countries separated by thousands of kilometres.

And thanks to communication satellites and their capacity to transmit to millions of homes, we find before us the option of making real the old dream of creating an Iberoamerican Audiovisual Space, with its own accent. Ultimately, digital satellite platforms offer us an opportunity to develop an audiovisual market in 'Spanish', composed of more than a hundred million homes, led by the creators, producers, and media groups of our own Iberoamerican countries.[16]

It is not as if Spain is the only nation wanting to bring the Spanish-speaking world together. For example, Latin American and Caribbean governments supported the development of a regional news agency. Correspondingly, over the relatively short time in which both Portugal and Brazil have become democratic nations, they have been willing to open up relations, which had lapsed considerably since independence. Thus, it was a former Brazilian minister of culture who was the prime mover in the creation of the CPLP (Comunidade dos Países de Língua Portuguesa – Community of Portuguese-speaking Countries) in 1996.

Yet the most ambitious extent of intergovernmental collaboration of this kind was reached in 1982 when the ministers of culture from Spain, Portugal, France, Italy, Mexico, and Brazil met to promote, in their words, 'co-operation between countries with a language of Latin origin'. It was left to the French (who, after all, had first invented the concept of 'Latin America'), to explore the possibility of building a 'Latin audiovisual space'.[17]

This initiative was prompted by concerns over the internationalization of both the television and film industries (hence the concept of 'audiovisual'), and came in the wake of the 1970s debate over cultural imperialism, a phenomenon by then seen to have become a problem for Europe as well as the Third World. While the scheme generated some excellent research,[18] and although France was later instrumental in ensuring that audiovisual production was not made subject to the free trade obligations under the GATT (General Agreement on Trade and Tariffs) when it was concluded in 1993, the initial impetus towards a Latin audiovisual space has not been sustained by the governments concerned.

However, if we set aside film, which requires a quite different line of analysis, it is notable that the activities of private entrepreneurial interests, at least in television, have gone much further than any intergovernmental collaboration in building up and co-ordinating international markets of Spanish- and Portuguese-speaking nations across the world. For example, perhaps the most durable and effective organization for international co-operation in television has been the OTI (Organización de Televisión Iberoamericana), which has had a close association with Televisa in Mexico, the country in which it was formed in 1971, as well as with some of the other major Latin American entrepreneurial channels such as Venevisión and the channels owned at the time of OTI's formation by Goar Mestre in Argentina and Chateaubriand in Brazil. An organization of broadcasting companies, public as well as private, OTI exists to co-ordinate the transmission of such premier international events as the soccer World Cup. Latin American entrepreneurs have maintained themselves as an international lobby group as well, in the form of AIR (Asociación Interamericana de Radiodifusión – Interamerican Broadcasting Association).[19]

Against the Flow

A comprehensive study of the audiovisual trade flows within the Iberoamerican geolinguistic region, drawing on 1996 industry-supplied data from Mexico, Brazil, Venezuela, Argentina and Chile, as well as Spain and Portugal, identifies Spain as one of the biggest importers of audiovisual products, second only to Brazil. Looking more widely, the vast majority (44 per cent) of all audiovisual imports in the national markets named was of films and programmes destined for broadcast television, followed by satellite and cable television services (especially important in Argentina) with 28 per cent, then 16 per cent for videos and 12 per cent for cinema. For all the regional trade in television programmes, the major traded product being the *telenovela*, only 6 per cent of total audiovisual imports came from within the region itself, the same amount as originating in Europe (and mostly imported by Spain and Portugal), with the overwhelming majority of 86 per cent coming from the USA. Even the figures for television programming alone (though including the important category of films bought for television) showed a massive preponderance (79 per cent) of US material, with Spain being the biggest market, accounting for half of all such imports.[20]

Just as audiovisual production and distribution in the USA has become dominated by a few major suppliers, pricing their products according to each national market, the same study found that in television programming exports from the region, five companies accounted for 94 per cent of programmes exported. In order of importance, these were Televisa, Globo, Venevisión, RCTV (also of Venezuela), and Spain's RTVE. Without citing any actual figures, however, the study reported that export sales still represent only a small percentage of the income of these companies. Not surprisingly, the distribution pattern of destinations for television programmes in particular varied little from that for audiovisual goods and services in general: 50 per cent to the region, 23 per cent to the USA, 9 per cent to Europe and 18 per cent to the rest of the world. Note, however, that just as the USA was shown to be the most important market outside the region for the main Spanish-language producers, the special importance of Portugal for Globo was seen in the fact that fully half of its regional sales go to SIC (Sociedade Independente de Comunicação).[21]

The same study found that the export of television services in the region (as distinct from programmes), mainly (70 per cent) came from Televisa and Multivisión in Mexico, presumably by virtue of their involvement with the Murdoch Sky and Hughes Galaxy DTH ventures respectively. Even though 90 per cent of the services exported from Iberoamerican countries went to other regional nations of the same language (the rest mainly to the Spanish-speaking networks in the USA), evidence of the geolinguistic cohesion of the region's trade, the study also showed that the US services have been able to cross the language barrier without much movement back in the other direction. This trend is likely to consolidate if, as the study predicts, the trade in services rather than programmes soon becomes the major form of audiovisual exchange.[22]

Convergence is more than a technological phenomenon: it occurs within the structure of the communication and information industries themselves, as telecommunication companies take up strategic holdings in more entertainment-based cultural industries such as subscription television, as noted in the case of Telefónica in Spain and Argentina, and as some of the very largest companies build vertically integrated structures for content production and distribution.

Such integration was formerly one of the more distinct features of the Latin American model of corporate organization, but now it is becoming internationalized. As became apparent with the Hughes's Galaxy DTH initiative in Latin America, and once again, in the case of Telefónica, these integrated structures can cross the former divide between hardware or 'carriage' (in these cases, satellite design, manufacture and management), and software or 'content' (television programme production and distribution).

It has been argued here that this kind of convergence has also transformed the international television business from an import-export trade in programmes as products, to a post-broadcast industry which provides not so much particular products but continuous transmission of services, whether delivered via cable or delivered direct to subscribers. Given that the US-based and other global corporations such as Hughes not only have taken over the technological vanguard in the region once held by PanAmSat, but also faced up to the content issue by extending into services in the regional languages, if post-broadcast services do come to eclipse programmes as the core of the television trade, then much of the comparative advantage once enjoyed by the major Latin American companies would be undermined.

Thus, the comparative advantage of language difference which the Latin American companies once enjoyed as a kind of natural monopoly is under threat. It is not only the new satellite technologies of digital compression and conditional access DTH reception which have brought this about: several of the global channels have gained their experience in the USA with the potential audience of 35 million Spanish speakers there, and the move into Latin America represents immense opportunities for them to exploit. At the very least, it is well worth their while to dub programmes produced in English. The prospect of the 300 million or more Spanish speakers of Latin America gives US producers an incentive to develop programming for the Latino market in the first instance, with Latin America, and Spain, as 'aftermarkets', now that the technology is available.

'The Hollywood of Latin America'

Such immense technological and structural transformation has consequences for how we understand communications theoretically, and this includes the implications for language and culture. Following the Spanish geographer Manuel Castells, David Morley and Kevin Robins argue that what Harold Innis called the 'space-binding' properties of communications media now are redefining space in terms of flows, rather than of places as such, although with key economic and cultural 'nerve centres' in the network of flows.[23] We can think of geolinguistic regions as prime examples of such virtual restructured spaces, in which new centres have emerged. These include not just Mexico City and Rio de Janeiro, the home bases of Televisa and Globo, but also Miami. Not only is it a strategically located centre for television production and distribution to serve both Americas, but Miami has assumed a mythical place in the Latin American 'collective imagination'.[24]

Miami's function as a node within the Latin audiovisual space of flows is primarily that of exchange between the American continents, which involves production as well as distribution, and distribution of programmes as well as of services. What Miami does can be understood by looking at which companies have located there, what they are doing, and why. First and foremost, there are the US Spanish-language broadcast networks, Univisión and Telemundo, which have had their operations centred in Miami since the late 1980s. In addition to producing for the US Spanish-speaking market, some programmes are sold and shown throughout Latin America, where both networks also have their own international cable services.

Nevertheless, the bulk of prime-time programming on these networks is made up of *telenovelas* imported from Latin America. US-produced *telenovelas* are rare, and have tended not to be successful with audiences. As we have seen, the handful of vertically integrated production-distribution enterprises that dominate the Latin American television industry produce for their own large domestic markets in the first instance. Yet increasingly they are looking to export markets to maximize the profitability of their investments. The 35 million Spanish speakers in the USA constitute a small but relatively affluent export market for them. Most significantly, Televisa of Mexico, whose corporate ancestors were instrumental in establishing Spanish-language television in the USA in the first place, has a contract with the leading US network Univisión to supply 40 per cent of its programming. Signed in 1992, this runs until 2017. Univisión obtains another 11 per cent from Venevisión, which is the other

Latin American network with a stake in Univisión. Telemundo, which is now owned by the US mainstream network NBC, is obliged to source its material more widely, and strike up co-production arrangements, most recently with Globo from Brazil and with Caracol/RTI of Colombia.[25]

Because both the networks buy programming from the major Latin American producer-distributors, those companies too are attracted to Miami, which also serves as a location for their regional production and distribution, and a forward base for distribution beyond the USA. These include the Cisneros Group, already mentioned, and Coral Pictures, the distribution arm of the Cisneros Group's major competitor in Venezuela, RCTV. Coral Pictures distributes RCTV's inventory and other programming in the USA and elsewhere, including Spain.

Finally, in addition to the US Spanish-language networks and the Latin American producer-distributors, Miami has attracted some of the major US-based global cable and satellite services discussed earlier: those that since the late 1980s have begun to offer channels in Spanish and/or Portuguese for the US Hispanic and Latin American markets, such as MTV Latino. In turn, the satellite companies that carry such channels also uplink from Miami, notably PanAmSat, which has a teleport just outside the city. Originally a Televisa initiative, PanAmSat is now the world's most extensive private satellite system for television, and carries Televisa and Cisneros Group signals in the region as well as the US cable channels and the Hughes DirecTV DTH service to Latin America.[26]

The presence of the various production and distribution companies in Miami helps to attract production and technical personnel, directors, writers, actors and other creative talent to live there. Production in Miami is facilitated by the availability of such people, as well as the strata of technical and other support services that production requires, such as casting agencies and post-production facilities. Thus, in the language of neoliberal competitive advantage and location theory, Miami forms a 'cluster', just as Hollywood does for the film industry.

At another level, for audiences, the imagery of Miami's American-tropical settings in the programmes produced there imparts a distinct aura to the place. Although it has been the Cuban immigrants who have made Miami a Spanish-speaking citadel of capitalism, the city's ethos has become more 'Latin-cosmopolitan' than Cuban. While this is a special advantage for the television industry, it also reflects Miami's wider appeal as a city with a skilled, bilingual, hybrid workforce and an urban environment that functions for the whole hemisphere of Spanish speakers in the Americas. It provides an interesting case for evaluating the relative significance of cultural *vis-à-vis* economic factors in the location of cultural industries such as television. Furthermore, in an era steeped in globalization's dictum that 'time and space have disappeared',[27] Miami serves as a reminder of the importance of regional factors in modulating globalization processes.

The Return of the Repressed

While there can be no doubt that the advent of digital television via satellite marks a whole new phase in the technological development of the medium and in the nature of television as an international business, it does not necessarily follow that it is about to replace broadcast television as we have known it at the national and regional levels. As long as DTH and even cable services are subscription services ('pay-TV'), and broadcast television remains free-to-air, we can expect there to be a significant socio-economic division between those who can afford to upgrade to the new modes of delivery, and those who cannot, particularly in developing countries.

Drawing on his own and other research in Latin America, Joseph Straubhaar maintains that there is a class factor in the now frequently observed mass preference for television programming which derives from one's own language and culture:

> New research seems to point to a greater traditionalism and loyalty to national and local cultures by lower or popular classes, who show the strongest tendency to seek greater cultural proximity in television programs and other cultural products. They seem to prefer nationally or locally produced material that is closer to or more reinforcing of traditional identities, based in regional, ethnic, dialect/language, religious, and other elements.[28]

On the other hand, for the elite strata of the region, the dictum of global marketing guru Theodore Levitt appears to hold true: 'globalisation does not means the end of segments. It means, instead, their expansion to worldwide proportions.'[29] Thus, Kenton Wilkinson's research on the Latin American television trade brings to light differences between the *telenovelas*, variety shows, sports, imported action series and movies programmed for mass audiences on broadcast television, and the much more internationalized material on the cable and satellite services subscribed to by the social elites: 'the regional program market is itself segmented according to characteristics of the target audience'.[30]

In other words, the mass audiences not only tolerate but rather enjoy seeing locally made programming (much of it not at all exportable), material which is nationally produced and distributed, and the characteristic generic programming of the region, such as *telenovelas* from the major exporters, though they do also watch films and series from the USA. The elites that subscribe to satellite and cable services get their MTV, HBO, CNN, Discovery, Disney, Playboy and other US-based services, but in Latin American versions, along with some Latin American channels such as ECO, and European feeds from Antena 3 and RTVE. This is a much more global, cosmopolitan mix, although with some local inflections, as in the case mentioned of MTV. Cultural stratification of this kind corresponds to the multiple levels of television flows identified by scholars such as Straubhaar and Wilkinson: the local, national, regional (that is, world-regional, including geolinguistic regional), and global. While there might appear to be a complex mix of choice in the middle of the scale, the extremes are clear, between local live shows on free-to-air television at one end of the range of offerings, and the global channels on DTH subscription services at the other. Anyhow, precisely because audiences are stratified, relatively few viewers would have the full range of choice.

Furthermore, it is worth emphasizing at this stage that, partly for this reason, the different levels are not mutually exclusive – that is, the build-up of global channels in Latin America does not drive out local, national and regional programming, any more than the rise of regional programming could ever have hoped to replace the global. Rather, consistent with world trends, 'the productive capacity of regional players has increased along with the total volume of programmes transmitted',[31] and as well, with the differentiation of audiences.

If Televisa and Globo had ever aspired to join the global league, rather than just maximize their advantages within their geolinguistic regions, this would have involved competing head-on with the entrenched US corporations on their home ground: the US market and the anglophone geolinguistic region as a whole. This they have never sought to do: Televisa's ECO might be modelled on CNN, but it did not set out to compete with it; Globo has concentrated on the fullest development of the *telenovela* genre, but does not have a film division.

While the Latin American corporations have cultivated their geolinguistic regional level niches rather than challenge the US-based majors at the global level, those niches themselves are now being forced open to competition as the global corporations have recognized their potential value, and gained experience and economies of scale in production for them. Thus, a service such as ECO, for which Televisa was prepared to sustain recurrent losses in order to develop on a regional basis, found itself being overtaken first by the now defunct CBS Telenoticias and then by CNN en Español. One reason given for this is that ECO's pan-regional perspective is actually less attractive to subscribers than the strategic 'global localization' combination of international and local news offered by the new services.[32] Again, while the inclusion of Televisa and Globo in the Murdoch DTH scheme, and Venevisión in that of Hughes, is a recognition of the Latin American companies' special strengths in being able to supply traditional entertainment programming to their region, this represents only a minor proportion of the whole bouquet that was offered in each case.

The pattern that emerges is that the US-based corporations have been quick to occupy the global level of distribution opened up by digital technologies, and they also have begun to penetrate the regional level, at least so far as the elite subscriber audiences are concerned. The Latin American corporations have been granted a limited but significant measure of participation in the new services at the global level, but have had to face the unwonted competition of global channels in Spanish and Portuguese at the regional level. We have seen, however, that by and large, they continue to dominate the regional trade in programmes for broadcast television as a relatively mass medium, and maintain their predominance over domestic competition in broadcast television within the national markets where they have their roots and still earn by far the bulk of their income.

The capacity of the Latin American corporations to build the geolinguistic markets which they have over the last few decades is largely due to their discoveries that they had a comparative advantage in being the largest producers in their respective languages, and that language and culture were 'market forces' – that mass audiences, at least, were attracted by linguistically and culturally proximate programming. If US producers and distributors are now in on the secret and threaten to cream off the more affluent subscription viewers with 'global localized' programming, such a turn of events probably means that the Latin Americans have no choice but to collaborate rather than to compete at the global level of televisual flows for elite audiences, while their hegemonies over mass broadcast audiences at the regional and national levels will remain secure for the immediate future.

Notes

1. David Crystal, *English as a Global Language* (Cambridge: Cambridge University Press, 1997), pp. 3–5.

2. Geohive Global Statistics: <http://www.geohive.com/cd/index/.php>. Consulted April 2003.

3. John Sinclair, *Latin American Television: A Global View* (London and New York: Oxford University Press, 1999); John Sinclair, ' "The Hollywood of Latin America": Miami as Regional Center in Television Trade', *Television and New Media*, 4(3) (2003), pp. 211–29.

4. Joseph Straubhaar, 'Asymmetrical Interdependence and Cultural Proximity: A Critical Review of the International Flow of Television Programs', paper presented to the Conference of the Asociación Latinoamericana de Investigadores de la Comunicación (São Paulo, August 1992), p. 14.

5. Rafael Roncagliolo, 'Trade Integration and Communication Networks in Latin America', *Canadian Journal of Communication*, 20(3) (1995), p. 337.

6. Alan Wells, *Picture Tube Imperialism? The Impact of US Television in Latin America* (New York: Orbis, Maryknoll, 1972).

7. John Sinclair, 'Mexico, Brazil and the Latin World', in John Sinclair, Elizabeth Jacka and Stuart Cunningham (eds), *New Patterns in Global Television: Peripheral Vision* (Oxford: Oxford University Press, 1996), pp. 33–66; Sinclair, *Latin American Television*.

8. Diane Goldner, 'MTV Rocks to Latin Beat', *Variety*, 19–25 May 1997, p. 22.

9. Media Research and Consultancy Spain, 'La industria audiovisual iberoamericana: datos de sus principales mercados 1997', report prepared for the Federación de Asociaciones de Productores Audiovisuales Españoles and Agencia Española de Cooperación Internacional (Madrid, July 1997), p. 14.

10. Sinclair, *Latin American Television*; Sinclair, ' "The Hollywood of Latin America" '.

11. DirecTV Latin America Corporate website: <http://www.directvla. com>. Consulted April 2003.

12. Francisco Hérnandez Lomeli, 'Televisa en España', *Comunicación y Sociedad*, 16–17 (1992–93), pp. 74–105.

13. Sinclair, *Latin American Television*; Vía Digital: <http://www.viadigital. es>. Consulted April 2003.

14. Sinclair, *Latin American Television*.

15. Ibid.

16. Díaz Argüelles, cited in Sinclair, *Latin American Television*, p. 148.

17. Armand Mattelart, Xavier Delcourt and Michèle Mattelart, *International Image Markets: In Search of an Alternative Perspective* (London: Comedia, 1984), p. ix.

18. Armand Mattelart and Michèle Mattelart, *The Carnival of Images: Brazilian Television Fiction* (New York: Bergin and Garvey, 1990).

19. Sinclair, *Latin American Television*.

20. Media Research and Consultancy Spain, 'La industria audiovisual ibero-americana', pp. 12–15.

21. Ibid., pp. 16–17.

22. Ibid., pp. 17–18.

23. David Morley and Kevin Robins, *Spaces of Identity: Global Media, Electronic Landscapes and Cultural Boundaries* (London: Routledge, 1995), pp. 26–9.

24. Carlos Monsiváis, 'Globalisation Means Never Having to Say You're Sorry', *Journal of International Communication*, 1(2) (1994), p. 124.

25. Daniel Mato, 'Transnacionalización de la industria de la telenovela, referencias territoriales, y producción de mercados y representaciones de identidades transnacionales', paper presented to the XXIII International Congress of the Latin American Studies Association (Washington, DC, September 2001).

26. Sinclair, '"The Hollywood of Latin America"'.

27. Marjorie Ferguson, 'The Mythology about Globalization', *European Journal of Communication*, 7(1) (1992), pp. 69–93.

28. Joseph Straubhaar, 'Beyond Media Imperialism: Assymetrical Inter-dependence and Cultural Proximity', *Critical Studies in Mass Communication*, 8(1) (1991), p. 51.

29. Quoted in Morley and Robins, *Spaces of Identity*, p. 113.

30. Kenton Wilkinson, 'When Culture, Language and Communication Converge: The Latin American Cultural-Linguistic Television Market', PhD dissertation (University of Texas at Austin, 1995), pp. 238–90.

31. Ibid., p. 236.

32. Michael Kepp, 'News Addicts', *Cable and Satellite Europe*, August 1997, p. 41.

CHAPTER 10

Adapting US Transnational Television Channels to a Complex World: From Cultural Imperialism to Localization to Hybridization

Joseph D. Straubhaar and Luiz G. Duarte[1]

§ THIS chapter examines the movement of many US television channels from being 'global' exports to regional adaptations or 'localizations', and beyond that to national adaptations in an increasing number of cases. The chapter looks at the globalization strategy of several US channels, which reflect key differences over how eagerly or grudgingly they embrace localization. The chapter examines the role of local or regional partners in enhancing or restraining localization, and examines the evolution of national and regional markets in terms of segmentation and competition. Theoretically, the chapter argues that many initial US channel strategies did in essence reflect a sense of cultural imperialism, but that adaptation to market demands has forced a change in strategy towards localization, indeed perhaps beyond localization to hybridization in the case of some channels. Most of the truly hybrid channels, however, are produced by national or regional actors, not global ones, whose localization strategies tend to be very conservative, unwilling to invest in unstable markets, perhaps also still underestimating the demand of national and regional audiences for cultural proximity and relevance.

An exploratory case study was conducted of the American pay television that ventured into Latin America in the 1990s. The US television networks who most committed to the Latin American market were shown to be linked to large conglomerates, focused on the top six country markets and co-operating to face strong competition from a handful of local players. These networks have developed a variety of adaptation strategies, including language translations, production and co-productions at the local markets, multiple transmission feeds and repackaging of programmes and graphic vignettes.

The evidence supports recent theoretical models in international communication that suggest an asymmetrical interdependence of industries and a trans-border flow based on audience demands for content in close proximity to their own culture. Global channels faced severe difficulties against local competitors, who continued to dominate the mass audience with greater local cultural appeal based in national production. Even in smaller Latin American markets, the imported television that gained a mass audience was imported from within the cultural-linguistic region, not primarily from the USA. Global channels emerged with specialized channels focused on globalized elites, niche audiences among the upper middle and upper classes.

Thanks to a wave of economic liberalization by new democratic regimes, multi-channel TV systems flourished in the 1990s, opening the opportunity for over a hundred new networks to reach this relatively untapped market. And the majority of these were from the United States. As new multi-channel television technologies arrived in Latin America and a barrage of new channels suddenly invaded the region, American media firms raced to mark their presence, bringing with them new concerns of an American invasion. Did these firms use their newfound audiovisual market space to dump amortized reruns of the lowest common denominator or did they seek a way to the hearts of Latin audiences by applying the principles of cultural proximity? How did audiences respond to renewed waves of imported US programmes on the new satellite and cable channels?

Although the American firms expected great success with Latin American audiences, the theoretical models developed by the early 1990s, like cultural proximity,[2] indicate that breaking into geolinguistic markets defined by language and cultural barriers would in fact be hard for these new channels despite the direct technological access to audiences that satellite technology gave them. The apparent tendency to adopt and adapt commercial media models, cultural forms and genres indicate that seemingly dependent countries do have the potential to talk back. Domestic media conglomerates have grown in Third World countries like Mexico and Brazil to compete with American media in the international market, making the relationship more interdependent and the flow less and less asymmetric. In this new scenario, the American media firms wishing to sell abroad may not be in such a hegemonic position any more. While in the past, media imperialism scholars could afford to view transnational media products as highly standardized commodity goods,[3] produced in a capitalist context, recent scholarship has been forced to recognize product adaptations to make media attractive to particular cultural groups.[4]

This chapter briefly reviews the general process by which firms venture overseas, outlining their stages of commitment to foreign markets. A major assertion of this body of theory is that companies tend gradually to 'become more local' as they step up their involvement abroad. Rather than mimicking their behaviour and offerings in the original domestic market, numerous marketing studies demonstrate the tendency of successful multinationals to adapt their strategies to the specific challenges of new local markets. The literature review dives further into the debate regarding whether firms should standardize or adapt their international operations. This leads to the fundamental proposal of this study: successful US television networks adapt their offerings to Latin Americans and, in so doing, break a pattern of classic imperialism. Rather than imposing a totally foreign cultural product, they demonstrate intent in satisfying audiences with products adapted to their needs and demands. Rather than classic imperialism, we find asymmetrical interdependence. Within a world capitalist system,[5] we find national and regional media firms gaining considerable market power against the giant global firms that entered the local markets via satellite and cable television technologies.

The Major Outside Television Groups Entering Latin America

Apart from some daring independent media corporations, such as Hallmark or Gaylord's CMT, the major players in Latin America are large conglomerates, the likes of Time Warner, Disney and News Corp. These media giants are committed to being there first and, with disregard to initial returns on investments, plunged significant investments to solidify their presence in the large and smaller countries. They took advantage of their prior experience in international operations to move quickly, sometimes matching, sometimes beating their traditional domestic competitors to the Latin markets. Such prowess, however, did not save these networks from going through difficult learning curves before they could become reasonably attractive to at least some segments of the Latin audiences. Although only minimal adaptations could be seen in their content – much of which is of a broad international appeal anyway – the outside networks eventually realized that simple transpositions of their domestic models were not enough to win the audiences over from powerful local broadcasters.

Before satellite technology permitted the entry of these new channels, major Latin American media conglomerates, such as Brazil's Globo, Mexico's Televisa and Venezuela's Cisneros groups, had already consolidated a dominance of broadcast television.[6] They were producing most of their own programming and exporting heavily to the rest of Latin America.[7] In addition to their existing dominance of broadcast television, the home team advantage enjoyed by these Latin American conglomerates guaranteed them some prime space in the limited installed distribution capacity of satellite and cable TV. Thanks to their natural knowledge of local audience and market demands, these players seem to have left only a complementary role to most foreign networks, which strive to find some profitable niche market for themselves. We will examine some of the adaptations promoted by US networks in their intense competition with each other and the locals. By the end of the 1990s, they set up a whole new translation-dubbing/subtitling industry, and started new satellite transmission feeds to break Latin America into Mexican, Argentine and Brazilian sub-regions.

From a Global One Programme Fits All to Increasing Localization

The development of the cable and satellite programming industries in Latin America tracks developments in theory about the globalization of television. In many ways, cultural imperialism theorists, international diplomats and the managers of major global conglomerates all had rather similar expectations of satellite technology. They all expected the technology to open the way for rapid expansion of direct provision of American and selected other developed world programming straight to large audiences around the world.

In 1972, about the same time that cultural imperialism theory had been made explicit by Schiller,[8] the United Nations Commission on the Peaceful Uses of Outer Space voted to require that any country wishing to broadcast directly from a satellite into the territory of another nation had to obtain permission, or prior consent, from that nation first.[9] In 1971, Schiller focused on the impact that 'American empire' was having on other nations via its control of mass communications. In 1974, Nordenstreng and Varis showed that most nations were importing most of their television, mostly entertainment from the USA,[10] which fed the New World Information and Communication Order debate in UNESCO and the ITU in the 1970s.[11] In 1985, Mattelart and Schmucler focused on how new media technologies, such as satellite TV, cable TV, VCRs and computers, could renew the impact of cultural imperialism by providing new channels that would privilege US and other developed nations' cultural exports.[12]

Interestingly, it seems that corporate executives expected something similar. In fact, much of the research by Schiller and Matellart was based on quotes from American trade and economic newspapers and magazines, which seemed to stress the strong expectations that many in business had for increasing American cultural exports with the new technologies. Major conglomerate leaders seemed to expect to reach broad global and regional audiences with satellite and cable TV channels that would essentially retransmit material they had already produced for the United States, Great Britain, etc. For example, in Asia, Star TV under Rupert Murdoch originally expected to be able effectively to draw broad Asian audiences with only five channels: MTV Asia (Viacom), British Broadcasting Corporation's World Service Television (WSTV), Prime Time Sports (a joint venture with the Denver-based Prime Network), entertainment and cultural programmes through Star Plus, and a Mandarin Chinese-language channel. He has since been forced to expand to dozens of localized channels to compete effectively in local markets.

These three major groups (policy-makers in international organizations, critical scholars and global conglomerate leaders) shared assumptions based on a strong technological and economic determinism. They felt that the new technology of satellite transmission across borders would automatically reinforce the reach and power of the major existing communications powers and corporations. They assumed that the export strength Hollywood enjoyed in television in the 1960s and early 1970s would continue over time and into new media, that large audiences simply awaited the more direct and convenient delivery of American programming through the new channels of satellite and cable.

In contrast, by the early 1980s, new scholarship was beginning to re-examine these trends in programme flow and challenge the theories that seemed to explain them. By 1981, Straubhaar had noted that Brazilian importation of American programming was tapering off slightly, but that the time Brazilian audiences spent with American programming was declining much more rapidly, paralleling the fact that prime time was increasingly full of Brazilian national production.[13] By 1984, Antola and Rogers used the same methodology to note that from the early 1970s to the early 1980s, US television exports were declining to the major Latin American countries, while intra-Latin American exports were rising, and viewing time in Latin America was shifting towards either national or regional production.[14] Empirically, these flow studies challenged major aspects of cultural dependency and imperialism theory, which had emphasized the power of American exports. Other studies were also challenging the presumed political-economic power of global actors over local ones. For Tomlinson, for example, the major weakness of cultural imperialism is that it 'does not explain how a cultural practice can be imposed in a context which is no longer actually coercive'.[15] As a result several new bodies of theory began to grow to provide alternative explanations at different levels of the complex process of television production, flow and reception.

At the level of audience studies, the flow studies showed an audience tendency towards a preference for national or regional television. This built on a growing tendency in cultural studies and audience reception studies to see audiences as active and powerful enough to make choices about what they wanted to watch,[16] that it was not enough to know what global entrepreneurs might want them to watch or to know what technology was making available to them. Two new theoretical approaches captured this tendency. One focused on a cultural discount that might be applied against cultural products like television which were in languages or cultures unfamiliar or uninteresting to the receiver.[17] Another focused on the concept of cultural proximity, that given a choice, people would make positive choices to prefer their own culture or similar ones on television. 'Audiences generally prefer programmes that are proximate to their own culture: national programming if the local economy allows, regional programming in genres impossible to produce locally. The US continues then to have an advantage in genres that Third World countries cannot produce, such as feature films, cartoons and action-adventure series.'[18]

A related body of theory was also growing that concerned the development of cultural linguistic or geocultural markets for television. In the early 1980s, Antola and Rogers had noted a tendency towards intra-Latin American trade in television.[19] An audience survey study in 1989 in the Dominican Republic noted a strong preference for regional Latin American programmes in several genres that that small nation could not afford to produce for itself.[20] By the 1990s, the term cultural linguistic market was being used to describe the intra-Latin American market for television, as well as other parts of the world, such as Asia.[21] The idea is that multi-country television markets develop, based on shared languages, shared historical experiences, geographical proximity and cultural proximity.

In the words of Sinclair:

> The world is divided in a series of regions, each with its own internal dynamic, besides its link to the global scale. Although mostly based on geographical realities, such regions are also defined by cultural, linguistic and historical links that go beyond their geographical space [...] Each geolinguistic region, as we can call it, is dominated, in turn, by one or two centers of audio-visual productions.[22]

As Sinclair notes, a major aspect of current geolinguistic television markets is the emergence of regional production centres. These tend to share a language and cultural background with the geolinguistic market they serve. Mexico exports television programmes to Latin America, Egypt to the Arab-speaking countries, India to South and Central Asia, and Hong Kong to Chinese-speaking populations around Asia. Many of these television programme export patterns were built up in the 1970s–80s, before satellites began to distribute channels to cable systems or directly to homes. So regional exporters were already established before global satellite operations started.

Furthermore, many of the more successful aspects of Hollywood programming formulas had already been adapted to local cultures by national and geolinguistic or geocultural producers. Robertson has observed that national cultures and institutions tend to absorb and localize for influence in a process that he calls glocalization.[23] The American programmes have been adapted everywhere in a dynamic cultural syncretism or hybridization.[24] The soap opera has morphed into the Latin American *telenovelas* and the old-fashioned Hollywood musicals received new accents in the Hindi cinema.

Logics of the Market?

Even so, cultural linguistic or geocultural markets for television might seem promising targets for global media entrepreneurs. There is some evidence that certain kinds of Hollywood genres and formulas maintain considerable appeal in many markets. The lowest common denominator of a universal appeal is considered more effective in some genres, like action-adventure, than in others, like soap opera or comedy.

Certainly, as this study shows, a number of global media firms have entered regional markets using satellite technology. We argue, however, that global entrepreneurial logic still seems to have been more focused on past success in exporting standard Hollywood productions and on new technological opportunities rather than on markets truly defined by culture and language. Most of the early regional satellite and cable television operated by global players such as Murdoch, Hughes and Turner seem to have focused first on what geographic area could be covered by a given satellite beam,[25] rather than what actually comprised a logical and coherent cultural linguistic market.

The literature on international marketing shows that for foreign firms entering into a local market a fundamental decision is to determine how much they are willing to adapt their products and procedures abroad or whether they want to stick to exporting a standard product everywhere.[26] Some think that a truly global standardization is both possible and desirable.[27] In the 1970s and 1980s, the growing interaction among people of all nations, spurred by cheaper and easier transportation, besides sophisticated communication technology, led many scholars to perceive a relative homogeneity between markets. According to Levitt, 'technology has been driving the world toward such commonality and the result is the emergence of global markets for standardized consumer products on a previously unimagined scale of magnitude'.[28] Marketing studies have highlighted the gains achievable through standardization, with economies of scale and the potential to enhance product quality.[29] Both of these were seen as significant advantages for Hollywood exports.[30] But standardization also has a major political and cultural effect, as pointed out by communications scholars of the imperialism school who warn of a resulting political domination and cultural homogenization.[31] As noted above, there is a notable correspondence between what some firms intended and what scholarly critics feared.

On the other hand, it seems that most contemporaneous marketers defend adaptation to the local market as a necessary step to satisfy what communications authors see as consumers' intrinsic need for cultural proximity elements in what the company offers customers/audiences.[32] Tamer Cavusgil suggested five stages of internationalization for companies: domestic marketing, pre-export, experimental involvement, active involvement and committed involvement.[33] Some Hollywood producers have remained at the level of experimental involvement, selling programming through middlemen or at meetings like NAPTE. Some Hollywood companies have become actively involved, systematically exploring a large number of foreign market opportunities, establishing buyer and legal requirements and locating local dealers. They abandon the middlemen, while expanding the volume of exports and new foreign markets. In the committed involvement stage, firms venture into other forms of involvement, such as local production via subsidiaries or joint ventures, significantly upping their commitments. This study looks at several global TV companies that took this step in satellite television in Latin America.

Most global firms do tend gradually to recognize a need to localize their global offerings to the culture of that market. Firms vary considerably, however, in their willingness to make such changes. It is cheaper, after all, simply to repackage and offer that which you already have available, whether that is feature films, news, entertainment series for television or music videos.

This study argues that global firms tend to have approached regional markets by making the most minimal adaptations they felt they could get away with. Since most audiences are more interested in cultural proximity, however, the result of minimal adaptation is also a minimal audience. In order to try to attract larger audiences, this study argues that global firms had to make increasingly larger adaptations to local cultures, reflecting the theories of cultural proximity and the predominance of cultural linguistic definition of markets.

Outside television networks at an early stage of involvement in the Latin American market tend to focus their efforts on the larger markets. They do not have a significant knowledge / previous experience of the market and usually export to a limited set of independent distributors in the largest markets without commitment of large resources. These networks may be following the competition and seeking strategic allies that will take the helm – and the risks. On the other hand, the experienced television networks expanding to Latin America with a strong commitment to this market will probably be less restricted in their country selection. They rely less on strategic alliances and invest heavily to supplant their offerings with locally produced fare.

The Latin American Context for Pay-TV Expansion in the 1990s

Initially, the 1990s seemed to be a good time for all kinds of global networks to expand into Latin America. Real wages, which had shrunk over the entire 'lost decade' of the 1980s, grew and consumers responded by unleashing a wave of pent-up demand in the marketplace. So the potential for consumption of pay-TV via satellite and cable seemed good.

In the 1990s, perhaps following Chile's lead, and under pressure from the USA, the World Bank and multinational creditors, most countries shifted towards a more deregulated, neoliberal model. Trade pacts, like NAFTA (Canada, USA and Mexico) and MERCOSUR (Argentina, Paraguay, Uruguay and Brazil), expanded, reducing restrictions on outside media. Many countries that had restricted satellite and cable TV began to let it expand. Furthermore, countries that had restricted foreign ownership of media and discouraged local joint ventures with foreign media firms began to reverse that trend.

Not all country markets in Latin America, however, looked attractive to outside firms. Even in the growth of the 1990s, the large discrepancies between the 'haves' and the 'have-nots' in Latin America continued. Between 1994 and the turn of the century,[34] the consumer market had grown by an astonishing 21 per cent – from

US$1,033.2 billion to $1,250.2 billion – but not everywhere. The seven largest economies in Latin America accounted for 93 per cent of that consumer market and, in spite of the 1995 market crash in Mexico, and continued problems and economic contraction in Venezuela, grew by 20 per cent over the same period.[35] Even more striking is the dominance of just three economies (out of eighteen major ones)[36] which, together, formed a consumer market of US$958.9 billion in 1997, or 77 per cent of the region's total consumer buying power: Argentina, Mexico and Brazil. Even with the collapse of Mexico and subsequent contraction in Argentina (the 'tequila effect'), total consumer buying power in Argentina, Mexico and Brazil grew by just under 20 per cent in the 1994–2000 period.

Brazil and Mexico are certainly the largest countries in the region, with vast territories and some of the largest and youngest populations in the world. UN data show that in area, Brazil is the world's fifth biggest country – larger than the continental United States – with bountiful natural resources. In population, it's number four world-wide, with nearly 170 million people; and its economy ranks among the top ten. In 1999, Brazil lured more foreign direct investment than any developing nation except China. It was a record US$31 billion from overseas to its factories, offices and other businesses; and economists have projected $28 billion more in 2000.[37]

It should be no wonder why the two pan-regional satellite networks operating in Latin America focused most of their resources on these two countries. Rupert Murdoch's Sky partnered with the largest media conglomerates in Mexico (Televisa) and Brazil (Globo) to create its direct-to-home digital television service. Hughes's DirecTV, in its turn, also ended up acquiring partners in these countries to be competitive in the largest markets in the region. An assortment of other variables, however, made Argentina and Chile just as interesting markets. Argentina's considerably smaller population enjoys a simple but effective commercial infrastructure, which allowed for higher literacy and consumption capacity (higher GNP/capita). Chile was an early champion of free markets and experienced tremendous growth and intensity in the past decade. Venezuela, on the other hand, has counted on oil exports to form a powerful class of consumers.

Within the specific television industry, the superior market potential of these countries comes out as the result of a more simplified rationale by global firms: 1) go after the largest countries; 2) check that they have a lot of TVs there; 3) make sure these TVs can be connected to a multi-channel system; 4) consider only those actually connected; and 5) verify how much money you can get out of these subscribers.

Brazil, Mexico and Argentina are indeed some of the largest countries in the region. They also present the largest number of TV households. The number of basic homes passed by wireline cable is also the largest there, as well as the proportion of multi-channel subscribers.[38] In the long run, the most profitable operations will also probably be in Brazil, Chile, Argentina and Mexico.

The smaller countries, however, can sometimes achieve higher penetration rates faster. Argentina, for example, is a medium-sized country with the highest cable penetration rate in the region (53 per cent of TV households) in the 1990s, while Brazil was expected to reach that rate in only fifteen years.[39]

Class Stratification and Cable/Satellite TV Markets

In most Latin American countries, the potential for most house-holds to buy satellite dishes, subscribe to cable TV, and pay anything extra for pay TV is severely limited by income distribution and social class stratification. (For example, in the Argentine economic crisis after 2001, quite a few Argentines dropped cable TV.) Consumers are limited by both economic capital (the ability to purchase access to the new television channels and systems) and by cultural capital (the ability to understand programming in foreign languages, limited knowledge of events covered in news and entertainment, limited awareness of what makes foreign jokes funny, etc.) as predicted by Bourdieu and applied to television in Latin America by Straubhaar.[40] While global media programmers and marketers may have been aware of the economic limits on potential subscribers, they seem initially to have missed the limits imposed by cultural capital on who would be interested enough in largely foreign content on pay TV to subscribe.

When marketers speak of social class in Latin America, they use a shorthand developed by national market researchers, which has spread to most of the region. The letters A, B, C, D and E are typically used to designate the household as upper-class (A) – the top 1 per cent to 5 per cent;[41] middle- to upper-class (B) – the next 10 to 20 per cent;[42] middle-class (C) – the next 30 to 50 per cent;[43] lower-class/

working poor/poverty (D), and subsistence or below poverty level (E) – combined to represent the remaining 30 to 50 per cent.[44]

In this measurement scale, Brazil had the largest concentration of the very attractive classes A and B by the turn of the century. Mexico had only 15 per cent as many as Brazil and Argentina only 10 per cent, while the remaining countries barely showed on the marketing radar. Indeed, most research shows that 80 to 90 per cent of multi-channel viewers in these countries are in A-B-C households, that is, the ones with purchasing power and also the education,[45] language ability and cultural knowledge to appreciate imported television channels.[46]

Levels of Market Commitment and Adaptation

The macroeconomic conditions of each country and the microeconomic status of their television industries presented here seem unanimously to point to Brazil, Argentina and Mexico as the markets with highest potential demand for American TV networks. Together with the second-level group, formed by Chile, Venezuela and Colombia, the 'Group of 6' have represented the truly attractive side of Latin America for foreign investors. According to the theories on the internationalization process of the firm, it should follow, therefore, that the least committed networks are operating actively only in these countries. The more committed ones, on the other hand, would be operating in many other countries, actively seeking several local companies and selling to a broader base of distributors.

Major Global Entrants into Latin America Competing with four large Latin American multimedia groups and six other significant local players, were some fifty US companies, as of 2000.[47] (Some companies have since dropped out of the market.) These companies seem to be agglomerated around a few American media giants as well: Time Warner (HBO, CNN, E!, TNT, Cartoon, Cinemax, Sony, AXN, Mundo, Warner), Discovery Communications (Animal Planet, People & Arts, Discovery Channel, Discovery Kids), News Corp (Canal Fox, Fox Kids, Fox Sports), Viacom (MTV, Nickelodeon, USA) and Disney (Disney Channel, ESPN). These are powerful multimedia conglomerates with global operations from which to draw expertise when faced with new challenges in Latin America.

The Time Warner strategy was to merge the former Turner global channels – CNN and TNT/Cartoon Channel – with their HBO International and Warner channels to make a four-pronged assault on the global market. Turner and Time Warner were both global television powers with the TNT/Cartoon Network and Warner channels, drawing upon their respective large libraries of cartoons and motion pictures. HBO International has already established itself as the leading subscription TV channel in the world; it has a family of pay channels and is available in over thirty-five countries. CNN International, a subsidiary of CNN, is also established as the premier global television news channel, beamed via ten satellites to over 200 nations and 90 million subscribers by 1994. The long-term goal for CNN International is to operate (or participate in joint ventures to establish) CNN channels in regional languages. CNN launched a Spanish-language service for Latin America in 1997, based in Atlanta.

Discovery's brand is now a popular commodity, present in CD-ROMs and websites, besides a chain of some 125 shops alongside a roster of television channels, including learning, travel, health, children and civilization. The BBC now owns a 50 per cent stake in all new Discovery channels outside the USA, including Animal Planet. The alliance has greatly spurred international growth, as Discovery celebrates more than ten years of branching into Europe, and five years into Latin America and Asia (see Table 10.1). Discovery has been particularly adept at targeting middle-class viewers in Latin America and elsewhere. Furthermore, its typical documentaries are more easily translated and dubbed than are many other kinds of content.

Australia-based News Corp owns almost 40 per cent of the European satellite service BSkyB and a similar service in Latin America, Sky Latin America. Sky Latin America is a partnership with two of the very largest regional broadcasters, TV Globo of Brazil and Televisa of Mexico. The Fox Channel is the primary asset of the global parent company, while the major partners contribute some degree of real localization inasmuch as they contribute original local material on some of their channels.

Viacom has targeted global growth, with a stated goal of earning 40 per cent of its revenues outside the United States. In the 1990s, Viacom was estimated to have invested between US$750 million and $1 billion in international expansion. Viacom's two main weapons are Nickelodeon and MTV. Nickelodeon has been a global powerhouse. MTV is the pre-eminent global music television channel, with MTV

TABLE 10.1 International satellite TV networks in Latin America, 2001

Network	Startup	Programming	Owners	Language	Uplink
Antena 3 International	Sep. 96	General entertainment	Antena 3, Multivision (Mex)	S	Mexico
BBC World	Aug. 96	News	BBC	E	Long Beach, CA
Bloomberg	Jul. 96	Business news	Michael Bloomberg	E	Long Beach, CA
The Box	Apr. 96	Music	CEA/The Box Worldwide	E/S	Buenos Aires, Argentina
Canal de las Estrellas	Sep. 91	General entertainment	Televisa	S	Mexico
Canal de Noticias NBC	Mar. 93	News	NBC	E, S	Charlotte, NC
Canal Fox	Aug. 93	General entertainment	News Corp	S, P, E	Atlanta, GA
Cartoon Network	Apr. 93	Kids	Time Warner/Turner	S, P, E	Atlanta, GA
CBS Telenoticias	Dec. 94	News	Viacom	S	Miami, FL
Cinecanal	Apr. 93	Movies	UIP, Fox, SACSA, Cablecinema	E/S	Atlanta, GA
Cinecanal 2	Oct. 96	Movies	UIP, Fox, SACSA, Cablecinema	E/S	Atlanta, GA
CineLatino	Dec. 94	Movies	Multivision (Mex)	S	Mexico
Cinemax	Dec. 93	Movies	Time Warner, Sony, Ole Comm.	S	Caracas, Venezuela
Cl@se	Jan. 97	Educational	Galaxy Latin America	S, P	Caracas, Venezuela
CNN International	Feb. 91	News	Time Warner/Turner	E	Atlanta, GA
CNN en Español	Mar. 97	News	Time Warner/Turner	S	Atlanta, GA
Country Music Television (CMT)	Apr. 95	Music	Westinghouse/CBS	S, P	Nashville, TN
Deutsche Welle	Nov. 92	News, documentaries	ARD	G/E/S	Cologne

Discovery Kids	Nov. 96	Kids	John Hendricks, Cox, TCI, Newhouse	S, E, P	Miami, FL
Discovery Latin America	Feb. 94	Documentaries	John Hendricks, Cox, TCI, Newhouse	S, P, E	Miami, FL
E! Entert. Television	Nov. 96	General entertainment	Comcast, Disney	E/S	Los Angeles, CA
ECO	1988	News	Televisa	S	Mexico
ESPN International	Mar. 89	Sports	Capital Cities, ABC	S, P, E	Bristol, CT
EWTN	Aug. 95	Religious	Eternal Word Network TV	S	Birmingham, Ala
Film & Arts	Apr. 96	Cultural, movies	Rainbow Programming Holdings	E/S, E/P	Miami, FL
Fox Kids	Nov. 96	Kids	News Corp	S, P, E	Atlanta, GA
Fox Sports Americas	Mar. 95	Sports	News Corp, Liberty Sports (TCI)	S, P	Denver, CO
GEMS	Apr. 93	Women's	Empresas 1–BC, Cox	S	Los Angeles, CA
Hallmark Entertainment Network	Nov. 95	General entertainment	Hallmark Entertainment de Mexico (franchise)	S	Miami, FL Mexico
HBO Olé	Oct. 91	Movies	Time Warner, Sony, Disney, Ole Comm.	E/S	Caracas, Venezuela
HBO Olé 2	Oct. 96	Movies	Time Warner, Sony, Disney, Ole Comm.	E/S	Caracas, Venezuela
Hispavision	Oct. 94	General entertainment	Television Espanola	S	Valencia, Spain
HTV	Aug. 95	Music	Robert Behar, Daniel Sawicki	S	Miami, FL
Infinito	Dec. 93	Documentaries	Imagen Satelital	S	Buenos Aires, Argentina
Inravision	N/A	Cultural	Colombia Government	S	Bogota, Colombia
Locomotion	Nov. 96	Kids	Cisneros TV Group, Hearst Corp.	S, P, E	Caracas, Venezuela

TABLE 10.1 International satellite TV networks in Latin America, 2001

Network	Startup	Programming	Owners	Language	Uplink
Multipremiere	Jul. 96	Movies	Multivision (Mexico)	E/S, E/P	Mexico
Mundo Ole	Nov. 96	Documentaries	HBO Ole Partners, Flextech	E/S	Caracas, Venezuela
MTV Latino	Oct. 93	Music	Viacom	S	New York, NY
Nickelodeon	Dec. 96	Kids	Viacom	S, P, E	New York
Playboy	Sep. 96	Erotica	Cisneros TV Group, Playboy	S, P, E	Long Beach, CA
RAI America	Oct. 92	General entertainment	RAI	I	Fucino, Italy
Ritmoson	Apr. 94	Music	Televisa	S	Mexico
Solo Tango	Jun. 95	Music	Imagen Satelital	S	Buenos Aires, Argentina
Sony Entertainment Television	Sep. 95	Series	Sony, HBO Ole Partners	S, P, E	Caracas, Venezuela
SUR	Apr. 92	General entertainment	Grupo Pantel	S	Lima, Peru
TeleHit	Aug. 93	Music	Televisa	S	Mexico
AXN (former TeleUno)	Mar. 93	Series	Spelling Satellite Networks	S, P	Mexico
Television Española (TVE)	Oct. 92	General entertainment	Television Espanola	S	Mexico
TNT Latin America	Jan. 91	General entertainment, movies	Time Warner/Turner	S, P, E	Atlanta, GA
TodoNoticias	Jun. 93	News	Artear (Clarin)	S	Buenos Aires, Argentina
The Travel Channel	Oct. 95	General entertainment, travel	Landmark Comm.	S, P, E	Atlanta, GA

Channel	Date	Type	Company	Languages	Location
TV5	Oct. 92	General entertainment	TV5-Europe, TV5-Quebec	F, S	Mexico
TVN Chile International (Canal 7)	Oct. 89	General entertainment	Television Nacional de Chile	S	Santiago, Chile
UCTV International (Canal 13)	Mar. 95	General entertainment	Univ. Catolica de Chile Corp. de TV	S	Santiago, Chile
USA	Apr. 94	General entertainment	Viacom, Universal	S, P	Buenos Aires, Argentina
Venus	Jan. 94	Erotica	Imagen Satelital	S	Buenos Aires, Argentina
Warner Channel (WBTV)	Sep. 95	General entertainment, family	Time Warner, HBO Ole Partners	S, P, E	Caracas, Venezuela
Weather Channel	Nov. 96	Weather	Landmark Comm.	S, P	Atlanta, GA
Worldnet/C-Span	1991	News	US Government	E/S	Washington, DC
ZAZ	Jul.96	Kids	Multivision	S	Mexico

Source: compiled by the authors from various sources. Languages: E (English); F (French); G (German); I (Italian); P (Portuguese); S (Spanish). Letters separated by forward slash indicate second audio programme.

Latin America and MTV Brasil, an early joint venture in Brazil with the dominant publishing company, Editora Abril.

DirecTV was the first major pay-TV operation in Latin America, extending the DirecTV brand of satellite television into the region, although the service was originally known as Galaxy Latin America. It was primarily owned by Hughes, which saw it as a logical extension of its satellite expertise. Like Sky Latin America, Hughes also developed this service with major Latin American partners, particularly the Abril Group and the Cisneros Group (Venezuela's largest conglomerate, owner of Venevision, one of the region's largest broadcast networks).

Disney has traditionally preferred to operate on its own, but CEO Michael Eisner has announced Disney's plans to expand aggressively overseas through joint ventures with local firms or other global players, or through further acquisitions. Disney's stated goal was to expand its non-US share of revenues from 23 per cent in 1995 to 50 per cent. Historically, Disney has been strong in entertainment and animation, two areas that do well in the global market. For the most part, Disney's success has been restricted to English-language channels in North America, Britain and Australia. Disney's absence has permitted the children's channels of News Corporation, Time Warner and especially Viacom to dominate the lucrative global market. Disney launched a Chinese-language Disney Channel based in Taiwan in 1995, and subsequently launched channels in France and the Middle East. In 1999, it also launched the Disney Channel in Latin America. With the purchase of ABC's ESPN, the television sports network, Disney has possession of the unquestioned global leader in sports. It was severely beaten by the competition, however, and today Disney relies more heavily on its share of E! Entertainment Latin America to mark its presence.

These conglomerates are directly or indirectly involved in the majority of American television networks currently reaching Latin America, and their wealth of experience in launching international operations is well known. It is worth noting, however, that some of the networks being launched by these conglomerates in Latin America constitute new product lines, not in existence anywhere else. In this sense, it could be said that the region is being used as a test market for some new concepts. A good example is the AXN Channel (focused on US action-adventure series), created by Sony after acquiring the

Teleuno operations in 1997, and launched in India and Spain the following year. While experience in internationally launching other product lines remains useful for these tests, the process in place is significantly different from a simple transportation of well-established networks. Sony demonstrated considerable commitment in launching a brand-new network first in Latin America.

On the other side of the spectrum, it is also important to observe that a few minor players are equally venturing into the region, with much less of a global operation to base their strategies. Gaylord, for example, launched the Country Music Television in Brazil[48] and Solo Tango in Argentina, despite comparatively much less previous experience in launching channels abroad. The Rainbow Media Holding followed suit with Film & Arts and Landmark Communications with its weather channels. It seems that these channels, however, have not always been as successful in getting there first and securing distribution deals with some of the major systems in each market. None of them figured in the top fifteen networks as of 1999 and most have failed already. They may have been just as (or more) committed to the region, but their lesser experience and resources put them at a disadvantage, reflected in their usually late entry in the market and consequential earlier stage in the internationalization process they are currently in.

Despite the size of these companies, it is interesting to note that they seem to have followed distinct modes of entry in Latin America. While most of the major Hollywood studios have secured a foothold in the region, some have just extended their international operations to include a Latin American office, with significantly less commitment than others, which have entered a variety of strategic alliances to offer more channels. The following sections compare those channels that have made minimal adaptation versus more extensive localization.

Minimal Adaptation A classic example of offering a standard cultural product across markets is the marketing of certain pay-TV channels in Latin America. While the number of interested viewers in each country is generally low, the sum of these small groups across the region provides the necessary mass of consumers to pay for broadcasting costs. And, since these people share common traits that led them to become a captive audience, it only makes sense to adopt a single, common marketing strategy to lure them.

The outside television networks penetrating Latin American markets only via one of the two pan-regional direct-to-home (DTH) satellite systems demonstrate lesser commitment than those engaged in multi-market cable affiliate relationship building. Both DirecTV and Sky Latin America maintain headquarters in Florida (USA) and offer a one-stop gateway to the region. Their American managers (in some cases US Hispanics) pose no cultural challenges and their superior channel capacity allows them to be more relaxed in the selection of networks to carry. In other words, negotiating with these multi-channel carriers presents little stretch to an American network's domestic operation.

Nevertheless, exactly because of such easiness, obtaining carriage agreement with one or both of these DTH systems can be considered a benchmark for a minimum commitment level, below which networks would be less-than-mature international players at this point. In this sense, an analysis of the line-up of these DTH operations offers a first cut to the list of committed networks.[49]

The worst case is Playboy, which really sold its international operations to Venezuelan Cisneros Group. Universal has joined the others, with a minor share of some movie channels (Telecine and LAPTV's four channels), and by opening an office to manage the two feeds of its USA Channel (now under new management). MGM has also invested in LAPTV and obtained financial support from United Global Com to operate in the region. Until the end of 1999, however, MGM Latin America operations consisted of some office space and a small staff within Globecast broadcast facilities in Miami, where it produced the shows for Casa Club and managed the Globecast feeds for MGM in Spanish and MGM Gold for Brazil. Interestingly, the less-than-full commitment by these enterprises may be reflected in their limited distribution.

Expanded Commitment Some increasingly higher levels of commitment would thus be attached next to those networks also pursuing deals with individual cable systems, and doing so not only in the major markets identified, but also in others as well.[50] An analysis of the channel line-up of key multiple systems operators (MSOs) in the six largest Latin American markets suggests some conclusion. Some networks, such as Discovery and MTV, were very visible for their widespread presence. Others such as Bloomberg, The Box, GEMS,

MGM, Playboy or TV Guide have a limited distribution in Latin America.

There are two other reasonable indicators of commitment that should be considered. While the total number of subscribers does not necessarily reflect the intensity of commitment by a network,[51] it could be construed as an indirect indication of presence in the overall region. The same few networks enjoy a larger number of viewers than the rest of the group. And, finally, it is important that some networks have developed distinct satellite transmission feeds to tailor their product to one or a combination of markets. This is particularly relevant in the case of Brazil, the only Portuguese-language market in the region, requiring Portuguese to replace Spanish in the audio/subtitles. The list of networks committed enough to their internationalization process in Latin America to create or adapt new networks for the region comes down to the following handful: Animal Planet, AXN, Cartoon Network, CNN International, CNN en Español, Discovery Channel, Discovery Kids, E! Entertainment, ESPN, Film & Arts, Canal Fox, Fox Kids, Fox Sports, Hallmark, HBO Olé, MTV, Mundo, Nickelodeon, People & Arts, Sony Entertainment, TNT and Warner.

Some studios, like Disney, Viacom's Paramount and Twentieth Century-Fox have followed similar strategies of hedging their bets by acquiring minor participations in various holdings, but have at the same time invested with full force on their own few networks. Disney, for example, maintained some minor shares in A&E Latin operations and the HBO Latin America Group, while its Hearst-supported ESPN branch launched three channels and co-founded a fourth in Brazil. Besides being a pioneer in Latin America, ESPN International has been a winner in distribution and revenues for many years now. After a trial run with a mock-up premium channel inside DirecTV's weekend line-up, Disney also moved to launch its own signature network, featuring Mickey and all the characters, who traditionally attract more Brazilians and Hispanics to its theme parks than any other nationality. Viacom's Paramount also has some shares of LAPTV's channels and its MTV branch has launched three networks, besides acquiring MTV Brasil. The MTV offices in Miami are staffed to support the equally successful Nickelodeon operations, and The Box later joined the roster, despite still having difficulties in obtaining larger distribution agreements. Fox, in its turn, has not only got some shares of LAPTV and Brazil's Telecine, but also launched four channels with minor financial support by Saban Entertainment Studio and invest-ment giant Liberty Media. Except for the TV Guide network, which was launched later, the Fox channels (Canal Fox, Fox Kids and Fox Sports) enjoy great success, with large distribution and revenues.

Warner and Sony have developed the most complex web of stra-tegic alliances. The HBO Latin America holding formed by these studios along with Disney and others is shared by Olé Communica-tions, which is financially controlled by Venezuelan group Omnivision and gathers the largest number of networks in Latin America. While each one has a different ownership share composition, these sixteen networks are all likely to be offered in one sales meeting to any local operator. It is no wonder that half of the best-distributed channels in the region belong to this holding company. In fact, it is important to highlight the importance of such holding companies in the Latin American pay-television industry.

The Logic of Adaptation and Localization Even though a strong case can be made for placing emphasis on reduced costs and competitive prices through standardization, 'lower costs are not the primary objective of firms; their primary objective is increased profitability'.[52] To the extent that standardization does not necessarily guarantee increased profitability, many other researchers tend to present adap-tation strategies not as a fallback from circumstances precluding standardization, but as a desirable and rather common goal of many firms and industries.[53]

The barriers to standardization may be even higher in the Latin American pay-TV business, which does not present any of the characteristics Cavusgil believes lead to standardization strat-egies.[54] The satellite and cable-based pay-TV industry *is* technology-intensive; the product *is* culture-specific; competition *is* intense; and the enterprises enjoy worldwide presence. Furthermore, it presents several joint ventures between firms in both developed and developing countries – a strategic alliance that requires bigger compromises and decentralization to work well.

One key issue in firms expanding commitment to Latin American operation is hiring national and regional staff. Firms find that they need more and more expertise on the region, although they also need people who can work within American-style corporate environments.

With an eye on the bottom line, many networks have promoted

some Latin-specific productions amid their lineups and geared up to increase the advertising time and sales infrastructure over time. The fashionably late realization that Brazil constitutes a significantly distinct market from the rest of Latin America has also forced a few operations to segment their efforts into various arenas: one for Brazil and others for the clustered countries, such as one for Mexico/Colombia/Venezuela and Central America and another for Argentina and the Southern Cone. For example, ESPN Sur is a dedicated Spanish feed serving all the region except Brazil and Mexico since December 1997. ESPN Sur has offices in Buenos Aires, where most of programming is generated, such as national polo, rugby, volleyball and basketball.[55] The Warner Channel has four feeds: West, South, East and Brazil.

These kinds of expansions and changes represent slow, sometimes even begrudged (given the cost of localization and separate programme feeds), but growing awareness by global managers and programmers that localization in cultural and linguistic terms will be necessary.

Expanded Commitment Some increasingly higher levels of commitment would thus be attached next to those networks also pursuing deals with individual cable systems, and doing so not only in the major markets identified, but also in others. Along with ESPN, the HBO Olé channels have figured in the top of the list for subscriber numbers. But the HBO operation seems to have committed a lot more resources to the region. Instead of a simple departmental unit, a completely separate company was formed, after striking alliances with Disney, Sony and various Latin partners. Moving away from the New York offices of Home Box Office Networks and its international distribution arm – HBO International – the HBO Latin America Group has set up headquarters in Caracas, Venezuela, besides some other regional headquarters in Mexico, Guatemala and Argentina. With the end of an ill-fated alliance with Editora Abril in Brazil, it has also moved to Miami, where it is likely eventually to roll back all its offices. The entire operation displays a significant participation of Hispanic professionals and, in particular, Venezuelan representatives, as the holding company is financially controlled by Venezuelan Olé Communications.

Besides adopting strategies of multiple regional feeds to serve various groups of markets, and time multiplexing, the HBO Latin

America holding commercializes many different networks: HBO Olé (East and West), HBO Olé 2, Cinemax (East and West), Cinemax 2, Mundo Olé, Mundo Brasil, Sony Entertainment Television (various feeds), AXN Channel, the History, the Warner Channel and E! Entertainment Television.

Nevertheless, one of the things that has challenged even relatively extensive localization, such as that by HBO, is the need to adapt further to capture lower-class viewers. HBO's networks complement each other. For instance, WB targets younger audiences not served by HBO's R-rated movies, which in turn are generally promoted by E! Entertainment news. Nevertheless, HBO's rigid commercialization policies always pushed for bundle sales, particularly after the creation of a premium package (HBO, HBO2 and Cinemax). This has made it difficult for the conglomerate to keep pace with the MSOs' strategies of targeting C social class groups with channels that are necessarily dubbed and with greater content variety, including more local content. The HBO Group has only later moved to offer the Warner Channel (which is 70 per cent dubbed in Portuguese)[56] as an individual channel for the C class in Brazil, in recognition that social classes A and B prefer Sony and E! channels.[57] Similarly, HBO Brazilian viewers are between eighteen and forty-five years old, belong to social classes A and B and prefer subtitling to dubbing.[58]

Confronting the Audience Realities of Social Class and Cultural Proximity

One of the most severe challenges for almost all imported channels in Latin America has been to get away from offering imported content that largely appeals to classes A and B, which comprise at most 15 per cent of the population. A survey conducted in São Paulo by the authors in 1989 showed that among classes C-D-E (over 80 per cent of the population), far fewer people were interested in the kinds of imported programming featured on these channels: imported feature films, American series, imported music videos, imported US and Japanese cartoons, international sports and international news. A series of in-depth interviews conducted by the authors from 1989–2000 confirms that this pattern of low interest in cable programming outside classes A-B continues throughout 2000.

Both past and current ratings research by Latin American firms tend to show the same pattern. The IBOPE 2000 ratings report indicated that 60 per cent of viewers remember only eight channels: AXN, Cartoon, Discovery, Fox, Sony, TNT, Warner and MTV. Nearly all those identified by the survey were from classes A-B. In fact, since the overall economic decline that began in many countries around 2000, cable/satellite pay-TV subscribers have dropped off, particularly among lower-class and working-class households, as economic capital among potential subscribers has declined (as reflected in 2002–03 ratings research).

Even worse for international channels, many of those even in classes A-B do not subscribe. For example, slightly fewer than 5 per cent of Brazilian households subscribe, well under the 15 per cent potential of classes A and B. The series of interviews conducted by the authors 1989–2000 show that even among classes A-B, many viewers prefer national programming. Quite a few who have the economic capital to subscribe do not have the cultural capital, including language ability and knowledge of US affairs, to enjoy the programming sufficiently to make it worth the marginal cost to them. Some who might prefer a certain small dose of international programming do not see it as worthwhile, given other uses for short funds. This is particularly true among classes B and C, for whom subscribing to cable probably means sacrificing something else.

A study among class C and D cable subscribers in a Rio *favela* (slum), Rocinha, showed considerable churn as people subscribed out of curiosity, particularly to cut-rate pirate operations, but often discontinued subscriptions when money was low or when they simply found that they did not watch that often. The study found that the main channels that held audience interest were movies and cartoons, which kept young children occupied.[59]

Competition with Local Powers

While many networks seem to have entered Latin America simply to follow – or pre-empt – their global competitors,[60] they have also found out that the power of local media conglomerates was not to be underestimated. The local competition includes some giant broadcast oligopolies, such as Globo of Brazil, Televisa of Mexico and Venevisión (Cisneros) of Venezuela, that produce original local material for most of their broadcast day. It also includes unexpected competition from the so-called 'boutique' channels developed by and for the local and national cable systems.

The Cisneros Group of companies (CG) has grown today to be the largest privately owned business in Venezuela and one of Latin America's top media companies. This family-led group of some seventy different companies is present in thirty-nine countries, including Argentina, Brazil, Chile, Mexico, Venezuela, Portugal and Spain. The core enterprises include Venevisión, Big Show Productions, Caribbean Communications Network, Chilevisión and DirecTV Latin America (see Table 10.1). In 1996, CG announced the formation of the Cisneros Television Group (CTG), headquartered in Florida, now merged into Claxson, and operating in the USA, Europe and Latin America. It started with three original channels distributed via its DTH platform: Locomotion (children), Playboy and Adultvision; the latter two a result of a US$80 million acquisition of an 80.1 per cent stake in Playboy International, which distributes the channels in Latin America, Japan and the UK.

Claxson currently broadcasts a total of twelve channels to Latin America and another six solely to the Southern Cone countries.[61] The 90 per cent acquisition of Argentine programmer Imagen Satelital in 1996 added cheaply produced content and six key Argentine channels: Space, I-Sat, Uniseries, Jupiter Comic, Infinito and Venus. In 1999, CTG continued its expansion by adding the Latin music networks MuchMusic in January and HTV in March.

TV Globo covers 99.84 per cent of Brazil with 113 broadcast and affiliate stations that sustain a 55–74 per cent audience share and absorb 75 per cent of all advertising revenues. It produces a total of 4,420 hours a year of programming exported to 130 countries, ranking Globo as the world's largest television programme producer. In pay-TV, Globo's owned or franchised MSOs accounted for 61 per cent of Brazil's total 3 million subscribers as of March 2000.[62] By 2003, however, foreign loans to build that cable infrastructure had almost brought the Globo Group to the edge of insolvency, despite healthy profits in most aspects of its business (broadcast television, newspapers, magazines, music and radio).

Globosat is the branch responsible for producing and commercializing eighteen cable channels (four of which are dedicated to Portugal), reaching 2 million subscribing households, or 70 per cent of the Brazilian territory through exclusive NET distribution. Taking full advantage of the synergy with its regular broadcasting departments and talents, Globosat makes use of cross-platform promotions: a single ad piece can run with discounts on Globo's newspapers, magazines, broadcasting and cable transmissions. The well-respected anchors of its open-TV news bulletins also appear on Globo News cable channel, sports acquired can be seen partly for free, partly on cable's Sportv. Documentary channel GNT has ratings comparable with Discovery's and Telecine's five outlets are strong competitors to HBO in Brazil. Multishow, USA Network, Canal Brasil, Shoptime and Futura (educational) complement the Globosat lineup.

Televisa is the largest Spanish-language television company in the world. But the US$1.8 billion Mexican media conglomerate of today is quite different from the empire built by Emilio Azcarraga Milmo since the 1950s. In a time when Mexicans had no option but to watch one of Emilio's four channels, the company developed a loyal following for its cheap soap operas and theatre-style variety shows.[63] Channel 2 ('Canal de las Estrellas') presented the largest variety in coverage; Channel 4 focused on news; Channel 5 targeted young audiences with children programming and series; and Channel 9 was born as a cultural outlet for the families. By the time state networks and other private television systems like TV Azteca appeared, Televisa had already established a strong foothold in Mexican life, exerting heavy political influence and expanding to a wide variety of media, such as newspapers, magazines, billboards, music, movies and sports. And it did not limit itself to Mexico, making early inroads into the US Hispanic market through Univision, Galavision and other ventures.[64] By 1996, the company had passed the US$1 million mark of programming export revenues from markets that included Spain and many other Spanish-speaking countries.

Televisa's SKY Mexico is a leader in DTH and Cablevision new broadband strategies are attracting new subscribers after years of disregard by the corporation. In the programming arm, VISAT is responsible for eleven channels: ECO (news), TeleHit, Bandamax, Ritmoson (music), Canal de las Estrellas, Galavision, Unicable (variety), Telenovelas (soap operas), de Pelicula, Cinema Golden Choice 1 and 2 (movies). Televisa channels still command most of the viewership in Mexico and thus most of the advertising dollars.

Local original cable channels are often developed to suit local tastes (national/metropolitan news channels, or vintage national movies, for instance) and are seldom seen outside the country. These should not be regarded as just curiosities, however, because their creation and continued existence reflect consumer demand for certain types of programming not offered by the market leaders. In fact, some of these boutique channels are surprisingly popular. A case in point is Cinema Golden Choice, featuring vintage Mexican movies.[65] In this sense, the American networks may be just competing among themselves for the remainder of the broadband not already taken by local players. Moreover, if the foreign channels can benefit from large international audiences to subsidize their products, the formula is also within the reach of Latin American conglomerates. Mexican producers take aim at the large and rich Hispanic audiences in the USA and Spain, while Brazilian Globosat programmer already markets its shows to some 600,000 extra subscribers in Portugal.

These Latin groups undoubtedly present a superior knowledge of their markets and cultures. They enjoy tremendous brand recognition and loyalty, having demonstrated their ability to be strong players in the pan-regional pay-TV industry. Their main shortcoming, however, has traditionally been in the financial arena. Besides being attached to weaker domestic economies (in comparison with the American networks), they have had many more difficulties in capturing the required investments in the open markets. In 1998, even the giant Globo had to fire some 500 employees after its cable systems incurred losses such as US$28 million in 1995 and US$13 million in 1996.[66] Even more severe losses since 2000 have necessitated even more cuts at Globo, which is suffering the effects of going into debt to finance cable expansion in the late 1990s.

Accept Your Niche?

An apparent general consensus among pay-TV professionals is that sports, movies and sex constitute the tripod upon which the industry rests. Even in these kinds of niches, however, various predicaments can be found. A good example is the acute competition in Latin American sports programming. The traditional leader in this segment had been ESPN, but Fox Sports caught up to it, and PSN is come and gone. None of them, however, has been well positioned to offer coverage of Latin America's favourite sport: football. As a result, a smaller niche has to be found within the sports niche itself. ESPN held the title of largest pan-regional programmer in Latin America for many years (Discovery Channel surpassed it in late 1999), with an incredible 95 per cent penetration of all the multi-channel universe.[67] Nevertheless, ESPN has never positioned itself as a Latin American sports channel, but rather an international channel offering all US sports in addition to some local fare. As a result, it was forced to scale back operations recently and even merge with competitors in key markets such as Brazil.

Even in sports, national broadcasters and national pay-TV operations seem to have advantages. In Brazil, Globosat has practically monopolized the football transmissions on pay-TV. First, it closed a millionaire deal with FIFA to secure exclusivity of the tournaments promoted by the international organization, including the coveted World Cup. In mid-1999, Globo closed a deal with the so-called Clube dos 13, which actually gathers sixteen of the top football teams in Brazil. In April 2000, Globo's DTH operation – Sky – further increased the group's football supremacy by closing an exclusivity deal with the now defunct PSN (Pan-American Sports Network), which had more than 60 per cent of its lineup dedicated to football.

If asked, most pay-TV subscribers seem to respond that the main reason they subscribed to any multi-channel system was to have more movies.[68] It is no surprise that most basic channels also reserve some portion of their prime time for this genre. WB, Sony, Fox, MGM, TNT and USA Networks are all competitors in this segment, along with HBO and Cinemax.

Again, however, the movie niche is not a given advantage for global groups. After TVA (Editora Abril) added HBO to its systems in 1994, Brazilian Globosat programmer launched its Telecine channel. While the impression is that HBO brings more favourite movies, the multiplex Telecine (1 to 5) presents a significant local challenge. As, it seems, already typical for Globo enterprises, it is slow to the market, but it maintains more independence from the foreign partners, which ultimately may produce a better fit to Brazilian demand. Rather than negotiate with HBO, which intermediates the distribution of movies from Hollywood studios, Globosat went directly to the font and associated itself with the seven top movie studios in Hollywood: Warner, Columbia, Universal, Paramount, Fox, MGM/UA and Disney. Since most of these studios now own competing networks of their own, Globosat has also distinguished itself from HBO by adding European fare as well as a recent channel for national cinema.

The news genre represents an added value to the typical class A-B Latin American multi-channel subscriber, who likes to be in touch with the rest of the world. Without a doubt, CNN has a strong position in the region, stemming from the time when it was not only alone in the market, but mostly free. It ended 1998 with some 7.5 million subscribers after losing a significant parcel to its sister operation, CNN en Español, launched in 1997.[69] Regional competition against CNN, Bloomberg or the BBC has been difficult. ECONews and Telenoticias in Spanish failed after several years. But some national satellite news channels, like Globonews, have done moderately well.

Kids' networks are probably actually the most dependable for global or outside operations. Overall, the Cartoon Network is the most successful network in the region. It ranks first among all cable networks in all genres and its increasing audience share has attracted advertisers, making it also one of the most lucrative in Latin America.[70] Its strongest competitors are Warner Bros (with 8.3 million subscribers),[71] Fox Kids and Discovery Kids (both trailing with 7.1 million) and Nickelodeon (with 6.5 million). This is a difficult genre for national competition, since cartoons are very expensive to produce and easy to dub into other languages.

Music shows a complex situation of both global interest value and strong national and regional competition. The Latin music industry is one of the strongest in the world and all competitors in this genre have to pay attention to local fare. For example, the Brazilian music industry is the sixth largest in the world and above 75 per cent of recorded music sales in Brazil are for local artists.[72] MTV is certainly a top-of-mind brand in this genre, where some eleven programmers compete in Latin America. It is the most viewed music channel and the most active one in all markets, with multiple feeds, local productions and strategic associations to develop various promotional activities in the region. Its positioning of rock for youngsters also sets it apart from competitors such as Claxson's HTV and MuchMusic, which are targeted to adult Hispanics with local rhythms, such as salsa, rumba, merengue, cumba and balada. HTV is one of Claxson's channels with the largest distribution, reaching over 6 million subscribers in 1999. It is among the top five music channels in Argentina, but it does not seem to present a strong attraction to Brazilians,[73] who are not traditionally in tune with Hispanic rhythms and tend to prefer more American or European fare. MuchMusic is an Argentine network, with some 3.2 million subscribers in that country.[74]

Conclusion

The observed strategies taken by companies in adapting satellite/cable television programming offered to audience demands seem to support communication models that indicate a consumer preference for cultural products closer to viewers' own cultural backgrounds. Straubhaar's cultural proximity model fits well with the study's findings.[75] While Brazilians seemed to be culturally closer to the United States than to their Latin neighbours, and Argentines are significantly different from Mexicans, a general demand for some level of adaptation to local or national culture was evident in all cases studied. Audiences want networks to talk in their languages, focus on the genres they prefer, show known names (local stars), and demonstrate interest for their market idiosyncrasies.

The comparison of global television channels entering Latin America showed that relatively few were moving quickly enough towards genuine localization to break away from an audience primarily composed of the relatively globalized elite who comprise classes A and B. Global companies are finding profitable niche markets among those groups, such as the 'Sony-maniacs' in Brazil who absolutely love watching US sitcoms on the Sony Channel, or fans of US action series who watch AXN. Those viewers, however, are far from the mainstream of the Latin American audience, which continues to watch national or intra-regional *telenovelas* (prime-time serials), variety shows, talkshows, game shows, reality shows, comedies, sports and music, as reflected in ratings data from across Latin America.

Cable and satellite services seem to become more popular in those areas where significant local programming is featured, either on local channels or on channels contributed to regional pay services by local partners. TV Globo and Televisa both offer national cinema channels, for example. Those actually compete with specific global channels, however, even though they might also encourage more nationally oriented viewers to sign up for the overall pay-TV packages that carry national, regional and global channels. While this might help Murdoch consolidate his Sky Latin America network by bringing in more subscribers, it might also provide more competition to the non-local channels that Sky predominantly carries.

Global pay-TV networks dominate some niches. Many pay-TV professionals think that sports, movies and sex constitute the base upon which the industry rests. Kids' cartoon programming and middle-class family documentaries, however, actually seem to have broader audience strength and fewer local competitors, whereas sports channel programming is very crowded and still predominantly national.

Seen from the audience perspective, cable and satellite TV, at least the pay-TV services offered by global media firms, have evolved to serve a highly segmented audience. Some in the global elite want global news, like CNN. Some want global sports. Relatively more want global music, preferably interspersed with national and regional music. An emerging upper middle and middle class seems perhaps most interested in documentaries and cartoons for themselves and their children.

Overall, localization has been limited among the channels that belong to global firms. Few have ventured beyond getting channels into languages or language variations that fit geographic regions within Latin America, such as HBO Olé or CNN en Español. Some have created local segments within their channels, a few documentaries for Discovery, a few cartoons, more music videos. Most genuine localization, however, is really a process of glocalization: the adaptation of global formulas by national or regional conglomerates. By far the most localized cable and satellite channels are those created by Globo, Televisa or Cisneros. They have created local news channels, movie channels and music channels that are now carried by regional pay-TV networks (Sky Latin America, DirecTV Latin America) in which they are partners. Those and other local channels are also carried by local cable systems. As cable penetration grows more massive, as in Argentina, the number of local channels grows, too. And vice-versa, if the major systems want to grow their audiences, they will have to increase the number of locally produced channels they carry.

Notes

1. This author acted as a participant observer in this study, working at DirecTV Latin America and establishing executive contact with many industry players in California and Florida over a four-year period, now working at Sony Pictures International.

2. Joseph Straubhaar, 'Beyond Media Imperialism: Asymmetrical Interdependence and Culture Proximity', *Critical Studies in Mass Communication*, 8(1) (1991), pp. 39–59.

3. Herbert Schiller, 'Not Yet the Post-imperialist Era', *Critical Studies in Mass Communication*, 8(1) (1991), pp. 13–28.

4. Joseph Straubhaar, 'Class, Genre and Regionalization of the Television Market in Latin America', *Journal of Communication*, 41(1) (1991), pp. 53–69; John Sinclair, Elizabeth Jacka and Stuart Cunningham, 'Peripheral Vision', in John Sinclair, Elizabeth Jacka and Stuart Cunningham (eds), *New Patterns in Global Television: Peripheral Vision* (Oxford: Oxford University Press, 1996), pp. 1–31; John Sinclair, *Latin American Television: A Global View* (Oxford: Oxford University Press, 1999).

5. Immanuel Wallerstein, *The Capitalist World Economy* (Cambridge: Cambridge University Press, 1979).

6. Sinclair, *Latin American Television*.

7. Joseph Straubhaar, Consuelo Campbell et al., 'The Emergence of a Latin American Market for Television Programs', paper presented to the International Communication Association Conference (Miami, 1992).

8. Herbert Schiller, *Mass Communications and American Empire* (New York: Empire, 1969).

9. Thomas McPhail, *Electronic Colonialism* (Newbury Park, CA: Sage, 1989).

10. Kaarle Nordenstreng and Tapio Varis, *Television Traffic: One-Way Street* (Paris: UNESCO, 1974).

11. McPhail, *Electronic Colonialism*.

12. Armand Mattelart and Hector Schmucler, *Communication and Information Technologies: Freedom of Choice for Latin America?* (Norwood, NJ: Ablex, 1985).

13. Joseph Straubhaar, *The Transformation of Cultural Dependency: The Decline of American Influence on the Brazilian Television Industry*, unpublished PhD dissertation (Fletcher School of Law and Diplomacy, Tufts University, 1981); Straubhaar, 'The Development of the Telenovela as the Paramount Form of Popular Culture in Brazil', *Studies in Latin American Popular Culture*, 1 (1982), pp. 138–50.

14. Livia Antola and Everett Rogers, 'Television Flows in Latin America', *Communication Research*, 11(2) (1984), pp. 183–202; Everett Rogers and Livia Antola, 'Telenovelas: A Latin American Success Story', *Journal of Communication*, 35(4) (1985), pp. 24–35.

15. John Tomlinson, *Cultural Imperialism: A Critical Introduction* (London: Continuum, 1991), p. 173.

16. James Curran, 'The New Revisionism in Mass Communication Research: A Reappraisal', *European Journal of Communication*, 5(2–3) (1990), pp. 135–64.

17. Colin Hoskins and Rolf Mirus, 'Reasons for the US Dominance of the International Trade in Television Programmes', *Media, Culture and Society*, 10(4) (1988), pp. 499–515.

18. Joseph Straubhaar, 'Beyond Media Imperialism', p. 15.

19. Antola and Rogers, 'Television Flows in Latin America'.

20. Straubhaar, 'Class, Genre and Regionalization of the Television Market in Latin America'.

21. Kenton Wilkinson, *Where Culture, Language and Communication Converge: The Latin-American Cultural Linguistic Market*, unpublished dissertation (University of Texas at Austin, 1995); Sinclair, Jacka and Cunningham, *New Patterns in Global Television*.

22. Sinclair, Jacka and Cunningham, 'Peripheral Vision', in Sinclair, Jacka and Cunningham (eds), *New Patterns in Global Television*, p. 2.

23. Roland Robertson, 'Globalization: Time-Space and Homogeneity-Heterogeneity', in Mike Featherstone, Scott Lash and Roland Robertson (eds), *Global Modernities* (Thousand Oaks, CA: Sage, 1995), pp. 25–44.

24. Néstor García Canclini, 'Culture and Power: The State of Research', *Media, Culture and Society*, 10(4) (1988), pp. 467–97.

25. Technically satellites have specific beams that are only large enough to cover regions or sub-regions. For market targeting reasons, satellite beams are usually contoured even more narrowly to countries or groups of countries.

26. Luiz G. Duarte, *Due South: American Television Ventures into Latin America*, unpublished PhD dissertation (Michigan State University, 2001).

27. Theodore Levitt, 'The Globalization of Markets', *Harvard Business Review*, 61 (May–June 1983), pp. 92–102.

28. Ibid., p. 92.

29. Michael Porter, *Competitive Strategy* (New York: Free Press, 1980); G. S. Yip, 'Global Strategy … In a World of Nations?', *Sloan Management Review* (Fall 1989), pp. 29–41.

30. Richard Collins, 'Wall-to-wall Dallas? The US–UK Trade in Television', *Screen* (May–August 1986), pp. 66–77.

31. Schiller, *Mass Communications and American Empire*.

32. Tamer Cavusgil, 'On the Internationalization Process of Firms', *European Research*, November 1980, pp. 273–81; Straubhaar, 'Beyond Media Imperialism'.

33. Cavusgil, 'On the Internationalization Process of Firms'.

34. The year Strategy Research Corporation (SRC) began tracking con-

sumer buying power in Latin America. SRC, now a Synovate company, is a full-service market research company serving the Americas and the Caribbean. Established in 1971, SRC has conducted over 7,000 studies, used by more than 1,500 multinationals.

35. J. A. Holcombe and A. Chiri, *Latin American Market Planning Report* (Miami, FL: Strategy Research Corporation, 1998).

36. (Argentina, Bolivia, Brazil, Chile, Colombia, Costa Rica, Dominican Republic, Ecuador, El Salvador, Guatemala, Honduras, Mexico, Nicaragua, Panama, Paraguay, Peru, Uruguay and Venezuela.

37. D. Hemlock, 'Brazil Soaring as a Trade Partner', *Sun Sentinel*, 16 July 2000, cover page.

38. Duarte, *Due South*.

39. Paul Kagan, *Kagan's Latin American Cable/Pay TV* (Carmel, CA: Kagan World Media, 1998).

40. Pierre Bourdieu, *Distinction: A Social Critique of the Judgment of Taste* (Cambridge, MA: Harvard University Press, 1984); Joseph Straubhaar, 'Choosing National TV: Cultural Capital, Language, and Cultural Proximity in Brazil', in Michael Elasmar (ed.), *The Impact of International Television: A Paradigm Shift* (Marwah, NJ: Lawrence Earlbaum, 2003).

41. The 'A' group consists of medium-sized business owners, high-level managers in large corporations, and professionals. Most have attained a college and postgraduate level of education, often in the USA or abroad. As a group, they control much of the means of production and wealth within a given country or market. They travel and vacation abroad frequently both with and without their families. Within their homes you will typically find two cars, three colour television sets with VCRs, a personal computer (between 50 per cent and 60 per cent in metropolitan areas), air conditioners, independent freezers and microwave ovens.

42. This upper-middle-class group aspires to join the SES 'A' class. They are typically employed as professionals, middle managers, small business owners with five or fewer employees, or teachers. This stratum has also benefited from recent economic trends – especially middle managers for businesses forced to go 'global'. They have completed the minimum of a high school education; most have a college education from a local institution. In their homes you will typically find one car, one or two colour TVs with VCRs, a microwave oven and perhaps a domestic maid whom they employ on a part-time basis. SES B households are rarely restricted in their purchase of goods and services, and are able to buy almost any brand of goods or service.

43. They are typically employed as small business owners without employees, skilled labourers such as chauffeurs and mechanics, and seamstresses. Most have completed primary school, some have a high school education. In their homes you will typically find one vehicle, although about 40 per cent do not own a car. Most have one TV, and about one-third have VCRs. They do not employ domestic help. This group is often referred to as Latin America's

'emerging middle classes'; however, they are also the most vulnerable to economic downturns, shocks and recessions. As a consumer segment, they are often restricted in the goods and services they can purchase, as well as the brands they are able to purchase.

44. Class 'D' (30 per cent) refers to the working poor, while 'E' (20 per cent) generally indicates a household living at or below the subsistence level (extreme poverty). They are typically employed in unskilled labour or services, often self-employed in the 'informal sector' of the economy. This is the only segment where both the male and female heads of household, and often their teenage children, are both working. They are considered 'traditional' in their market orientation, and are heavily restricted in the goods, services and brands they are able to purchase.

45. A. Canto and M. Quinoy, 'Multichannel Advertising Grows Rapidly in Latin America', *Latin Cable and Satellite Networks Guide 2000*, July 2000, p. 12A.

46. Straubhaar, 'Choosing National TV'.

47. Duarte, *Due South*.

48. Its partnership with TVA (Brazil), although ended, was none the less valuable to project CMT with local content. The channel has since gone off the air.

49. Ibid.

50. Ibid.

51. Due to the concentration of the MSO industry in various markets, a deal closed with a few operators could secure a large number of subscribers at a relative low effort. Furthermore, total numbers do not distinguish between major and minor markets.

52. S. Samiee and K. Roth, 'The Influence of Global Marketing Standardization on Performance', *Journal of Marketing*, 56 (April 1992), p. 6.

53. K. Simmonds, 'Global Strategy: Achieving the Geocentric Ideal', *International Marketing Review*, 2 (1985), pp. 8–17.

54. S. T. Cavusgil, S. Zou and G. M. Naidu, 'Product and Promotion Adaptation in Export Ventures: An Empirical Examination', *Journal of International Business Studies*, 24(3) (1993), pp. 479–506.

55. Jimena Urquijo, *Latin American Cable and Satellite Program Networks* (Carmel, CA: Paul Kagan Worldwide, 2002).

56. It is a general belief among programmers that the lower the social class targeted by the network, the more important it becomes to dub all shows.

57. Edianez Parente, 'HBO Brasil recheia seus canais básicos com novas atrações', *Pay TV*, 6 (October 1999).

58. F. Parajara, 'E! deve ter sinal exclusivo para o Brasil em julho', *Pay TV*, 6 (April 1999).

59. Bethany Lynn Letalien, *Does Pay Television Viewership Diminish*

Cultural Proximity? Evidence from a Rio de Janeiro Shantytown, unpublished MA dissertation (University of Texas at Austin, 2002).

60. Although no network would confess to it in interviews for this study!

61. Urquijo, *Latin American Cable*.

62. M. Cajueiro, 'Highlight: Globo Organization', *Variety*, 28 August 2000.

63. E. Malkin, 'Televisa: Turnaround, Take Two', *Business Week*, 17 August 1998.

64. S. Robina-Bustos, 'The Hemispheric Village: The Case of Televisa', *Mexican Journal of Communication*, 2 (1995), pp. 107–20.

65. R. Soon, 'Latin American Cable Channel Line-ups', *Zona Latina*, 8 September 1997, <http://www.zonalatina.com/Zldata20.htm>. Consulted May 2000.

66. L. Reis, 'Dificuldades fazem Globo descer do Olimpo', *O Estado de S. Paulo*, 7 November 1998.

67. It has the highest penetration of any channel in Argentina (88 per cent); in Brazil it used to be carried by 100 per cent of the multi-channel operators and it is in most of Mexico.

68. Duarte, *Due South*.

69. NBC, Telenoticias, ECO (launched March 1989) and CVN were already in the market when CNNE was launched.

70. Duarte, *Due South*; Urquijo, *Latin American Cable*.

71. Subscriber numbers are for 1999, as most of these networks have since reached full distribution with cable penetration over 70 per cent.

72. Edianez Parente, 'MTV quer ampliar distribuição paga e lançará novo canal', *Pay TV*, 5 (September 1998).

73. HTV is available in Brazil via DTH.

74. Urquijo, *Latin American Cable*.

75. Straubhaar, 'Beyond Media Imperialism'.

Notes on Contributors

Asu Aksoy is a research associate in the Department of Media and Communications, Goldsmiths College, University of London. She recently undertook research on Turkish migrants in the context of the UK Economic and Social Research Council's Transnational Communities programme. She is presently involved in an EU Fifth Framework project, 'Changing City Spaces: New Challenges to Cultural Policy in Europe'.

Jean K. Chalaby is senior lecturer in the Department of Sociology, City University, London. He is the author of *The Invention of Journalism* (1998) and *The De Gaulle Presidency and the Media: Statism and Public Communications* (2002) and has published extensively in leading journals on a range of topics related to the media. He recently founded the Centre for International Communications and Society with Professor Frank Webster.

Joseph Man Chan is professor at the School of Journalism and Communication, the Chinese University of Hong Kong, where he served as a former director. His publications cover international communication, political communication, and media development in Greater China. Among the books he has co-authored or co-edited are: *Mass Media and Political Transition: The Hong Kong Press in China's Orbit* (1991), *In Search of Boundaries: Communication, Nation-States and Cultural Identities* (2001) and *Global Media Spectacle* (2002). He has served as a president of the Chinese Communication Association and a visiting scholar at Harvard, Oxford and UC Berkeley.

William Crawley is co-director, with David Page, of the Media South Asia Project based at the Institute of Development Studies, University of Sussex. He has worked as a media trainer and consultant in Sri Lanka and Bangladesh, and has contributed articles to academic journals in the UK and India on South Asian history, politics and broadcasting. He worked for many years as a writer, broadcaster and editor for the BBC World Service. As head of the BBC Eastern

Service from 1986 to 1994, he was responsible for ten Asian-language services, broadcasting to South and West Asia and to Burma.

Luiz G. Duarte is a journalist and telecommunications consultant for the Latin American pay-TV industry, with services to companies like DirecTV Latin America and Sony Pictures Television International. His PhD in mass media, including a specialization in international marketing, is from Michigan State University. He actively participated in the launch of direct satellite services in Latin America and publishes in both the trade and academic press.

Graham Mytton worked for many years in the African section of the BBC World Service, and was then in charge of its global audience research. He has written several books and articles on African media, and audience and market research. He is now an independent consultant and trainer in audience and market research, with an emphasis on using the techniques of marketing and market research for the promotion of non-commercial developments in health, education and the alleviation of poverty.

David Page is co-author, with William Crawley, of *Satellites over South Asia: Broadcasting, Culture and the Public Interest* (2001). He spent twenty years working in the BBC World Service as a producer and editor of programmes broadcast to South Asia and Afghanistan. After leaving the BBC, he served as the media training co-ordinator for the European Union's Med Media programme. He has lectured in South Asian politics at Oxford and London universities and is the author of *Prelude to Partition* (1982). He now works as a consultant on communication and development issues.

Kevin Robins is professor of communications, Goldsmiths College, University of London. He is the author of *Into the Image: Culture and Politics in the Field of Vision* (1996), and (with Frank Webster) of *Times of the Technoculture* (1999). He is presently involved in an EU Fifth Framework project, 'Changing City Spaces: New Challenges to Cultural Policy in Europe'.

Naomi Sakr is a visiting lecturer in the School of Communication and Creative Industries, University of Westminster, and consultant in media, governance and the Middle East to several international organizations. She is the author of *Walls of Silence: Media and Censorship in Syria* (1998), *Women's Rights and the Arab Media* (2000), and

Satellite Realms: Transnational Television, Globalization and the Middle East (2002).

John Sinclair is a professor in the School of Communication, Culture and Languages at Victoria University of Technology, Melbourne, Australia. He has held visiting professorships at the University of California, San Diego and the University of Texas at Austin, and the Universidad Autónoma de Barcelona. His published work includes *Latin American Television: A Global View* (1999), from which the material in his contribution to this book is largely drawn. He has also co-edited and co-authored *New Patterns in Global Television: Peripheral Vision* (1996), and *Floating Lives: The Media of Asian Diasporas* (2001).

Joseph D. Straubhaar is the Amon G. Carter, Sr, centennial professor of communication at the University of Texas at Austin's Radio-TV-Film Department and also the director of the Brazil Center within the Lozano Long Institute of Latin American Studies. He previously taught at BYU and Michigan State University. His PhD in international communication is from the Fletcher School of Law and Diplomacy, Tufts University. He worked as a foreign service officer in Brazil and Washington and he has published extensively on international media studies and on the digital divide.

Ruth Teer-Tomaselli is professor of culture, communication and media studies at the University of Natal, Durban, South Africa. Her research interests include the political economy of broadcasting and telecommunications in Southern Africa, programme production on television, community radio, and the role of media in development. She is a member of the board of governors of the South African Broadcasting Corporation and holds an Orbicom professorship, the worldwide network of UNESCO chairs in communication.

Daya Kishan Thussu teaches transnational communication at Goldsmiths College, University of London. He has worked for the Press Trust of India and was for four years associate editor of Gemini News Service, a London-based international news agency. He has a PhD in international relations from Jawaharlal Nehru University, New Delhi. He is the co-author of *Contra-Flow in Global News* (1992), editor of *Electronic Empires – Global Media and Local Resistance* (1998), author of *International Communication – Continuity and Change* (2000), and co-editor of *War and the Media: Reporting Conflict 24/7* (2003).

Andre-Jean Tudesq is emeritus professor at Université Michel de Montaigne in Bordeaux, where he has taught contemporary history and media studies. He has published numerous books and articles on African media, notably *Feuilles d'Afrique* (1998), *L'Espoir et l'illusion: action positive et effets pervers des médias en Afrique subsaharienne* (1998), *Les Médias en Afrique* (1999), and *L'Afrique parle, l'Afrique écoute* (2002).

Index of TV Channels and Satellite Platforms

General Index